1980

THE REFERENCE SHELF

EMERGING CHINA

edited by **THOMAS DRAPER**

THE REFERENCE SHELF
Volume 52 Number 1

THE H. W. WILSON COMPANY
New York   1980

THE REFERENCE SHELF

The books in this series contain reprints of articles, excerpts from books, and addresses on current issues and social trends in the United States and other countries. There are six separately bound numbers in each volume, all of which are generally published in the same calendar year. One number is a collection of recent speeches; each of the others is devoted to a single subject and gives background information and discussion from various points of view, concluding with a comprehensive bibliography. Books in the series may be purchased individually or on subscription.

Library of Congress Cataloging in Publicaton Data

Main entry under title:

Emerging China.

   (The Reference shelf ; v. 52, no. 1)
   Bibliography: p.
   SUMMARY: A compilation of articles depicting China in transition with emphasis on the renewed relationship with the United States, the modernization of the economy, and the history, culture, and beliefs of the Chinese people.

   1. China—Addresses, essays, lectures.
[1.   China—Addresses, essays, lectures]
I.   Draper, Thomas.   II.   Series: Reference shelf ; v. 52, no. 1.
DS706.E45   951.05'7   80–400
ISBN 0–8242–0644–4

PRINTED IN THE UNITED STATES OF AMERICA

CONTENTS

868.5
R332
5-2-1

89442

PREFACE

Remote through most of its history by reason of culture and distance, and totally inaccessible to Americans after the Communist takeover in 1949, China is now emerging as an active participant in global affairs. This largest country on earth—one billion people on four million square miles—was so isolated in the 1960s that its only ally was the tiny ultra-Marxist state of Albania. From a policy of hermetically sealed independence, China began in the 1970s to seek help from abroad in the form of treaties and alliances that would further its aim to transform itself into a powerful modern state by 2,000.

The emergence of China on the international scene was prompted in the late 1950s not only by national ambition, but also by the erosion of Sino-Soviet relations and ideological conflict (Russia's divergence from Stalinism). This loosening of ties to its former Communist partner led to renewed relations with its former "capitalist opponent," the United States. In 1971, world recognition came for the People's Republic of China (PRC), when it became a permanent member of the United Nations with a seat on the Security Council. The first contact between the United States and the PRC occurred in the same year in the form of a table tennis match. This event, which was called "ping-pong diplomacy," was the prelude to President Richard M. Nixon's historic visit to Peking in 1972, and the signing of the Shanghai Communiqué, by which the United States agreed to recognize the PRC as the legitimate government of the Chinese mainland.

After the death in 1976 of Mao-Tse-tung, his successors began in earnest to steer the nation away from the constant social upheaval of the Cultural Revolution and toward rational economic modernization. In spite of reported disagreements within its leadership, China has cemented its ties with the United States by trade agreements, cultural exchanges and, most important of all, full diplomatic relations.

Many questions about China's economic goals and the stability of both its leadership and national policies remain. Despite the fact that rapprochement now permits visits by American government officials, journalists, and tourists, China is still for most Americans *terra incognita*. The present compilation—twenty-seven selections from magazines, newspapers, and government documents—is an attempt to give the reader a picture of China today.

Section I deals with a changing China, both at home and on the world scene, and its relations not only toward the superpowers but also toward its continental neighbors, particularly Vietnam and Tibet.

Section II describes the process of normalization of relations between the United States and China—how the countries reached their present level of reconciliation after twenty years of non-recognition and sometimes conflict. Among the articles in this section are several suggesting that the Carter administration has been overly soft in acceding to China's wishes, at the expense of loyalty to an old friend, Taiwan.

A number of articles in Section III focus on China's drive to modernize, while others evaluate the current economic plan and speculate on the chances of China being able to become the world's third superpower.

The fourth and final section presents a range of articles about life inside China according to Westerners' reports: improved status of women, the aged, population control, the arts, medicine, religion, law, and belief systems.

Most of the articles in this compilation employ the traditional Wade-Giles system of spelling Chinese names in English, but a few use the newer Pinyin system, in which Peking becomes *Beijing* and Mao Tse-tung is *Mao Zedong*. Where an article uses the Pinyin spellings, the more familiar Wade-Giles version is supplied in brackets.

The compiler wishes to thank the authors and publishers who generously contributed to this volume and granted permission to reprint their publications.

THOMAS DRAPER

November 1979

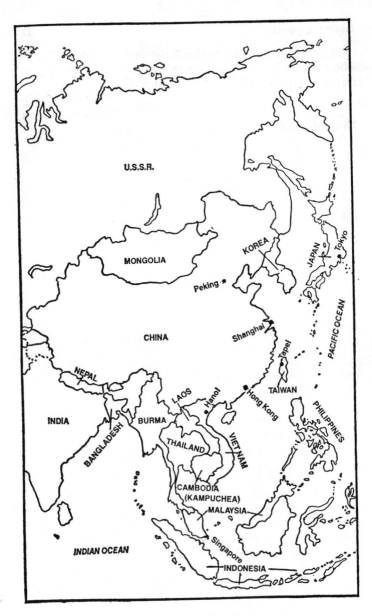

China and Surrounding Areas

I. EMERGING GIANT

EDITOR'S INTRODUCTION

The articles in this section attempt to provide an overview of China's current role in world affairs, and to trace the many historical influences and events that have caused the country to embark on a new path in foreign relations.

In the first article, the Foreign Policy Association editors describe some of the history of U.S.-China relations: going back to the Open Door policy (1900), ping-pong diplomacy (1971), and the Shanghai Communiqué (1972). In the second article, Harold Hinton, a China expert, provides a broad survey of Chinese history from the thirteenth century, in the course of which he cites the events that have precipitated China's recent turnabout—including the failures of the Great Leap Forward and Cultural Revolution, the rift with Russia, and Mao's waning influence.

The next two articles, both published in the *Nation*, concentrate on China's 1979 invasion of Russia's ally, Vietnam, an event triggered by Vietnam's earlier invasion of Cambodia. Owen Lattimore, a distinguished sinologist, provides historical background for the invasion, particularly the traditional Chinese attitude toward neighboring peoples and minorities. James Aronson, a journalist and teacher who visited Peking in 1979, reports the mood in that city as being one of concern that the border fighting might be only a prelude to wider conflict and that the United States and Russia seem to be on a collision course.

Frank Ching, writing in the *Wall Street Journal*, suggests that China may not only be relaxing its grip on Tibet, which it conquered in 1960, but that it is also beginning to encourage religious tolerance of all minorities within its borders.

DEALING WITH CHINA[1]

"There lies a sleeping giant. Let her sleep, for when she wakes she will shake the world."

With these words over a century and a half ago, Napoleon Bonaparte cautioned the Western world against intruding into the affairs of history's oldest and largest continuous civilization. His advice was not heeded. In the 20th century, its sleep troubled by internal social decay and the ever more massive intrusions of the great industrial powers, the Chinese giant awoke with a start.

We are now in the 30th year since Mao Tse-tung's Communist revolution swept the Chinese mainland. Yet the rest of the world, and especially the United States, still anxiously wrestles with the same question: How to deal with this restless colossus? How to accommodate the rising power of the most populous nation in history—about 950 million people, nearly a fourth of humanity?

By Western standards, the People's Republic of China (PRC) is still a "developing" nation, with an economic product of less than $1 a day per person and a population overwhelmingly rural. Yet it has thermonuclear missiles with a range of over 3,000 miles; an army of 3.8 million soldiers; vast size and natural resources. Its annual economic growth has averaged around 7 percent for 30 years despite many political convulsions. It is already a major power in Asia and wields some influence beyond the region.

Post-Mao China Emerges

Since Mao's death in 1976, the PRC's new leaders have vowed to speed up their country's technological modernization and to propel China by the year 2000 into the top ranks of world powers. Among China watchers, such bold an-

[1] Excerpts from chapter in *Great Decisions 1979*, by the Foreign Policy Association editors. p 34–43. Foreign Policy Association. Copyright 1979 by the Foreign Policy Association. Reprinted by permission.

nouncements are received with caution but not dismissed. Indeed, it was partly the knowledge of China's vast potential that underlay President Richard M. Nixon's decision in 1971 to end 22 years of U.S. ostracism of the Communist government in Peking.

Of the great civilizations of human history, perhaps the most self-contained over thousands of years was that which began in the great river valleys of China long before the Christian era. Contacts, peaceful and otherwise, with the outside were many, but outside influence, especially from the West, was slight. Meanwhile China itself, after long ages of alternating war and peace, gradually became unified under a succession of imperial dynasties.

At last, in the 19th and 20th centuries, the massive intrusions of more-dynamic and technically proficient nations into this vast Chinese realm decisively ended its isolation. China and America now have to learn to deal with each other. Yet it would be hard to imagine two high civilizations separated by more forbidding barriers of language, culture and contrasting experience.

The Chinese World View

Four elements are basic to the way China views the world. First is the legacy of *cultural ethnocentrism,* often amounting to arrogance, that was a hallmark of the Confucian Middle Kingdom for some 2,000 years. As a powerful empire surrounded by smaller, weaker neighbors, China treated all non-Chinese as "barbarians" lacking in philosophical and social refinement. While China's leaders no longer view the outside world with such contempt, this legacy can be seen in the determination of Maoist China to be self-reliant and avoid "contamination" by foreign ideas and cultures.

A second key to the Chinese world view is *resentment of foreign imperialism.* In the mid-19th century, it was the commerce-seeking West that shattered China's isolation. Britain and France, seeking to extend their commercial privileges in China—including a thriving illegal trade in opium—made short shrift of China's primitive coastal defenses in the 1840s and 50s. The Chinese emperor was forced to sign a series of "unequal treaties" granting extraterritorial concessions within China to Britain, France, Russia and other powers for their commercial and missionary activities. (Epitomizing proud China's humiliation was a sign posted in a park in the foreign quarter of Shanghai early in this century: "No dogs or Chinese allowed.") Finally, between the 1890s and the 1940s, imperial Japan launched a series of aggressive wars which, until its final defeat in World War II, made it the most massive foreign presence in a war-ravaged China.

When Mao's Communists came to power on the mainland in 1949, they eliminated what remained of foreign control except for the coastal colonies of Hong Kong and Macao, which are still under British and Portuguese rule respectively. But the bitter memory of foreign domination lives on and goes far to explain Peking's endless denunciations of actions in Asia and elsewhere that it regards as imperialist—or, in the case of its Soviet neighbor, "hegemonist" (seeking domination). It also explains why China's leaders are so dedicated to overcoming the weakness that made China a tempting target for aggression. As Mao put it: "If, in the decades to come, we don't completely change the situation in which our economy and technology lag far behind those of the imperialist countries, it will be impossible for us to avoid being pushed around again."

A third, and newer, element in the Chinese world view is the *revolutionary ideology* of Marxism-Leninism, introduced by the Chinese Communists. It gives China's anti-imperialism a global application in support for wars of "national liberation" to complete the decolonization of the "third world." Although Mao modified many doctrines of Marx and Lenin, he never abandoned their teaching that armed revolution is the only way oppressed peoples can throw off the "imperialist yoke" and take their destiny into their own hands.

Finally, to these three elements which spring from

China's own history must be added a fourth which is common to all nations: the pursuit of *national security and self-interest*. Such calculations have often obliged the PRC to cooperate with ideological opposites on the ancient principle "the enemy of my enemy is my friend." During China's border conflict with India in the early 1960s, the PRC allied itself with Pakistan, a conservative military dictatorship. And a decade later, on precisely the same principle, feeling itself threatened by the Soviet Union, it entered into a tactical relationship with its old archfoe, the United States.

America's Response to China

Through the 19th century the United States—despite the booming mid-century clipper ship trade across the Pacific and a rising influx into China of American missionaries—remained a minor factor in the troubles of China. As the century ended, however, U.S. concern over exclusive European spheres of influence led to the famous Open Door policy of 1900. Its original aim, achieved in large measure, was to obtain from the powers possessing "treaty ports" and other concessions pledges of equal access for the trade of the United States and other nations.

But the policy soon acquired a far broader aim—to preserve what remained of China's territorial integrity from further foreign encroachment. This proved easier to say than to do. When Japan flagrantly violated the Open Door by invading China in the 1930s, the American response was one of great concern but little action. Only when Japan attacked the U.S. directly at Pearl Harbor in December 1941 did the United States ally itself with "free China" against Japanese aggression. From 1942 to 1945, major U.S. military aid flowed to the beleaguered Chinese Nationalist armies of Generalissimo Chiang Kai-shek.

To Chiang, however, the No. 1 enemy was not Japan but a force of which most Americans were then only dimly conscious—the armed Chinese Communist movement which had grown strong in rural northern and central China under Japanese occupation. Chiang resisted U.S. attempts to restore a united Chinese front against Japan and kept his powder dry for a showdown with the Communists, which began as soon as Japan was defeated in 1945. In this new conflict, the U.S. continued to aid its wartime Nationalist ally even while attempting to reconcile the two sides. Both military and diplomatic efforts failed. In 1949 Chiang led the defeated remnants of his government and army into their present stronghold, the island province of Taiwan. On October 1 of that year, the People's Republic of China raised its banners in Peking.

The triumph of the Chinese Communists—then allied with our cold-war adversary, the Soviet Union—was received in the United States with shock and dismay. President Harry S. Truman, waiting for the picture to clarify, held off a decision on whether to seek diplomatic relations with the new regime or retain relations with the Nationalists on Taiwan.

Only months later, in June 1950, North Korea's surprise attack on South Korea set off a train of events that determined the American course in favor of Taiwan. The impact of these events on China policy was twofold. First, President Truman, the same day he ordered U.S. troops into battle in Korea, sent the Seventh Fleet to patrol the Taiwan Strait lest fighting be renewed there—thus frustrating the Communists' hope of completing their unification of China by "liberating" Taiwan. Second, the United States, in its counteroffensive in Korea, pursued the North Koreans almost to the Chinese border—whereupon a Chinese Communist army poured into Korea and engaged the Americans and their allies in heavy combat.

Whether Peking's purpose in Korea was aggressive, as the U.S. then charged, or defensive, as historians now tend to believe, the result was to freeze attitudes between Washington and Peking into near-total hostility for more than two decades. President Dwight D. Eisenhower's Secretary of State, John Foster Dulles, saw Chinese communism as a "temporary, passing phenomenon," and sought to hasten its passing by nonrecognition, military containment and economic embargo. He organized an annual campaign to block the seating of Peking's representatives in the United Nations, arguing that "the Chinese Communist regime does not conform to the practices of civilized nations; has not been peaceful in the past; and gives no evidence of being peaceful in the future." In 1954 he negotiated a mutual defense treaty with the Nationalist government on Taiwan, pledging U.S. aid against a Communist invasion. This treaty is now the main bone of contention in normalization discussions between Washington and Peking.

For their part, China's new leaders responded in kind, branding the United States as the "leader of the forces of global imperialism" and, in the words of Mao, "the most dangerous enemy of the people of the world." The mutual enmity continued almost to the end of the 1960s, especially while China was going through the internal convulsion of the Cultural Revolution which began in 1966.

How the Freeze Ended

What finally led to the thaw was a rapid deterioration in China's alliance with its far more powerful neighbor, the Soviet Union. The partnership had been fraying since 1960, when Soviet technical aid to China ceased. In 1968, the Soviet invasion of Czechoslovakia raised ominous thoughts in Peking. If this could be done to an ally in the name of "defending socialism," what was to prevent a Soviet invasion of China? Then a bloody border clash between Chinese and Soviet troops in March 1969 raised Chinese fears almost to the level of hysteria. "Dig tunnels deep, store grain everywhere, and never seek hegemony," Mao ordered the Chinese people. Some reports say a Soviet threat of nuclear attack on China in the summer of 1969 added to Peking's forebodings.

The decision to turn toward the United States was made less difficult by another event of 1969: President Nixon's gradual withdrawal of U.S. troops from Vietnam. "U.S. imperialism" now seemed on the wane in Asia, no longer a major threat to the PRC. Under these circumstances, the view gained ground in China that a limited relationship with the United States was possible as a counterweight to Soviet pressure.

The United States, too, saw several advantages in a limited thaw with the PRC. It would increase U.S. diplomatic leverage in dealing with the Soviet Union and with Japan. Peking might help arrange a negotiated settlement in Vietnam. There could be Sino-American trade and cultural, scientific and technical exchanges—and hope for a stable balance of power in Asia.

The first small bombshell burst in April 1971, when an American table tennis team, then visiting Japan, was invited to make an unscheduled stopover in Peking for "friendly competition." Coming after a generation of public hostility, the gesture created a sensation and gave the world a new phrase: ping-pong diplomacy. Three months later, after a secret visit to Peking by his national security adviser, Henry A. Kissinger, President Nixon announced to a stunned American public his acceptance of Chinese Premier Chou En-lai's invitation to visit the PRC. "There can be no stable and enduring peace without the participation of the People's Republic of China," said the President. He had therefore initiated steps "to open the door for more normal relations between our two countries." He added words of reassurance for America's ally on Taiwan ("Our action . . . will not be at the expense of our old friends") and for a suspicious Soviet Union ("It is not directed against any other nation"). But the key word in his announcement was another addition to the diplomatic vocabulary: normalization. Reassurance or no, it was a word bound to arouse anxieties in both Taipei and Moscow.

As a corollary to this dramatic shift, Washington abandoned in 1971 its 22-year opposition to a PRC presence at the UN. Seeking to salvage something for its ally, the U.S. proposed an idea it had long resisted—a dual-representation formula, giving the Security Council veto power to the PRC but preserving UN membership for the Republic of China. The attempted compromise failed. By a vote of more than 2 to 1, PRC delegates were recognized as "the only legitimate representatives of China," and "the representatives of Chiang Kai-shek" were expelled.

Shanghai: Creative Ambiguity

On February 21, 1972, President Nixon, Dr. Kissinger, a large official delegation and an army of reporters and TV camera crews descended on Peking for what Mr. Nixon would later call "the week that changed the world." The week's activity was divided between TV spectaculars for a watching world and tough diplomatic bargaining.

Diplomatically, the outcome was a document that became famous as the Shanghai communiqué. It contained clear language on everything except the most contentious point—Taiwan.

"Progress toward the normalization of relations between China and the United States," said the communiqué, "is in the interests of all countries." Contacts and exchanges would be developed in science, technology, culture, sports and journalism. Trade would be developed. And the two governments would "stay in contact, through various channels, including the sending of a senior U.S. representative to Peking from time to time" to exchange views on "issues of common interest."

When it came to the nub, Taiwan, the communiqué split into two parallel tracks, Chinese and American. At the heart of the Chinese section was a forthright reaffirmation of Peking's standard position that "the government of the People's Republic of China is the sole legal government of China; Taiwan is a province of China . . . ; the liberation of Taiwan is China's internal affair in which no other country has the right to interfere; and all U.S. forces and military installations must be withdrawn from Taiwan." But as to the consequences if the U.S. still rejected this position, the Chinese text was discreetly silent.

On their side, the Americans steered an artfully ambiguous middle course designed to maintain the favorable climate without giving in on vital points. The United

States, said the communiqué, "acknowledges that all Chinese on either side of the Taiwan Strait maintain there is but one China and that Taiwan is a part of China," and "does not challenge that position." This formulation stopped short of endorsing these assertions but was a sufficient acknowledgement of them to save Peking's face and thereby remove a threat of failure that had hung over the delicate negotiations from the outset of the Nixon visit.

In another partial concession, the Americans affirmed their "ultimate objective" of withdrawing "all U.S. forces and military installations from Taiwan" in the context of "a peaceful settlement of the Taiwan question by the Chinese themselves." Meanwhile, U.S. forces on Taiwan would be reduced only "as the tension in the area diminishes"—a phrase generally taken to mean the end not only of the Vietnam war but also of PRC military activity directed against Taiwan.

Thus, in the careful diplomatic architecture of the Shanghai communiqué, neither side got all it wanted. But through deliberate ambiguities and an "agreement to disagree," the Taiwan issue was kept from killing the new relationship in its infancy.

The Honeymoon—and After

The public celebrating and TV coverage during the Nixon visit to Peking seemed an occasion for exclusively happy thoughts. The PRC, about which little but bad news had appeared in the U.S. media for two decades, was now portrayed as a dynamic, thriving nation, its people hard-working and happy, its pandas delightful, its acupuncture a cure for every ailment. CBS News anchorman Walter Cronkite, who had once dubbed Mao's Cultural Revolution "a monument to madness," was now seen amusedly trying to spear Chinese snow peas with a set of chopsticks. The New York *Times,* which had once called the PRC "the most totalitarian regime of the 20th century," was represented by its ranking columnist James Reston, who likened the Chinese revolution to an old-fashioned American "cooperative barnraising." Under the impact of such news and views, a Gallup poll found 23 percent of the American public responding favorably to mention of "Communist China"—quite a jump from the 5 percent approval recorded five years earlier. (A year later, the 23 percent had jumped again to 49.) And when, just three months after the Peking visit, China's Soviet adversary signed a strategic arms limitation agreement with the same President Nixon, the "opening to China" seemed more than ever a diplomatic triumph for the United States.

In this atmosphere, Washington and Peking began a three-year diplomatic honeymoon. In 1973, with at least the tacit consent of Peking, what appeared to be a negotiated settlement of the Vietnam war was achieved and U.S. forces on Taiwan were duly reduced. The trickle of U.S.-China trade increased dramatically; exchanges of scientific and cultural groups began; the annual handful of American tourists to China became an appreciable number. Perhaps most important, the two countries established permanent diplomatic liaison offices in each other's capitals, headed by senior officials of ambassadorial rank. Although the only full-fledged Chinese embassy in Washington remained that of Nationalist China, the new step clearly looked toward a full normalization—presumably including the end of U.S. diplomatic and military ties with Taiwan. Some reports say the Chinese had been promised that this action would follow Mr. Nixon's reelection in 1972, and that it was only prevented by the Watergate disaster and, later, the military collapse of South Vietnam.

In 1975, signs appeared that the honeymoon was coming to an end. The cause was the same thorny issue—Taiwan. That March, the printed program of a Chinese performing arts troupe about to tour the United States contained the title of a song, added at the last minute: "Taiwanese Compatriots, Arise! We Shall Certainly Liberate You!" When the Chinese refused to delete the song, the State Department cancelled the tour. But the Chinese had made their point. Soon afterward Peking laid down three essential conditions for normalization: U.S. derecognition of the Republic of China; total removal of U.S. forces from Taiwan; and termination of the mutual defense treaty.

Meanwhile, U.S. ties to the Nationalist regime continued to flourish. Trade with Taiwan amounted to $3.6 billion, far above the 1971 level, and continued to zoom. U.S. military sales, although of types generally viewed as defensive, had been stepped up since 1973. The Nationalists had opened three new consulates in the U.S., while a senior career diplomat was appointed as the new U.S. ambassador in Taipei.

Clearly, Peking was becoming impatient with a situation in which the Americans had contrived simultaneously to enjoy détente with the PRC and flourishing relations with Taiwan. In the Shanghai communiqué the U.S. had seemed to say "One China, but not now." The Chinese were now saying, in effect: "If not now, when?"

The Shadow of the "Northern Bear"

What kept the posthoneymoon letdown from growing more serious was apparently the same overriding fact that had first turned Peking toward Washington: its fear of the Soviet Union. As long as the mighty United States could be relied on to restrain Soviet ambitions, the Chinese—so Washington appeared to calculate—were in no position to sever their new American connection, Taiwan or no Taiwan. But would this remain true indefinitely? Some Asia watchers thought not, and foresaw a frustrated China turning once again toward Moscow—with potentially disastrous consequences for our Japanese alliance and other vital U.S. interests.

It was with both Taiwan and the Soviet Union in mind that the PRC invited President Gerald Ford to Peking in December 1975. Mr. Ford's host, Vice Premier Teng Hsiao-ping, warned of the need for strength to restrain the Soviet Union, which he said "bullies the soft and fears the tough." The United States, the President answered, would follow "its own policies and methods." Détente with the Russians, in other words, was still fundamental. Equally reserved on Taiwan, Mr. Ford conceded a "possibility" of severing diplomatic relations with the Republic of China if he won the 1976 election. But, he added, in line with the Shanghai formula, this would depend on prior peaceful resolution of differences between Peking and Taipei. . . .

CHINA SINCE THE MONGOLS[2]

. . . The Mongols ruled China from 1280 to 1368, taking the name Yuan dynasty. Already disliked by the Chinese in a number of ways, the Mongols had but slight respect for Confucianism and the civil service examinations and systems, factors which led to even greater opposition by the Chinese, particularly the upper classes. The rulers were actually religiously tolerant, and permitted small communities of Franciscan missionaries to introduce Christianity into several parts of coastal China.

Both the Mongols and Christianity were expelled from China in 1368 in a great upheaval with strong anti-foreign sentiment. The new dynasty which came to power, the Ming (1368–1644), at first ruled firmly and energetically, creating a powerful empire, but a period of decline began about 1500. Japanese pirates began to increase their activities along the coast. Internal weakness became an increasing problem which was transformed into an even greater liability by the rise in power of the Manchu rulers to the north. In 1644, a combination of domestic rebellion and Manchu might was sufficient to overthrow the Ming dynasty; within a few decades the Manchus had subdued all of China.

The new rulers took the name Ch'ing dynasty, but are more easily remembered by their Manchu name, which avoids confusion with the earlier Ch'in dynasty. Although Chinese culture was by this time largely static to a degree

[2] Excerpt from the chapter, "China," in *The Far East and Southwest Pacific 1979*, by Harold C. Hinton, Ph.D., professor of political science and international affairs. An annual issue in The World Today Series. Copyright 1979 by Stryker-Post Publications, Inc., Harpers Ferry, W. Va. All rights reserved.

that made basic changes all but impossible, under the Manchus, the country was once again united and became rapidly powerful. In an effort to consolidate their positions, the Manchus ruled through existing Chinese institutions, including the very formal civil service with its Confucian orientation; for this reason, and others, they became accepted rapidly by their Chinese subjects. After an initial period of wise and successful rule, the Manchus indulged themselves in a period of energetic, but arbitrary and costly activity in the late 18th century, which undermined the power of the dynasty and caused the beginning of its decline.

Europeans, principally British, started to seek Chinese silk and tea in the 18th century, but had little to offer in return at first that interested the Chinese and consequently their efforts presented few problems to the Manchus. In the late 18th and early 19th centuries, two developments occurred which led to dramatic changes in China's relations with the Western powers. The British discovered that opium, grown in their possessions in India, could be sold at a handsome profit in China; at the same time Britain underwent its Industrial Revolution at home, making it possible to manufacture cheap cotton textiles and other goods in much greater quantities than before. The Manchus made an unsuccessful effort to prevent the importation of opium—the failure of their effort was caused by widespread smuggling when legal means of marketing the narcotic were closed.

The Industrial Revolution, particularly in Britain, not only created economic wealth, but also furnished a base for a greater military power. Determined to promote the sale of huge quantities of textiles and other products, and also to "legalize" the sale of opium in China, the British fought a series of small wars with the Manchus beginning with the Opium War of 1839–1842. Incidental goals were to exempt foreigners from the cruel criminal laws of China, abhorred by European Christians, and to open dependable diplomatic relations. The British achieved their purposes. The other major powers, including the United States, also profited from the efforts of Great Britain, by means of the "most favored nation" clause in their commercial agreements with China. Under this principle of international trade, all nations were granted the same advantages which China had accorded to its "most favored nation," Britain. At the insistence of various Christian mission organizations from a number of countries, the Manchus were forced to permit the re-entry of the Christian teaching into China.

Under a series of treaties, which were and are termed "unequal treaties" by the Chinese, signed under pressure in the last half of the 19th century, China lost a large degree of its sovereignty. Its best ports were carved into foreign "concessions" which were administered by foreign consulates and were places where non-Chinese could live and carry on business with a minimum of interference from Chinese officials. At the end of the century, near the close of this period, since termed one of the "diplomacy of imperialism," much of China was carved up into foreign "spheres of influence" by virtue of some further "unequal treaties" forced upon the Manchus. In each of these, a particular Western power (with the exception of the United States) was granted sweeping and exclusive economic rights in its area, coupled with a great degree of political influence.

Russian domination was established in Manchuria, but the fertile southern portion of that region went to the Japanese in 1905 after they defeated the Russians in a brief conflict. The Germans established themselves in the province of Shantung; the British became the major power in the Yangtze valley region; the Japanese controlled Fukien Province and the French asserted their dominance over Southwest China. Outside what had been China, the states which had paid tribute to the Manchu emperors also became colonies, or spheres of influence, of Britain, France, Russia and Japan. Russian influence became paramount in Outer Mongolia, now known as the Mongolian People's Republic, and penetrated into Sinkiang in the 1930s. The British became a powerful influence in Tibet, remaining so until 1947.

These losses of territory and authority were dramatic demonstrations of China's basic backwardness and weakness by the standards of Western powers, and were an insult to the sense of national pride of the Chinese. The economy of the coastal regions, traditionally more wealthy than the interior areas, was almost dominated by foreign trade and investment, the introduction of manufactured goods, and new industrial techniques and economic organization along European lines. The awkward process of modernization was thus started, but brought China the pains that usually accompany this process. Missionaries and Chinese who studied Western culture and ideas spread them widely, undermining the basic confidence of a growing number of people in the truth and wisdom of many aspects of traditional Chinese culture. Most important, the values of Confucianism were substantially weakened. These developments created somewhat of a cultural vacuum, into which a variety of foreign influences flowed.

Millions of Chinese rose in revolt against the Manchus in the mid-19th century under the leadership of a religious figure in Kwangsi Province who incorporated some Protestant Christian elements in his teachings and founded the short-lived Taiping Kingdom. This rebellion was quelled largely due to the loyalty to the Manchus of able Chinese officials devoted to the traditions of Confucianism. The revolt ultimately resulted in reforms and modernization within the official hierarchy.

Following the death of I-chu (also known as Emperor Hsien-feng) in 1861, his wife, referred to as the Empress Dowager, was co-regent during the reign of her son, Tung-chih (1862–1874) and wielded considerable influence during that period. Her son died without heirs, and the throne then passed to her nephew Kuang-hsu in 1875, but this remarkable woman, Tzu-hsi, wielded actual power until her death. Ruthless, able and extremely conservative, she embodied the tradition cherished by the Manchu court officials who clung to the security of the past. She was able to imprison her nephew-Emperor when threatened by his attempt in 1898 to modernize the government and the country.

At the popular level, there were several anti-foreign and anti-Christian outbreaks of violence in the years following 1870. Both sentiments joined to provide discontent resulting in the 1900 Boxer Rebellion, which was encouraged by influential members of the Manchu court. A joint military expedition, in which the U.S. took part, was sent in by the Western powers and soon crushed the rebellion. The Empress Dowager, shaken by defeat, granted her reluctant assent to certain innovations in the imperial government, but her life, and the effective control of the Manchu dynasty, ended in 1908.

During the last part of the 19th century, as the power of the Manchus continued to decline, there came into the political life of China a slowly growing number of people who knew something of the political ideas of the West. Although they did not attain high official status, they became aware of the need for China to adopt Western political and technical ideas in order to preserve the identity of China as a state in the world, and in order to perpetuate those elements of the Chinese culture that could be salvaged. These early reformers were not unified; their disunity prevented them from achieving any real influence on the Manchu court until it was too late. Because of their inability to obtain positions of leadership within the official government, reform leadership passed to the more radical elements in this group.

The most important of the radicals was Sun Yat-sen, who dedicated himself to the overthrow of the Manchus, and to the modernization of China along semi-Western lines. Although he was able to attract a relatively large following, Sun was not really a major intellect and was almost totally lacking in political skills. When Tzu-hsi died in 1908, the Manchu court installed the two-year-old Pu Yi. He reigned until 1912 through regents appointed by the court; he was later to become "Emperor" of Manchukuo (Manchuria) as a Japanese puppet, using his English name of Henry Pu Yi.

When revolution unseated the Manchu court in 1912, Sun Yat-sen became Provisional President of the new Republic of China. His rule was brief—he resigned in a few months in favor of the more powerful Yuan Shih-kai, a former Manchu official. In the following years he devoted himself to the forming of a political party, the *Kuomintang* (*National People's Party*) and to drawing up plans and a political theory for the modernization of China.

The *Kuomintang* broke with Yuan in 1913, but the party was easily suppressed because it had almost no real power. After a short time Yuan attempted to make himself the first emperor of a new dynasty—it was this step that aroused intense opposition, and he died in 1916 without achieving his ambition.

Following the death of Yuan, China literally disintegrated into a score of petty states run by individual military governors, usually referred to as "warlords." They had little governing ability and their rule was almost uniformly oppressive. The legal government of China in Peking continued to be recognized diplomatically by the foreign powers. In reality this "government" was an ever-shifting combination of one or more warlords, sometimes under the influence of one or more foreign nations, possessed of no power beyond the personal power of its leader or leaders. Communications were extremely poor and there was a thin scattering of modern arms in the outlying regions, making it almost impossible to achieve any genuine national unity. Sun Yat-sen set up headquarters in southern Canton, and tried in various ways, without success, to overthrow the shadow government at Peking and to unite the country under the *Kuomintang*.

In addition to the trend towards economic modernization in the cities and coastal regions durng the 1920s, there was a marked growth of nationalism among the Chinese, who sought an end to foreign influence in their country and an identity in the world community. In 1919 the government was in the hands of a group under Japanese influence to the extent that it was willing to sign the Treaty of Versailles, turning over what had been German territory and interests in China to Japan, rather than recognizing Chinese authority. An outburst of patriotism led by students, which became known as the May Fourth Movement, prevented the actual signing of the treaty. The people of China, particularly the youth, desired the end of foreign influence and internal disunity and came to believe that these goals could only be achieved through a major political and social revolution. Some chose the *Kuomintang,* and a smaller number joined an infant communist movement.

The *Chinese Communist Party* was founded in 1921 by young, leftist, nationalist Chinese, most of whom were students. The movement quickly came under the control of the Third International, more familiarly known as the *Comintern* led by Russia under its energetic revolutionary leader, Lenin. The picture became even more complicated when the *Comintern* decided to enter into an alliance with Sun Yat-sen's *Kuomintang* and ordered the local Chinese communists to do the same. This unstable union was produced by a common overwhelming desire to expel Western and Japanese influence from China and to eliminate the power of the warlords.

To accomplish these aims, the *Comintern* reorganized and greatly strengthened the *Kuomintang* through money and military aid, but it also hoped that communists could gradually acquire control over it by infiltrating top positions, and by putting pressure on the party through communist-dominated labor unions. The plan made considerable progress at first while the party was led by the politically inexperienced Sun Yat-sen, but after his death in 1925 he was succeeded by General Chiang Kai-shek, who became alarmed at the threat of Soviet domination of China and the more immediate threat of an ill defined "social revolution." He determined to head off these threats by military force, which he began in 1926 and 1927, by breaking with the *Comintern,* the Chinese communists and the left wing of his own party. He was able to seize Peking, the nominal capital of

China in 1928, and then proclaimed the new Republic of China at Nanking under the control of the *Kuomintang*. Actually his regime controlled only the eastern provinces of China, and was faced with tremendous problems: a large army that had to be fed, floods, famine, political apathy and backwardness, and continual pressure from the Japanese. Manchuria was seized by Japan in 1931–32; the territory was renamed *Manchukuo* and the deposed Manchu pretender to the throne in China, Henry Pu Yi, was installed as a puppet ruler for the conquerors who then undertook a widespread industrialization of the area.

The communists had certainly lost a battle, but were not defeated. Areas of communist control began to emerge in Central and South China by 1930. Chiang Kai-shek, beset with all of these problems, made probably the poorest choice of possible remedies: increasingly conservative and oppressive measures that ultimately lost him the support of increasing numbers of educated Chinese. It is possible, on the other hand, that had he not been diverted by a Japanese attack in the pre-World War II years that he would have succeeded in establishing some sort of stable and comparatively modern China with a right-wing government. It is very likely that he would not have been overthrown by the communists.

In the enclaves controlled by the communists, a leader gradually emerged in the late 1920s and early 1930s: Mao Tse-tung. The pathway to success was difficult—in 1934 the communists were forced by overwhelming *Kuomintang* military pressures to evacuate their base areas in Central and South China. After a long dramatic foot march led by Mao, they took weary refuge in the more remote and desolate regions of Northwest China.

Japanese forces invaded eastern China in 1937; the weakened condition of the communist movement in China prompted the Soviet dictator Stalin to urge the communists to form into another alliance with the *Kuomintang* in order to resist the Japanese. Mao Tse-tung probably saw an opportunity not only to resist the Japanese, but to overthrow the *Kuomintang* after it had been weakened by the Japanese, and made the agreement which was urged. The expansion of the communists from that time forth was actually at the expense of not only the Japanese, but also the *Kuomintang*, referred to also as *Nationalists*. The Japanese conquered the prosperous coastal regions of China, depriving the *Kuomintang* of its major economic and political bases. Driven into the hills and mountains of southwest China, it became more conservative and more subject to corrupt influences.

Inflation and weariness sapped the strength of the *Kuomintang*, enabling the Japanese to inflict some further heavy defeats on it as late in World War II as 1944. In the areas which they controlled, the Japanese were unable to prevent the communists, more skilled in the art of guerrilla warfare than the Nationalists, from infiltrating and setting up base areas within territory that was supposed to be Japanese. Partly in retaliation for this resistance the Japanese committed terrible atrocities against the Chinese people in the occupied areas, driving many into sympathy with the communists and thus assisting them to seize political control on an anti-Japanese, if not openly anti-*Kuomintang* platform.

Increasing numbers of Japanese soldiers were withdrawn from China starting in 1943 because of the defeats that were being suffered in the Pacific war. This permitted the communists to expand rapidly, so that by the end of the war they controlled nineteen base areas, some of which were quite large, in various parts of China, principally in the North and Northwest.

The elimination of Japanese troops and control of China at the end of the war brought about a frantic flurry of political and military activity by both the *Kuomintang* and the communists. The U.S. was the major political power in the Pacific area at this time, and it attempted to bring about some sort of settlement between the two so that there could be an end to civil strife. The talks, conducted under the encouragement of U.S. General George C. Marshall, the special envoy of President Truman, completely broke down in 1946 because neither side had any real desire for an agreement, but preferred a trial of armed strength.

The *Kuomintang* was plagued by the basic inability of Chiang and his colleagues to deal with China's very serious problems: inflation, corruption and loss of political unity. The military leadership employed very poor strategy and tactics against the communists, so that the *Kuomintang* lost almost all the major battles at the same time the home "front" was deteriorating to the point of collapse. By the end of 1949 the *Kuomintang* was driven to the island of Taiwan, also known as Formosa. The Chinese communists under Mao then controlled all of mainland China except for the then independent state of Tibet. They proclaimed the Chinese People's Republic and changed the name of their capital to Peking from Peiping, as it had been called by the Nationalists.

In 1950–51, the Chinese communists invaded Tibet. Although there was some initial resistance, the "roof of the world" was brought under Chinese control; the Dalai Lama, spiritual leader of the Buddhists, who also was vested with rather wide governing powers, soon was a figurehead. He fled Tibet in 1959 after some unsuccessful uprisings against the Chinese in the eastern part of the region; the people continued to be deprived of a leader to whom they traditionally ascribed divine powers and character.

The "People's Liberation Army" brought the new regime to power, and it remained important as a defense against possible enemies, both external and internal. The *Chinese Communist Party* has been the real instrument of Mao and the regime; its members hold all important public offices and it is the only political force since the Manchus that has demonstrated itself able to hold China together. Mao Tse-tung played an apparently overpowering role, and with his colleagues' consent, he made himself into a dictator whom all Chinese, especially the young, are taught to worship to a degree that would have created envy in the heart of the previous emperors.

The combination of Mao, party and army held together quite successfully until about 1965, and achieved a number of results that were impressive, considering the backwardness from which the country has only started to emerge in the 20th century. The people doubtless have regarded the regime as the only hope of escape from the long nightmare of civil and foreign war, general chaos and abject poverty, and therefore have given it a good deal of popular support. The communists restored the defunct economy and launched an impressive program of heavy industrialization with Soviet technical assistance and equipment. The small plots of farmland were collectivized into larger acreages patterned after the farms of Soviet Russia, not only to promote progress toward "socialism," but to give the government greater control over the people and output of the rural areas. In short, China progressed from rampant disorganization toward a centralized, autocratic and rationally administered state. Traditional Chinese culture and society were forcefully changed in directions desired by the communists, with widespread, fundamental and seemingly impossible effects. It must be remembered also that the Chinese, with only insignificant exceptions, had never esteemed the values of personal liberty developed and cherished by the people of Western nations.

In its foreign relations, the Chinese regime initially established an alliance with the Soviet Union, then led by the conservative and aged Stalin; it also entered into diplomatic relations with all communist countries and with a number of nominally neutralist others. The United States, which had become protector of the Nationalists on Taiwan, refused to recognize Mao's government, which in turn had shown little interest in diplomatic relations with the U.S. With only slight success, the Chinese communists initially tried to promote revolutions elsewhere in Asia, but retreated from this policy somewhat in the mid-1950s in order to be in a better position to cultivate the friendship of the neutral Asian nations.

When communist North Korea was threatened with total

defeat by the United States, the Chinese provided "volunteer" soldiers to fight for their communist ally against the predominantly U.S. forces of the U.N. battling on behalf of the South Koreans. The inability of large forces of Chinese troops to win a decisive victory against the U.S. in 1951 demonstrated to the Chinese communist hierarchy that the U.S. was dangerous if directly challenged, and more important, that the Soviet leadership was not willing to risk its own destruction on China's behalf in the event of an all-out Chinese-United States clash.

In the mid-1950s, policy differences and political tensions began to appear between the aging Mao and some of his underlings who were more rational than he. Clinging to the ideals of his youth, Mao seemed to believe fanatically that a sort of continuous revolutionary process throughout China, conducted largely by the young people who have been indoctrinated in, and taught to revere Mao and his "thought," was absolutely necessary for progress. Some of his colleagues began to prefer a more conventional and bureaucratic approach to political control and nation building.

In 1956, probably to strengthen his own political position, Mao launched a series of major policy changes in both the domestic and foreign areas, culminating in something called the "Great Leap Forward" in 1958. This effort resulted in herding the peasants, by propaganda and other pressures, into "people's communes," where they were worked to the point of almost utter exhaustion. Crude "backyard furnaces" were promoted to boost iron production, but actually were almost totally useless since the small quantity of metal they produced was inferior and economically worthless. All of these programs were failures, and they seriously strained China's relations with the Soviet Union, then the only source of economic and military aid, to a point that the Soviet leader Khrushchev cut off all aid by 1960. During this period of turmoil Mao engaged in another futile gesture—the shelling of the islands of Quemoy and Matsu, controlled by the Nationalists, close to the China mainland in the Straits of Taiwan (Formosa). Whatever his original intentions had been, nothing more than an artillery and airpower duel occurred, which nevertheless alarmed other nations because of another possible Chinese-U.S. confrontation.

The end result, after economic setbacks and failure to succeed in doing any damage to the Nationalists in the off-shore waters, was that instead of being stronger, Mao was somewhat weaker. On the other hand, he was able to persuade his colleagues to rally around an anti-Soviet policy. The Soviet Union was accused of being as great, if not a greater political enemy than the United States. The task of struggling against the supposed imperialistic designs of the U.S. was hopefully assigned to other infant revolutionary movements in Asia, Africa and Latin America.

The revolutionary zeal of the Chinese, and their tendency to urge youthful and nationalistic movements to greater tasks than were possible, with endless quantities of advice and of Mao "thoughts," coupled with quantities of arms did not produce the desired results. Right wing, moderate nationalist, and socialist leaders of Asia and Africa became rapidly aware of the not very serious threat, and took steps to expel Chinese agents. The prospects for revolution in Indonesia and in sub-Saharan Africa, which had seemed promising in the years 1963–1965, began to decline.

The leadership in Communist China, partly as a result of the lack of success elsewhere, for a time became very insistent that the conflict in Vietnam must continue at almost any cost until a major political setback could be inflicted by the Vietnamese communists on the United States. But, at the same time, the Chinese were quite satisfied that the actual fighting was by the North Vietnamese and their supporters in South Vietnam, and they preferred to remain on the sidelines as a supplier of military aid and as a cheerleader. Accordingly, Peking was distressed when Hanoi began negotiating with the United States in 1968. By 1969, however, the Soviet Union mounted increasing pressures in the dispute concerning the borders separating the two nations; there was a military build-up by both sides along the border and some limited conflict. In what appeared to be an abrupt reversal of policy, Peking began to show interest in improving its relations with the United States and because of this, came to favor the signing of a ceasefire agreement by North Vietnam and the U.S. It even seems to have put some pressure on Hanoi to this effect (but behind the scenes) in 1972.

Since about 1958, growing Chinese political pressures on the Soviet Union, which were calculated to prove the correctness of Mao's brand of communism and the error of the Soviet brand, have produced serious and fundamental tensions not only between the Soviets and the Chinese, but between many communist bloc nations. After the fall of Khrushchev, who actually handled the revolutionary impatience of the Chinese rather clumsily, his more practical successors offered China a limited agreement, which was spurned by Mao. By virtue of this refusal, Mao seemed to have worsened his relations with some of his more influential supporters who prefer a less antagonistic attitude toward Russia and toward the United States, particularly in view of the possibility, however remote, of a major war with the United States.

By the last half of 1965, the aging Mao, impatient and convinced that the time was at hand to silence, refute and overthrow his critics within the party and among the communist nations, and also to put his stamp indelibly on the Chinese revolution for an indefinite future, manufactured the "Great Cultural Revolution." His first obstacle, the reluctant municipal boss of Peking, P'eng Chen, was overthrown by a combination of political pressures and military threats by the end of May 1966. Mao then relied upon the revolutionary young people, organized into "Red Guards" and enjoying the support of the army under the command of Mao's companion and designated heir, Defense Minister Lin Piao. The Red Guards attacked and terrorized Mao's real and imaginary opponents in the universities, in the party structure and anywhere else they were thought to be found. In some cases, persons were declared to be anti-Mao whether or not they in fact were such, in order to provide a continuing series of targets at which the "Great Cultural Revolution" could focus and fire, and thereby continue its existence.

Early in 1967 it was necessary for Mao to urge the army to intervene in order that chaos might be averted, but also to keep the "Great Cultural Revolution" moving. The army quickly discovered that both of these tasks were incompatible, and increasingly began to emphasize the restoration of order at the expense of the restlessness encouraged by the unruly Red Guards. In the late summer of 1967, Mao was brought, willingly or unwillingly, to endorse this turn towards a more conservative view. After that time, the impact of the "Great Cultural Revolution" on everyday life lessened. During 1968, the army acquired more and more local power, and with Peking's consent, it broke up many of the Red Guard units.

It appeared during 1969 that a moderate coalition led by Premier Chou En-lai and some of the military (with the possibly reluctant consent of the semisenile Mao) was trying to restore domestic stability and more nearly normal foreign relations. Chou felt it advisable, after several months of Soviet threats, to enter into negotiations on the mutual border dispute and other matters relating to the state, downgrading disputes concerning communist theory. By the end of 1970, it appeared that the negotiations had resulted in a deadlock partly because of Soviet suspicion of what appeared to have become a "co-equal" among communist states.

The year 1970 saw real, although uneven, progress toward stability in China's internal and foreign affairs. The establishment of diplomatic relations with Canada in late 1970 gave Peking an important post in North America from which it could observe and perhaps influence developments at the United Nations and in the United States.

An important event of 1971 was the purge of Defense Minister Lin Piao and some other military leaders, apparently at the initiative of Premier Chou En-lai, who wanted to decrease the political influence of the armed forces and eliminate an arch opponent of better relations with the United States. In the same year, Nationalist China was expelled from the United Nations and the People's Republic of China became the official representative of the Chinese nation.

Since 1969 a re-emergence of bureaucratic controls has resulted in discontent on the part of radicals who cling to the revolutionary ideals of the past. A period of political ferment reflecting this dissatisfaction began in the summer of 1973 and has since continued.

The moderates launched a campaign in mid-1974 in the interest of economic growth to curb the power of the radicals. Premier Chou En-lai initially appeared to be still in charge, even though he retired to a hospital in mid-1974; he possibly sought to conserve his energies, survive Mao and ensure that an early demise on his own part did not give radicals an opening to resume the initiative.

A new state (not party) constitution abolished the post of Chairman of the Republic (chief of state) in January 1975; it made a few other changes, none of them basic. It was adopted by the National People's Congress (China's version of a parliament) which met for the first time in ten years. This was one of several signs that political conditions were returning to normal after the turmoil of the Cultural Revolution.

The death of Chou En-lai on January 8, 1976, deprived the world of one of its most astute statesmen and placed the future of the moderates in Peking in jeopardy. Vice Premier Teng Hsiao-ping, Chou's main assistant since 1973, apparently antagonized the radicals and did not remain in office for long, leaving the scene in April 1976, presumably with Mao's approval. The new premier announced at that time, however, was not a radical, but a compromise choice. Hua Kuo-feng's record suggests a closer affinity with the moderates than the radicals. A major earthquake in mid-1976 tightened the political ties between Hua and the army, which handled most of the relief work.

Mao, frail and senile, died on September 9, 1976; his death removed the main shield of the leading radicals including his widow, Chiang Ching; they were purged by Hua a month later. The so-called "Gang of Four" was accused of fomenting disturbances and riots in various provinces during 1976; even after their purge, propaganda against them continues unabated. Teng Hsiao-ping has been "rehabilitated" and again is second in command to the premier. The apparent trend toward stabilization of the new regime was indicated by the successful holding of a Party Congress in August 1977 and a National People's Congress in February–March 1978.

Because of concern over Soviet military increases along the Chinese-Soviet border, China exhibited increased interest in improving its relations with the United States in the hope of having a diplomatic counterweight. To the surprise of Americans, China extended an invitation to an American ping pong team to visit in April 1971. This was quickly followed by ex-President Nixon's visit in 1972. In its propaganda, however, China continues to be critical of U.S. policy, especially in the Far East. Former Secretary of State Kissinger visited China for the seventh time in November 1974; an invitation was extended to President Ford in late 1975, which was accepted; he made the trip in December of that year.

Peking has become seriously concerned over what it considers an inadequacy of United States efforts to cope with the Soviet Union's expansionism, both in the Far East and on a worldwide basis. On the other hand, Peking was pleased when it succeeded in reaching an agreement with the United States to "normalize" their relations on December 15, 1978. At the same time, the United States terminated its diplomatic relations with the Republic of China on Taiwan. . . .

Culture

The fundamental and lasting institutions of family life and farming completely dominated Chinese popular culture for thousands of years; this was certainly true throughout most of Asia, but these two foundations were developed to a higher level within China. Agriculture combined the careful cultivation of cereal grains, skillful efforts to control water by the construction of levees and irrigation ditches, and the return of all available fertilizer, including human waste, to the soil. This permitted production of great yields with a high nutritional content, which in turn permitted a rapid rate of population growth. The family was the basic social unit—above it stood the village, governed usually by the heads of the leading families; contact with central government officials was avoided by the leaders with varying degrees of success.

Traditional upper class culture was also based on the family and on the group of related families which together formed a clan. Ancestor worship, involving sacrifices to dead forebears, who were not considered to be actually divine, began among the upper classes and spread to the lower during the Chou period. The wealthy avoided manual labor and regarded literacy and education—especially in the Confucian tradition—ownership of land, and public service as the highest social goals and symbols of status. This upper crust, dominating education, government service and land ownership, was not so exclusive that the lower classes were entirely excluded from it. Unlike India, China had no caste system as a part of its culture, but in reality, it was almost unheard of for a person of peasant origin to acquire enough education, wealth or influence to move to the top of the social scale.

The scholarly elite, as this upper class may be called, developed an almost unbelievably complex writing system derived from the priests of the Shang era. Learning this was a major undertaking, and over the centuries it became the medium of almost every type of literary effort, except for the epic poem, which never emerged in China. Other varieties of verse, as well as history, plays, novels, essays, encyclopedias and other writings were produced in enormous abundance. The poetic works of Mao Tse-tung, composed with skill, are a modern counterpart of these ancient and more recent literary efforts. About 900 A.D. a form of printing was developed: a character or page was carved in reverse on a block of wood, which was then used as a stamp. It has been estimated by some that under this system, up to the time of the 18th century, more literature had been printed in Chinese than in all of the other languages of the world combined.

In spite of tendencies toward conservatism and anti-foreignism, traditional Chinese culture was probably the richest, and certainly the longest lived and most continuous of the great civilizations, ancient and modern, of the world. It was relatively free from the religious bigotry and intolerance that was evident in much of Western history. In contrast to the principles of decaying despotism of France under the Bourbon kings, the Chinese philosophical expressions greatly impressed well-educated Jesuit missionaries who came to China in the 18th century. Through their writings, the French writer and philosopher Voltaire communicated some of the Chinese ideals to the educated of Europe.

The decline of the traditional Chinese political system in the late 19th and early 20th centuries also brought a decline in the vitality and self-confidence of most of the traditional Chinese cultural values. Education was increasingly altered to conform to Western ideals; literature began to be written more and more in the vernacular, or conversational language, rather than in the old, difficult and formal literary language. During the 1920s, the ideals of Marxism gained ground among intellectuals, but not always in the form of communist doctrine.

At the level of the uneducated, the solidarity of the family was greatly weakened by the beginning of economic progress toward industrialization which created jobs for women, drawing them away from their families to the factories in the cities. The Japanese invasion in 1937 and the ensuing chaos uprooted millions of people and heavily contributed to the further breakdown of the traditional social and cultural order.

The communists have exploited this fluid and unstable situation to press ahead toward their own goals of a new culture and a new society, to be achieved, to a large extent, by overhauling the educational system. This has produced a new generation of Chinese heavily indoctrinated in the desired ideals and cast in a completely new mold. The fundamental purpose of all of this is to break down the traditional ties of family and religion, as well as other values that have interfered with the purposes of the regime. The ultimate desire is that every Chinese be willing, and indeed eager, to do what the state wants of him, to encourage others to do the same, to report on them if they do not, and in general to exist to contribute to the often-changing programs and goals of the leadership.

Progress toward these goals has been faster in the cities, where indoctrination and control are easier than in the countryside. However, some progress has been evident among the peasants. The Peking dialect of Mandarin (northern Chinese) is being taught in all schools, several hundred of the most complex written characters have been simplified, and the regime has shown a more than passing interest in the development and introduction of an alphabetical writing system. Literacy is now much more widespread than before the advent of the communists, but the ability to read, as well as the school system, are both basically used to indoctrinate and propagandize the people along the lines indicated above, rather than to encourage creative and independent thought.

The regime permits the people almost no contact with the outside world, with the exception of closely guarded diplomatic missions. It almost appears that this aspect of the country's anti-"imperialism" is a revival of anti-Western sentiment along the lines of the conservative Manchus and of the Japanese Tokugawas; it is certain that this absence of contact provides even greater opportunities for indoctrination to the communist regime.

On the island of Taiwan, the basic cultural pattern is that of the moderate intellectual classes of China of the first half of the 20th century. To this has been added a large degree of modernization and adoption of Western customs, as a necessary adjunct to American military and former economic support. The inner circles of the nationalist regime have grown conservative with age, but are actually realistically practical for the most part.

Economy

In terms of the percentage of the people involved and the value of the product within the whole economy, agriculture has always been and is now the most important industry in China—vitally necessary to feed some 800 million people. Food crops, especially cereal grains have been emphasized rather than livestock raising and dairying. In recent years, commercial crops such as cotton have received more attention in order to supply textile and other industries which process raw materials. Fishing, both at sea and in the inland waters, is also widespread and contributes valuable protein to the diet of the Chinese.

Mining and lumbering have grown, permitting a corresponding growth of modern heavy and light industry; however, much of China has been deforested over the centuries. Uranium, mined in the remote regions of outer China, has permitted the explosion of atomic and hydrogen bombs, and there is a small, but effective, offensive missile industry which has provided the means to deliver this form of destruction to other countries.

Modern industry began in the treaty ports and consisted principally of textile and metalworking plants. The communist regime is trying to rapidly modernize, diversify and expand China's industry. Beginning in 1950, foreign trade, which had been mainly with Japan and Western nations, was shifted sharply to the Soviet Union and to the communist nations of Eastern Europe. However, with the collapse of the "Great Leap Forward" in 1960 and the beginning of the tensions that brought an end to Soviet aid, the government of Mao Tse-tung redirected its trade toward Japan and Western nations, with the most notable exception of the United States. Australia and Canada have supplied large amounts of their surplus grain, particularly in the lean years of Chinese farm production. Since China's intervention in the Korean War, all Western countries have refused to ship materials which would directly support a military effort. By exporting food and water to the thriving British Crown Colony of Hong Kong, Communist China earns several hundred million dollars each year in foreign currency which is used to help pay for its imports.

Since it is communist, the regime of China believes in rigid, centralized, economic planning and control. During the first three years of its power from 1950 to 1952 it rebuilt what had been destroyed during the preceding years of war and laid the foundations for economic progress in a "socialist" direction. One of its major successes in this respect was the wiping out of the rural landlord class and the turning of land over to the peasants, but only for a short period. In 1953, with substantial Soviet assistance, the first "Five Year Plan" was launched which stressed the construction of communications and transportation, particularly railways, and heavy industry centering around iron and steel production. This was also the period when agriculture began to be collectivized, whereby the individual peasants tilled their combined plots with more modern techniques, and with a small amount of the great quantities of farm machinery that had been promised.

The second "Five Year Plan" was launched in 1958, but was quickly replaced by the "Great Leap Forward." This was a period in which the planning and statistical apparatus that the regime had created was wrecked and replaced by a hodgepodge of senseless and impossible goals which were to be achieved by a "quota" system of uncoordinated production. The hope was that there would be a great economic surge, but the whole thing was a dismal failure that led to a crisis in agriculture and to an end of Soviet aid. Following this there was a period of relaxed control and recovery during which heavy industry was de-emphasized, and the peasants were given slightly more of the basic comforts of life. The economy began to recover in 1962, and a third "Five Year Plan" was launched in 1966, but information on progress under this scheme is scanty.

China's leadership evidently believes that with reasonable luck and an absence of political disturbances, methods can be devised to feed the growing numbers within the country, and at the same time to industralize the nation. Mao Tse-tung, however, apparently did not understand the need for stability; his "Great Cultural Revolution" provided turmoil which was economically damaging, although not as destructive as the "Great Leap Forward." The end of the cultural revolution in 1968 was followed by a resumption of solid, although unspectacular, economic growth.

At the National People's Congress of February–March 1978, the regime adopted a new "Ten Year Plan" for economic development that appears to set some unrealistically high targets. In early 1979, it was found necessary to "suspend" contracts with Japanese firms worth $2.5 billion.

The Future

As is true in nations of the world with large populations of basically poor people, the race in China between the growth of population and the supply of goods will continue to be a close one. The annual increase in China's population has been equal to the entire population of Australia. Intensive efforts at birth control are underway to minimize population growth. The increasing capability of delivering nuclear destruction on the real and imaginary enemies of the regime is already widely known.

Desires for security and predictability will probably lead in the long run to a government less devoted to international and internal adventures. The reverence for the institution which Mao's person had become will probably survive.

The question of the legal status of Taiwan will remain a thorny one. It would not be surprising if (in order to insure survival of the Chinese on Taiwan as a nation) the Kuomin-

tang dissolved itself and the leadership announced that
after a generation, the Chinese and Taiwanese have integrated as "one people."

CHINA'S HISTORICAL HEGEMONY[3]

As the news about guerrilla resistance in Kampuchea
[Cambodia] and the Chinese thrust ("incursion" in Kissinger-Nixon language) into Vietnam comes off the wires
and flickers on the screens, we are left to try to fit the pieces
together in a way that makes sense. Even serious commentators know so little about issues, historical precedents and
traditional patterns of behavior in that part of the world
that the only comparison they have come up with is to the
unilateral Chinese tidying up of the India-Tibet frontier,
by military force, in 1962.

Our journalists also remind us of the Chinese insistence
that the Russians have, since Czarist times, repeatedly en-
croached along the Siberian frontier on territories that once
upon a time belonged to China. Not only in the North, but
also in the deep South, where it is the Chinese who have for
centuries been expanding, we need a much longer historical
perspective to bring immediate events into focus.

In Peking in 1972 I was given a Foreign Office brochure,
intended as background reading for anyone interested in
frontier disputes between China and Russia. Precisely, even
elegantly, with a minimum of words, it wove together several themes:

(1) For more than 2,000 years the Chinese have lived
in a multinational polity: the Chinese themselves forming
the majority, and such minorities as the Tibetans, the oasis
peoples of Sinkiang or Chinese Turkestan, the successive
historical peoples of Mongolia (Hsiungnu, Sienpi, the
Northern Turks, the Mongols themselves), the successive

[3] Article entitled "Great Wall and Jungle: China's Historical Hegemony," by
Owen Lattimore, professor of Chinese studies, Rutgers University. *Nation*. 228:257,
273+. Mr. 17, '79. © 1979 by the Nation Associates, Inc. Reprinted by permission.

peoples of Manchuria (which the Chinese justifiably prefer to call the Northeast, since even the Manchus never had a term meaning "Manchu-land").

(2) In this multinational world, the state power was at times held by one of the minority peoples. This means that the "conquests" of China by the Mongols in the 13th century and the Manchus in the 17th century were not conquests resulting from invasions by foreigners: they were the outcome of civil wars within an already existing polity.

(3) By corollary, the Chinese themselves, in more than 2,000 years, never engaged in imperialism—an interpretation that will raise the eyebrows of most historians, Marxist or non-Marxist.

(4) On the other hand the Russians have always been imperialist, conquering and exploiting non-Slavs whose cultural heritage and political evolution had nothing in common with the history of the Russians themselves.

Here the Chinese neglect a phenomenon of primary importance. Nineteenth-century travelers, especially the British, when commenting on Russian relations with Asian peoples, remark over and over again on Russian "racial tolerance." This "tolerance," I think, can be accounted for by the fact that in South Russia there was for centuries an ebb and flow of war and of periods in which Slavs were ruled by Turkish-speaking peoples, alternating with periods in which Turkish tribes were ruled by Russians. After each turn of fortune, the sons of chiefs on the winning side took as wives the daughters of defeated chiefs, while commoners often intermarried with commoners. It was out of this alternation that there developed a Russian attitude toward ethnicity that had more to do with class than with "race." No wonder that British travelers were astonished. Quite a few aristocratic Russian families were proud of their partly "Tatar" descent, and the great poet Pushkin had a maternal great-grandfather who was an Abyssinian general in the Russian service, ennobled by Peter the Great. No Peer of the Realm in the House of Lords ever boasted that on one side he was descended from an Indian Rajah.

While the Chinese of today postulate a multinational polity of which the beginning is not known, which is assumed always to have existed (and the Kuomintang in its day made the same assumption), there is also a differentiation that has been observed throughout history: the peoples north of the Great Wall have always been classified as *wai*, "outer," and the Chinese within the Great Wall as *nei*, "inner," with the "outer" undisguisedly rated as barbarous and the "inner" claiming a monopoly of civilization. China's Great Wall has always been the symbol of this inner-outer division, and like the garrisoned Rhine-Danube *Limes* of the Roman Empire, it has always been thought of as defending civilization against barbarism.

This emphasis on defense makes it necessary to state a simple, opposing truth: neither Chinese nor Romans, retreating in the face of aggressive barbarians, dug in on a fortified line to save civilization. On the contrary, Chinese and Romans, each exploiting a geographical environment that had recognizable characteristics, built up the highest civilizations of their times. They expanded to take in all the terrain that could be profitably exploited by the techniques they already had, until they reached a zone—the depths of Mongolia, the depths of Germany—which because of costs of transportation and distances from metropolitan markets could not be integrated with the urban-rural *oikumene*. Further expansion would mean diminishing returns —too much military expenditure, too little additional revenue. That was where they dug in and why they dug in. Their "defense lines" were in fact the limits which they themselves set on their own expansion.

It was in this phase that "barbarian aggression" began, as a secondary phenomenon. The barbarians wanted all the products of civilization that they could get, but they did not have enough purchasing power. Civilization would take from them gold and a few luxury articles (fine-quality furs, jade, amber), but these did not make for bulk trade, and pre-industrial civilization had only a limited demand for the barbarian surplus production of skins and hides, livestock and wool. Unable to buy all they wanted, the barbarians tried to get as much as they could by force—border raids, blackmail, invasion and conquest from time to time. The Chinese and Roman response to the barbarian response was to lay on an occasional military incursion to "teach the natives a lesson" (a formula that is coming into use again today) ; to enlist some barbarians as mercenaries (as the British enlisted transfrontier Gurkhas and Pathans in special regiments of the Indian Army); to grant one tribe favorable treatment in order to stir up the jealousy of another tribe. The Roman formula was *divide et impera;* the Chinese formula was *i i chih i,* "use barbarians to control barbarians."

The Northern Reaches

It was in the vague northern reaches of what is now being presented to us as the multinational Chinese polity that the Russians began to appear in the late 1500s and increasingly in the 17th century. Who were these Russians? Here the Soviet historians have not made the clear case that ought to be made. The early Europeans, beginning with the Jesuits, and the Russians themselves, had no doubt that China had been conquered by non-Chinese, the Manchus. An early Jesuit wrote a history of the conquest under the title *De bello Tartarico.* Rather soon, however, both Europeans and Russians began referring to a Chinese Empire and an Emperor of China. The frontier peoples, however, never accepted this blurring. For them it was quite clear that the Manchus had separately conquered China, Mongolia and Tibet, and ruled them, indeed, to the very end, under separate sets of bureaucratic institutions. With the overturning of the Manchu throne in 1911, therefore, Chinese, Mongols and Tibetans ought to have been free each to go their own way. (It was the complexity of Great Power politics, including secret treaties between Czarist Russia and Japan, rather than China's own power, that frustrated or delayed this outcome.)

It was of decisive importance that the Russia that was

looming on the horizon was a Russia that had survived wars with Sweden, Poland and Turkey and was coming into its own as a great power. The Czar needed new revenues for a strong, centralized state. East of the Urals, private ownership of serfs was therefore forbidden (though many peasants were still listed as "state serfs"). The Czar did not want new sources of revenue to be intercepted by private landlords. Private enterprise and small-scale capitalism began to flourish. Small, thinly scattered Siberian tribes had about as poor pickings as the North American Indians, but more advanced peoples, like the Buryats and Yakuts, did rather well, some of them achieving an infant capitalism that flourished beside the adolescent Russian capitalism. In fact, by the end of the 19th century, when farm machinery became available, it was often Buryats who got the agencies to sell American machinery to Russians. As this kind of economic evolution went on in frontier territory where the few Chinese traders were still at the stage of barter and usury, the tribesmen who were neither Chinese nor Russian tended generally to prefer the Russians.

At this point we can turn to China's other major frontier, the "jungle" margin of expansion in the south. Not having the advantage of a Chinese Foreign Office pamphlet to describe the geography and define the issues here, I am forced to refer to my own work of nearly forty years ago (*Inner Asian Frontiers of China,* New York, 1940), in which I described the peoples to the north of China as "non-Chinese" and those with whom they were in contact in the south as "pre-Chinese" or "not yet Chinese."

What I meant was this: We have enough archeological evidence to be sure that in neolithic times there was agriculture in humid South China as there was in drier North China. It was practiced by peoples who were, probably, of the same general ethnic stock as the "true" Chinese. Their agriculture certainly ranged from intensive rice farming to slash-and-burn jungle hillside cultivation. Because of the monsoon climate there was a great deal of jungle. Techniques of ditching, draining and irrigation could be developed more quickly and easily in the open North than in the jungly South, but when developed and applied to the South there was a rich reward in double cropping and high productivity. It was, therefore, the Northerners who tended to encroach on the Southerners, converting a population that they at first regarded as backward and inferior into "standard" Chinese. As this integration took many centuries, and language changed while the forward movement was going on, we can account historically for the fact that dialects are more numerous and more different from one another in the South than in the North. It is as if we had in England a zone in which the population began to speak English at the Beowulf stage, then a zone of Piers Plowman speakers, then one of Chaucerians and one of Shakespeareans.

Moreover, because of the basic affinities of agricultural life, even when the crops grown are different, the social and cultural influence and intellectual prestige of China radiated on beyond the zones actually integrated into the Chinese polity. On the "unassimilable" North, for example, the historical impress of Confucianism was amazingly slight, but in the South it penetrated all the way down through Indochina. Ho Chi Minh came from the kind of Vietnamese family in which Confucian scholarship was regarded as part of a gentleman's education.

The Southern Reaches

Although the Chinese did not claim the direct rule of Indochina, they were fully aware of the range and force of their prestige. They took it for granted that Indochina came within the sphere of their cultural and intellectual hegemony, and entitled them to ascendancy in judging questions of political philosophy. "Hegemony" is not a polite word today, but here, used with due respect, it is the only word that fits.

China's frontier with Laos and Vietnam was drawn to accommodate French imperialism. It runs through populations of whom some, on the Chinese side, are not yet fully integrated into the Chinese polity (a few speak languages that are classified as Mon-Khmer or Thai), while on the Laos-Vietnam side there are, besides ethnic Chinese elements, many who have been affected, to different degrees, by the Chinese culture, the Chinese outlook. It is therefore silly (though fashionable) to reduce the political cross-currents of that part of the world to "the historic hatred of the Vietnamese for the Chinese."

It is particularly silly because Ho Chi Minh, in creating the Indochinese Communist movement, was acutely sensitive to French colonial policy, which encouraged distrust among North and South Vietnamese, Laotians, Kampucheans and mountain tribal minorities. To counter colonial imperialism, he worked for the maximum of unity. He left an important legacy—hard to measure, but vitally important. When the appalling Kissinger-Nixon policy devastated Kampuchea and installed Lon Nol as trusty, and then Kissinger-Nixon-Westmoreland skedaddled, abandoning Kampuchea altogether, they left it open not to a Communist revolution but to a medieval *Jacquerie*. The Kampuchean peasantry were like a well-bred, gentle dog that has been ordered to do this, ordered to do that, kicked, beaten, cursed until it turns not just savage but crazily savage. Pol Pot is just one man, a brutal killer, but a brutal killer produced by an American-made situation.

In such a situation there are bound to be a few survivors of the old Ho Chi Minh revolutionary movement. Would not such men, faced with more than they can handle in tragically rent and torn Kampuchea, be likely to remember old revolutionary comrades in Vietnam, with whom they once worked and whom they learned to trust, and ask them for help? Obviously, no single factor like this could explain all the tangled elements that confront one another in Indochina; but it is better than assuming that the only Kampucheans working with the Vietnamese are "puppets," "proxies," "surrogates." To believe that is to resign oneself to a C.I.A. level of intelligence. (Although, of course, to report that is the way to get promoted.)

And the Russians? The first thing to do is to drop the childish, cops-and-robbers notion that the Soviets (here I prefer "Soviets" to "Russians," because the Soviet Union is a multinational state, and one in which the non-Russian nationalities are multiplying faster than the Russians) operate only through sinister agents who bemuse dimwitted Asians and use them as the cannon fodder of a new imperialism. Soviet policy today is obviously, sometimes a bit puzzlingly, cautious. They seem to act only when they feel that there is a sizable element of the population (something more than a clique or a faction) that will not crumble if supported. Moreover, they also often restrain, or counsel restraint. They pulled out of Somalia when they thought the Somalis were going too far. And when the tide is running against them, they have a knack of pulling out before getting mired down that might even be envied by American supporters of Diems, Lon Nols, Shahs—and who next?

WAR TALK IN PEKING[4]

What does a journalist do when he's in another town and wants to get the feel of things? He looks up some local journalists. That is what I did when I arrived in Peking last month, as a relatively new hand in China (I was here in 1976), just as the Vietnamese border situation was ready to blow. I rode around the city with them in small China-made cars, ate with them (food quality as high as ever) and talked for hours about the changes taking place in every area of life and work. Mainly I inquired about Vietnam.

My Chinese journalists have a composite anonymity in this story. They preferred not to be mentioned by name, not because they were worried about talking with me (everyone is talking in Peking these days) but because they have a modesty not characteristic of many of their American coun-

[4] Article by James Aronson, professor of communications, Hunter College; Peking correspondent. *Nation.* 228:328–30. Mr. 31, '79. © 1979 by the Nation Associates, Inc. Reprinted by permission.

terparts. But if they took their persons off the record, what they had to say was not, and it may help to place the China-Vietnam dispute in perspective. It conveys, without any editorial intrusion on my part, China's point of view—a synthesis of the talk in Peking.

War is very much on their minds, but not the one with Vietnam. Rather, they are concerned about the "sharper and sharper conflict between the two superpowers." They see war as practically inevitable—"so long as imperialism exists"—between the United States and the Soviet Union. But, contrary to what many in the West believe, they do not and would not welcome it.

They believe that the best way for the world to block a new war is through an understanding of Mao Zedong's [Tse-tung] Three Worlds theory. According to this theory, when capitalism developed into imperialism, and divisions and defeats occurred among the imperialists, a "Second World" of capitalist and has-been imperialist countries took form. Among them are Japan, Britain, France, Belgium, Australia and Canada. Add the underdeveloped and developing countries (the Third World) and you have Chairman Mao's Three Worlds.

But even among the remaining imperialist countries there are divisions, and these should be encouraged. "We must distinguish," the Chinese say, "between the United States and the Soviet Union even though they are both superpowers, whatever else we may call them. At least one (the United States) is willing to say that it is opposed to hegemonism. The United States, however, is in a defensive position, and the main threat of war lies with the Soviet Union. The people of the world should unite and deal with this threat."

How? They do not spell it out. They are determined not to tell other nations how to shape their policies; but they do say that when the people of the world "fully understand the danger," they will join with China in seeking to isolate and contain it at its source—both the "larger hegemonist" on the world scene (the Soviet Union) and the "regional hegemonist" on the Southeast Asian scene (Vietnam). This was Mao's view, they say: "One line, one front." And it formed the "strategic basis" of Vice Premier Deng Xiaoping's [Teng Hsiao-ping] visit to the United States. The Chinese believe that the theory is "scientific and sound."

Why do the Chinese feel that the United States and the Soviet Union are on a collision course to war? Their response bristles with statistics: "Despite the SALT talks, the supply of nuclear bombs has not decreased. On the contrary, in the last years the United States has doubled its stockpile, and the Soviet supply has gone up five times. But the question of nuclear weapons now is one of quality, not quantity. The two superpowers are in a struggle to the death. They discuss these lethal weapons endlessly and haggle over details. Each side seeks to restrict the other, but neither side will get what it wants. What difference does it make if a plane carries twenty or eighty weapons? The talks are ineffectual. Both sides see this but seem impelled to go on. Meanwhile, there are absolutely no restrictions on conventional weapons."

The Soviet Union and the United States, the Chinese believe, have placed Europe at the top of the strategic list. There has been "no relaxation of vigilance by either side in Europe for thirty-three years." The basic difference, however, is that the Soviet Union is "strengthening its ability for sudden attack," while the United States is stepping up its defenses: "Once something stirs in Europe, war will burst." But, they caution, "it may not happen there." They elaborate on this theory with a long list of allegations about Soviet activity around the world:

In northeast Afghanistan, the Soviet Union is increasing its strength. . . . Its Pacific fleet has increased to 440 ships (the United States has fifty). . . . Its control reaches all the way down to the Indian Ocean. . . . There's the question of Chad. . . . In January and February of last year there was Somalia. . . . In April there was Yemen—both countries lost their heads of state by assassination, and the border war followed.

And now Japan, which faces a grave threat, and the dispute over the islands. We cannot exclude Moscow starting something if the conditions are right. It is necessary for Japan to maintain its defensive alliance with the United States. The Japanese could lose their country. You feel that sounds too exaggerated? Then what about Kampuchea? We know what occupation means, and we are prepared to ally ourselves with anyone willing to resist this great arc of danger.

The Chinese charge that the Soviet Union's strategy calls for fomenting unstable internal conditions. "Its methods are ruthless—murder, sabotage and treachery to achieve its aims. The C.I.A. was small potatoes compared with the K.G.B. Anyone who shows the slightest sign of independence is to be gotten rid of. They make use of mercenaries from dependent countries to serve their purposes."

In Peking the references to Cuba are not oblique. They give short shrift to the idea that the Cubans are in Africa of their own free will, out of a sense of solidarity with (for many Cubans) their African ancestors: "The Cubans are lackeys fed and led by the Soviet Union. The Russians buy half the crop of Cuban sugar at four times the world market price—28 cents rather than 7 cents. With a population of nine million, Cuba has 40,000 to 50,000 of its troops abroad —one-fourth of its armed forces. The Cubans are selling their labor and their lives to the Soviet imperialists."

Finally, in chronological fashion, the talk reaches Vietnam. For Americans who were deeply involved for ten years or more in the resistance to the war in Vietnam, it is difficult—sometimes impossible—to cast Vietnam in the role of enemy—anyone's enemy. But in Peking the view, based on the record as they present it, is different. Vietnam, the Chinese say, has become an *agent provocateur*. They dismiss the "traditional" hostility between the Vietnamese and the Chinese as a convenient ploy for pseudohistorians and lazy journalists. Of course imperial China did terrible things to the Vietnamese, they agree, "but they are not dealing with imperial China any longer—this is the People's Republic of China." They note that Premier Zhou Enlai [Chou En-lai] even apologized in person in Hanoi for crimes 2,000 years old, "but the Vietnamese go right on memorializing these events."

Having said this, the Chinese add that Vietnamese animosity did not rise suddenly in the last year or two; it was there "even when they were under siege by the United States imperialists. But we ignored that and helped them anyway." After the Vietnamese victory in 1975, the Chinese say, relations became worse. They speak of this with a sense of hurt, as though a member of the family had turned renegade. They note that China helped the Vietnamese liberation movement to the tune of $8 billion, "when our own people went without necessities so we could assist them in their struggle." They express no regret for the help given: "It was a just struggle."

They concede there are disputed areas at the border, and contend that China has offered repeatedly to negotiate—despite innumerable border violations by the Vietnamese—but, they insist, the Vietnamese have refused to discuss the problem. They note that 200,000 Chinese have left Vietnam since last April—driven out, they say. Who drove them out? "They blame us, but surely we could not drive people out of Vietnam; that would be impossible."

My Chinese journalist friends portray the Vietnamese leadership as "rascals, political hoodlums in the international arena . . . sticking up their tails and proclaiming they have the third greatest military machine in the world." They are, however, conscious of Vietnam's military strength and capability, given its store of American, Soviet and even Chinese weapons—the last, the journalists tell me, used against their former allies in the border fighting. What about the Vietnamese charges of Chinese aggrandizement? They hoot in derision: "Who are they to talk? They have taken over Laos, swallowed Kampuchea and pose a threat to all Southeast Asia. We don't want an inch of their territory. All we want is for them to stop behaving like rascals."

Then, finally, back to the larger picture: "If we allow the Soviet Union, Cuba and Vietnam to control strategic points, conditions for world war would become ripe. If we oppose it, we push back the threat of war." Clearly, in their view, the Vietnam action fell into this category. It was a delaying action. To them Kumpuchea was not only an outrage but will ultimately be a "quagmire" for Vietnam. They see the Russians with fewer and fewer friends around the world because of increasing suspicion about Soviet intentions. And what about the United States?

"During the recent period," they say, "China and the United States have normalized relations, and since Vice Premier Deng's visit, there has been a quickening of normalization. It is of tremendous importance. The thirty years of hostility were a historical mistake."

The new American hand in China, an old hand in America in the battle against the cold war, digests that. Aloud he asks whether, as so many friends of China in the United States feel, the new trade agreements do not pose a peril to the Chinese revolution. Smiles and a small pause. Then: "We have not forgotten our own experience of imperialism. But this is not the old China. We are a poor country and we must modernize for the sake of our own people. Of course there are risks, but they must be taken. And remember, there is a distinction between modernization and Westernization."

This is said without challenge or bravado, but with a determination which is eloquent. That same sense of quiet determination pervades the atmosphere of Peking. I find that everyone talks about Vietnam but there is no crisis mood. Crowds flock to see Chaplin in *Modern Times* as well as to the Peking Opera where the Monkey King conquers the White-Boned Devil (who bears an interesting resemblance to Mao's widow, Jiang Qing [Chiang-Ch'ing]).

To those concerned about the corruption of China's great traditions, I can report no McDonald's in the environs of Tian An Men, but I did have a superb Peking duck at the Peking Roast Duck Restaurant in Liu Li Chang. I did have a Coke—my first in ten years—but I had to cross into American territory to get it. The day the Liaison Office turned into an Embassy, our hosts served Coke and cookies. I can easily wait another ten years.

CHINA LOOSENS GRIP ON MINORITIES[5]

The tall, brawny Tibetan, silver dagger dangling from his belt, throws himself on the floor of the Jokang Temple before the image of the Buddhist goddess of mercy. Clutching his prayer beads in one hand, he murmurs his prayers and then rises, only to prostrate himself again for more prayers.

Such scenes in the temples of this Buddhist holy city have become commonplace again this year, after two decades of religious and ethnic suppression by the Peking government. After 1959, when the Dalai Lama fled to India with 100,000 Buddhist followers, the suppression of religion in Tibet increased to the point that some temples and monasteries were destroyed and Tibetan Buddhists were persecuted for even carrying prayer beads. The five-star national flag replaced the prayer flags that used to fly from Lhasa's rooftops.

Now, as the scene in Jokang Temple indicates, the Peking government has been easing its restrictive policies toward ethnic minorities. The turnabout is part of the government's drive for a united domestic front to promote economic modernization and social stability.

Victims of Radicalism

Because of their religious beliefs and traditions, members of China's ethnic minorities were among the major victims of the radicalism that led to the Cultural Revolution of 1966. Although the "minority nationalities," as Peking calls them, account for only 6 percent of China's 960 million people, they occupy more than half the land area, in-

[5] Article entitled "Tibetans' Observance of Buddhism Returns After Long Repression," by Frank Ching, Peking correspondent. *Wall Street Journal.* p 1+. Ag. 22, '79. Reprinted by permission of the Wall Street Journal, © Dow Jones & Company, Inc. 1979. All rights reserved.

cluding strategic and mineral-rich regions bordering the Soviet Union, India, Mongolia and Vietnam.

Besides Tibetans, China has 54 other ethnic minorities, ranging from the Heches in Heilungkiang, who number under 1,000, to the Chuangs in Kwangsi, who are 12 million strong. In June, after two years of study by Chinese ethnological specialists, the Jinuo people in Yunnan Province were officially recognized as a separate minority.

China's moderation of its policies toward the ethnic minorities began after the purge of the so-called Gang of Four in 1976. The old regime now is said to have violated the Communist Party's policy of respecting the cultural heritage and religious beliefs of all nationalities.

While Peking's rule over Tibet and other minority areas remains much firmer than it was 20 years ago, a new tolerance is clearly exhibited towards their customs and religious practices. Members of minorities also are being trained as officials and administrators.

Small Chinese Population

The changes are more noticeable in Tibet than elsewhere in China because the population here is relatively cohesive, with a separate language, religion and tradition. Hans, or ethnic Chinese, account for only about 6 percent of Tibet's 1.7 million people.

Although few people here are willing to discuss the political changes openly, most are silently accepting the new freedom with the same stoicism that they accepted the former curbs. Many are again fingering their prayer beads on the streets, as well as worshiping in the temples.

The change in government policy became evident earlier this year. In March, it was announced that Jokang Temple, Tibet's holiest, and that the two largest monasteries were being reopened to the public. Since the flight of the Dalai Lama, Tibet's 2,700 monasteries have been reduced to about 10 and the number of monks has declined from 100,000 to 2,000. As far as can be determined, no young men have entered the monkhood since 1959.

Before some temples and monasteries could be reopened this year, about $500,000 was spent on repairs to buildings, relics and murals damaged or destroyed in the Cultural Revolution. But the ruins of other temples can still be seen on hilltops around Lhasa. A small cave-temple on Yaowangshan, or "Medicine King Hill," is almost inaccessible but can be reached by climbing the rocky slope. Inside, the faces of dozens of statues have been gouged out, and paint has been splashed over others. The temple is deserted, but a blackened depression at the base of the main statue indicates there have been recent offerings.

In another conciliatory move in March, the government released the last 376 prisoners who took part in the rebellion that led to the Dalai Lama's fleeing the country in 1959. And in April, the government announced that 2,300 Tibetans would be paid a total of $5 million to complete reparations for estates taken over in 1959.

Now, government officials in Tibet are saying that the Dalai Lama and all other Tibetans living in exile, mostly in India and Switzerland, are welcome to return.

"We welcome compatriots abroad, including the Dalai Lama," says Raidi, a Tibetan who is deputy head of the regional government. "A long separation from home isn't a good thing. It is up to him to decide. If he wants to come and take a look and leave again, that is all right. If he wants to stay, it can certainly be considered."

Although the Dalai Lama, now 45 years old, has recently emerged from his citadel in northern India and is planning a trip to the U.S. next month, it is far from clear that he considers China's political climate warm enough for his return to Tibet. His return, for one thing, could be taken as a tacit endorsement of the Peking government's policies. And the government, however liberal it may profess to be, still has its limits.

It may ultimately be unwilling, for example, to permit a new generation of lamas, or monks. The official government position is that young Tibetans aren't interested in becoming lamas. Indeed, the few lamas at the remaining monasteries appear to consider the end of lamaism inevitable. "If young men don't want to become lamas, lamaism will vanish," says Losang Pingchu, the 61-year-old head lama at Jokang Temple.

The government has organized classes for the remaining lamas to study Marxism-Leninism and the works of Mao Tse-tung. Gandunjiacuo, the lama in charge of spiritual work at Drepung Monastery, said to be the world's largest monastery, tells visiting reporters that "in the final analysis, materialism will triumph over religion." While he still believes in Buddhism and reads the sutras, he says, he now feels that Marxism-Leninism embodies "the truth."

Although the lamas theoretically administer the monasteries, the government actually controls the monasteries and allocates about $1.5 million a year for their upkeep.

Religion in Other Areas

It isn't only in Tibet that China's new accommodation to religion is evident. Ningxia, in Northwest China, recently reopened 158 mosques so that the Hui people, who are predominantly Moslem, can practice their religion. Churches, mosques and temples are being reopened in Canton. And a Chinese delegation consisting of Buddhists, Christians and Moslems . . . [took] part in an international conference on religion and peace scheduled for Princeton, N.J., starting August 29.

In Tibet and elsewhere, ethnic minorities have been exempt from the government's birth-control campaign—and the Tibetan population increase has outpaced that of China as a whole. There are 1.6 million Tibetans in Tibet today, up 440,000 from 1949. Over the past 200 years, Tibet's population is said to have dropped by six million, largely because so many young men in earlier years chose the monastic life, which was economically secure.

The Chinese government is currently taking a firm hand in trying to develop Tibet and other minority areas. It has increased state subsidies and investments in the areas and is allocating more resources, manpower and technical support for development of such things as minerals and industry.

Gains in Education

Impressive gains have been made in education here in recent years. (Tibetan textbooks are used in schools, and Chinese is taught as a second language.) A rise in literacy is reflected at the Tibet Daily newspaper, which has a circulation of 38,000 today, up from 5,400 in 1964.

According to Mr. Raidi, the deputy in the regional government, 65 percent of the government's cadres, from the commune level up, are Tibetans. The rest are ethnic Chinese, whose representation in the government, however, is still disproportionately large.

Animosity between the Tibetans and Chinese is still evident here. "They are an ignorant lot," a Shanghai technician says of his Tibetan co-workers. "They not only can't read Chinese, many of them don't even know Tibetan." He acknowledged, however, that some Tibetans at his wool-spinning mill spoke the Shanghai dialect as well as Mandarin, the official Chinese dialect. He himself, after 13 years in Tibet, spoke no Tibetan.

II. THE U.S. AND CHINA

EDITOR'S INTRODUCTION

Normalization of relations between the United States and China, although thought by many to be long overdue, has generated a great deal of controversy, most of it centered on the abrogation of our treaty commitments to Taiwan.

Harry Harding, in a selection from his book, *China and the U.S., Normalization and Beyond,* examines the benefits and drawbacks of normalization from both the Chinese and American viewpoint. In the second selection, Terry Lautz provides historical details concerning Taiwan, from his book, *Asia: Half the Human Race.* The next three articles are all critical of the government's handling of the Taiwan issue. Robert Elegant, writing in *National Review,* is concerned that Taiwan might turn to the U.S.S.R. as an ally, while George Will, in an article from the Washington *Post,* believes we paid too high a price in concessions to the Chinese. Peter Kovler's article in *Commonweal* is critical of our attitude toward Vietnam and the Chinese invasion.

The last article, by a former deputy assistant secretary of state, discusses the new weight that the China relationship might bring to the balance of military power between Russia and the United States.

NORMALIZATION AND BEYOND[1]

Suddenly and dramatically, on December 15, 1978, President Jimmy Carter announced the normalization of rela-

[1] Excerpt from book entitled *China and the U.S., Normalization and Beyond,* by Harry Harding Jr., associate of the China Council of the Asia Society and consultant to the Rand Corporation; recently back from China. Foreign Policy Association. '79. Reprinted by permission.

tions with the People's Republic of China (PRC). The President revealed that the United States would recognize Peking as the sole legal government of China on January 1, 1979, and would establish an embassy in Peking on March 1. At the same time, the President disclosed that the United States would end formal relations with the Republic of China on Taiwan at the beginning of 1979 and would terminate its mutual defense treaty with the island at the beginning of 1980.

The administration's agreement with China met with a wide range of reaction in Congress and among the American people. Senator Frank Church, Democrat of Idaho and now chairman of the Senate Foreign Relations Committee, described it as a "gutsy, courageous decision." George Bush, former director of Central Intelligence, chairman of the Republican National Committee and once U.S. representative in Peking, responded that Mr. Carter's initiative "has not only diminished American credibility in the world but has also darkened the prospects for peace." U.S.–China relations have become once again the subject of lively debate and discussion. . . .

China Policy in Context

. . . Since the death of Chairman Mao Tse-tung in September 1976 and the purge of the radical Gang of Four one month later, China's new leaders have launched an all-out effort to modernize the country by the end of the century. After much discussion and debate, the Central Committee of the Chinese Communist party decided in December 1978 to endorse this plan and to subordinate most other political activity to it. As stated in an editorial in the authoritative *People's Daily* on December 25, 1978, "there must be no 'political movement' or 'class struggle' which deviates from this central task and damages modernization."

The changes in Chinese society produced by the modernization program have been nothing short of breathtaking. New leaders, committed to modernization, have assumed office at both the central and provincial levels. Most of the egalitarian programs in education and science that Mao promoted during the Cultural Revolution have been dismantled. Policy toward industrial management and economic planning has been substantially transformed. And, in a development that could be of major significance, some Chinese have begun to discuss the need for increased civil rights and greater political democracy. At the same time, China's leaders have also decided that extensive economic, scientific, and educational relations with the United States, as well as with Western Europe and Japan, will be indispensable to the modernization effort.

These domestic developments in China pose opportunities for the United States, but they also present us with many uncertainties and potential dangers. On the one hand, China's determination to modernize its civilian economy and its armed forces suggests that, for good or ill, China will play an increasingly active role in international and regional affairs in the decades to come. Good relations with such an emerging China would therefore be of obvious benefit to the United States. Conversely, if this modernization trend continues, China will be a more formidable adversary should Sino–American relations deteriorate.

On the other hand, the rapid pace of domestic change in China, viewed in the context of the past century of internal instability, raises the possibility that the dramatic developments of the last two years may be reversed. The departures from the policies and principles of the Cultural Revolution, and from the ideological legacy of Mao Tse-tung, may well arouse opposition from some segments of the Chinese people, as well as within the Communist party. China's new program of rapid modernization will undoubtedly benefit some sectors of society more than others and produce rising expectations that cannot be met. The advanced age of Vice Premier Teng Hsiao-ping (born in 1904), the principal architect of China's modernization drive, and of some of China's other economic planners, makes it almost certain that China will have to pass through another period of leadership succession in a few years' time.

U.S. POLICY IN TRANSITION: DIFFICULT CHOICES

Just as China is changing, so too is the United States. Over the last several years there has been an increasing demand for reformulating America's relations with the rest of the world. Neither the anticommunism of the Cold War nor the Soviet–American détente of the late 1960s and early 1970s seems to provide a sufficient basis for American foreign policy in the post-Vietnam era. While most observers agree that there can be no single "grand design" that will supply the answers to all foreign policy issues, there still seems to be a widely felt need for organizing principles that will provide consistency for American foreign policy, justify American actions abroad, and gain the necessary support from the American people. Our policy toward China, therefore, cannot be considered in isolation from this broader foreign policy framework. One meaning of "normalization," in fact, is that whatever organizing principles we choose as the foundation of our foreign policy must now be applied to China.

The tension between idealism and realism has complicated the search for a new framework for American foreign policy. One of the most controversial aspects of the Carter Administration has been the President's determination to give greater attention to broad moral purposes in American foreign relations. Thus, the promotion of international human rights has been declared to be one of the most important foreign policy goals of the Carter Administration. So has the limitation of the arms race—not only of nuclear weapons, but also of the transfer of conventional armaments around the globe. Critics have frequently responded that these goals are lofty and noble, but that they sometimes conflict with the more immediate security interests of the United States. At times, they point out, American security requires that we maintain good relations with authoritarian governments, or that we undertake to strengthen the military forces of our allies.

These dilemmas will be particularly sharp with respect to China. Do our interests lie in promoting a modern and prosperous China, which would warrant our granting Peking substantial economic and technological assistance? Or do violations of human rights in China require the United States to take a more critical and distant stance toward Peking? Do the security of China and the global balance of power suggest that the United States should contribute to the modernization of the Chinese armed forces? Or would such a policy be inconsistent with our attempts to restrict the global arms race? China, in short, may be another instance in which the American government, and the American people, will have to make difficult choices among conflicting interests and goals in foreign affairs.

ASIA: POTENTIAL CONFLICTS

The new Sino–American relationship must also be seen in the regional context. Both sides now have extensive parallel interests in Asia. The Carter Administration has said that it wants China to be stable, strong, and secure. China wishes the United States to remain involved in Asian affairs. Neither wishes the Soviet Union, or any other country, to establish domination—or, as the Chinese call it, "hegemony"—over Asia.

But beyond these parallel interests, there are significant differences between Chinese and American policy in the Asian–Pacific region. In Southeast Asia, although both countries support the emergence of a strong association of non-Communist states in the form of the Association of Southeast Asian Nations (ASEAN), whose members are Indonesia, Malaysia, Philippines, Singapore, and Thailand, the PRC appears more hostile toward Vietnam than the United States. Along the oil-rich coast, China has offshore territorial disputes not only with Vietnam but also with Japan, the Philippines and South Korea, raising the possibility that the United States might some day have to choose sides between China and one or more of our traditional Asian allies. On the Korean peninsula, although both Peking and Washington have a common interest in avoiding another outbreak of war, they remain closely linked to opposite sides in the dispute. Perhaps most important, China and the United States still have different interests with regard to Taiwan. It would be naive to assume, therefore, that Chinese and American interests in Asia are congruent. Important differences of principle and emphasis remain, and may become more apparent in the post-normalization era. The task will be to manage and, if possible, resolve the differences while building on the similarities.

DÉTENTE AND THE GLOBAL BALANCE

Finally, U.S.–China relations must also be placed in the context of the global balance between the United States and the Soviet Union. For the past several years, Washington has been committed to a policy of détente with Moscow and has sought areas of cooperation wherever possible. But China's view of the Soviet Union is considerably different, describing it as a "hegemonic" nation seeking world domination, criticizing any action which might be considered "appeasement" of Moscow, and calling for an international united front to resist Soviet expansion wherever it occurs.

In the view of some analysts, the Sino–Soviet dispute gives the United States the advantage of being able to play Peking against Moscow in order to gain the greatest possible leverage over both. But the strained relations between China and the Soviet Union also place the United States in an awkward position at times. To cooperate with China in opposing Soviet "social imperialism" would arouse Soviet fears of encirclement, and would almost certainly damage Soviet–American relations. Indeed, Moscow has already warned the United States in the strongest possible terms against joining China in an "anti-Soviet axis." Yet whenever Washington pursues détente with the Soviets, Peking denounces the United States for engaging in "appeasement" of Moscow.

Thus, any improvement in American relations with one Communist power is likely to arouse suspicion and concern on the part of the other. It may be true, as some officials of the Carter Administration have pointed out, that the United States no longer has to choose between China and Japan in formulating its Asian policy. But this regional dilemma may simply have been replaced by a knottier problem on a global scale: will it be necessary to choose between China and the Soviet Union, or will it be possible to maintain good relations with both? . . .

Normalization

In its unilateral statement, issued at the time of the normalization of Sino–American relations, the Chinese government pointed out that "The question of Taiwan was the crucial issue obstructing the normalization of relations between China and the United States." Peking's analysis was correct. Any assessment of normalization must therefore begin with a brief history of the relationship between the United States and the Nationalist Chinese government on Taiwan, and then examine the ways in which the Carter Administration has decided to alter that relationship.

In 1949, when the Nationalists fled the mainland and established their capital on Taiwan, the United States continued to recognize them as the legitimate government of all China and spurned the Chinese Communists' overtures to establish diplomatic relations. While continuing its economic aid to Taiwan, however, the United States refused to provide the Nationalists with military assistance in their struggle with the Communists. In President Harry S. Truman's words, the United States had decided not to "pursue a course which will lead to involvement in the civil conflict in China."

The outbreak of the Korean war led the United States to change course. In June 1950, President Truman interposed the Seventh Fleet in the Taiwan Strait, both to prevent a Communist invasion of Taiwan and to discourage the Nationalists from an assault on the mainland. Four years later, during the Eisenhower Administration, the United States signed a mutual defense treaty with the Nationalist government and thereby assumed a formal commitment to defend Taiwan. In a long series of ambassadorial discussions in Geneva in the mid-1950s, Washington tried unsuccessfully to persuade Peking to renounce the use of force in dealing with Taiwan. In fact, the United States provided extensive military assistance in 1955 and again in 1958 to help Taiwan defend the small offshore islands of Quemoy and Matsu against the threat of a Communist attack.

Despite occasional initiatives by both sides, relations between Peking and Washington remained deadlocked through the 1950s and 1960s. Then, in the early 1970s, both countries came to recognize the advantages of rapprochement. President Richard M. Nixon believed that improved relations with China could prod Moscow further toward détente, and could even help extricate the United States from the Vietnam war. Mao Tse-tung and Premier Chou En-lai, for their part, believed that an opening to Washington could strengthen China's position against the Soviet Union, with whom relations had seriously deteriorated in the late 1960s. The new common ground between Peking and Washington was symbolized by President Nixon's trip to China in February 1972, and by the joint communiqué signed in Shanghai at the end of the President's visit.

The Process of Normalization

Besides indicating that China and the United States had similar views on a number of international issues, the Shanghai communiqué also committed both countries to full normalization of diplomatic relations. To facilitate this, both sides made important compromises on the Taiwan question. In the Shanghai communiqué, for example, the United States pledged that it would eventually withdraw all its military forces from Taiwan, as long as there was the prospect of a peaceful solution of the Taiwan question. A year later, in 1973, the PRC and the United States agreed to establish liaison offices even while Washington maintained formal diplomatic relations with Taipei. But Washington and Peking could still not agree on two remaining issues:

the future of the mutual defense treaty between the United States and Taiwan and the disposition of the American embassy in Taipei. Full normalization of relations, therefore, was not immediately achieved.

Over time, the PRC made clear its conditions for establishing diplomatic relations with other countries. Foreigners could continue to have unofficial economic and cultural relations with Taiwan, but foreign governments would have to recognize Peking as the sole legal government of China. When applied to the United States, these general conditions had specific implications. The United States would have to (1) end diplomatic relations with Taiwan, (2) terminate its mutual defense treaty with the Nationalist government, and (3) withdraw all its troops and military installations from Taiwan. Debate over China policy in the United States promptly focused on whether or not the three Chinese principles could form the basis of an agreement.

China and the United States conducted intensive negotiations over normalization between September and December 1978. The final agreement was embodied in three documents, all released on December 15–16: a joint communiqué by Washington and Peking, a unilateral statement by the Chinese government, and a unilateral statement by the United States. Further details were provided in Chairman Hua Kuo-feng's remarks at a Peking press conference, President Carter's address to the nation on December 15, and background briefings by American government officials. Together, these indicated that the Carter Administration had accepted China's three principles for normalization. But the United States had also insisted on, and obtained, significant concessions from Peking.

Ending diplomatic relations. The United States agreed that the American embassy in Taipei and the Chinese Nationalist embassy in Washington would both be closed. Moreover, Washington agreed that its continuing commercial and cultural relations with Taiwan would be maintained "without official government representation" on the island. But the Carter Administration also announced plans to establish an unofficial agency on Taiwan that would be able to perform most of the functions of an embassy, and to permit Taiwan to establish a similar organization in Washington. Presumably, these agencies will be modeled after those which Japan and Taiwan established after they severed formal diplomatic relations in late 1972.

Terminating the defense treaty. In establishing normal diplomatic relations with Peking, the United States agreed to terminate its mutual defense treaty with Taiwan. But it insisted, in accordance with the provisions of the treaty, that Taipei be given one year's notice. The treaty will therefore remain in effect until January 1, 1980.

Even though the defense treaty will be terminated, Washington expressed its continued "interest in the peaceful resolution of the Taiwan issue. . . ." It stated that "the United States is confident that the people of Taiwan face a peaceful and prosperous future . . . and expects that the Taiwan issue will be settled peacefully by the Chinese themselves." While the PRC's unilateral statement continued to insist that the resolution of the Taiwan issue "is entirely China's internal affair," and while Peking did not renounce the use of force in dealing with Taiwan, the administration argued that Peking made two important concessions. First, the Chinese refrained from taking any exception to Washington's statement about expecting a peaceful solution of the Taiwan question; and second, they referred to the "reunification" of Taiwan and the mainland, rather than using the more militant term, the "liberation" of the island.

Withdrawal of American troops. Withdrawal of the remaining American military forces from Taiwan was always the least controversial of the three Chinese terms for normalization, for the troops had long since ceased to be essential to the island's defense. The Carter Administration's agreement to withdraw the remaining personnel—some 700 advisers and support troops—within four months therefore surprised no one.

The administration's principal achievement was its insistence on continuing to sell defensive arms to Taiwan. The Chinese formally objected to this American decision. In his press conference in Peking on December 16, Chairman Hua Kuo-feng, in response to a question, said that a continuing military relationship between Washington and Taipei "does not conform to the principles of normalization, is detrimental to a peaceful settlement of the Taiwan question, and will exercise unfavorable influence on security and stability in the Asia–Pacific region." But Hua went on to say that disagreement on this point would not prevent normalization of Sino–American relations. In Hua's words, "The two sides had differing views, but nevertheless, the joint communiqué was reached."

It was later revealed that the question of arms sales to Taiwan had, in fact, been the main sticking point in the discussions between Washington and Peking. Hua's remarks indicate that the two sides simply "agreed to disagree" on this issue. But, by so doing, the Chinese tacitly acquiesced to an important American demand.

THE GREAT DEBATE: THREE ISSUES

The announcement of the normalization decision aroused immediate controversy. In view of the long debate over China policy in the United States, this was not surprising. Congressional reaction varied. Some members of Congress, among them Senate Minority Leader Howard H. Baker, Jr. (R–Tenn.), described it as the betrayal of an old friend: "The Taiwanese have been a good and faithful ally, and we certainly owe them more than this." Others supported the President's initiative. Senator Alan Cranston (D–Cal.), for example, called it a "very positive step toward world peace." Public response to normalization was also mixed, and perhaps somewhat inconsistent. According to a New York *Times*/CBS poll, 45 percent of the American public opposed the President's decision to break diplomatic relations with Taiwan, while 32 percent supported the move. At the same time, the public opposed, by 58 percent to 26 percent, the administration's decision to continue arms sales to Taiwan. Mail received by the State Department, on the other hand, overwhelmingly supported continued military sales.

In essence, the debate over normalization has involved three separate issues:

(1) *Was the decision made after adequate consultation with the Congress?* In July 1978, by a vote of 94 to 0, the Senate adopted an amendment requesting that it be consulted prior to any change in American relations with Taiwan. Many members of Congress, even those who supported the terms of the normalization agreement, charged that they were not adequately consulted in advance of the President's decision and complained that normalization was announced while Congress was in recess and most members were away. Still other congressmen have claimed that the President had no legal authority to terminate the mutual defense treaty with Taiwan without obtaining congressional approval. Charging Mr. Carter with "an outright abuse of presidential power," Senator Barry Goldwater (R–Ariz.) and several other members of Congress have filed suit in federal court, challenging the President's right to terminate a treaty without approval by two-thirds of the Senate [Carter's action was affirmed by Court of Appeals, 11/30/79].

In response, the administration's supporters have argued that the President acted both legally and responsibly. The administration insists that there is ample precedent for a President to terminate a treaty without receiving the consent of Congress. And, more generally, it claims that its consultation with Congress was adequate under the circumstances. In an interview with Walter Cronkite a few days after normalization was announced, President Carter pointed out that he had had regular discussions with individual congressmen on China policy ever since coming to office, and that he therefore had a good understanding of congressional opinion on the question. Some observers outside the administration have expressed agreement with the President. Hugh Sidey of *Time* magazine has called the

China decision a "textbook model" of how a President
should balance the need for congressional consultations
with the need for private diplomacy. "In fact," Sidey says,
"several members of Congress were consulted in an ambiguous manner that did not reveal the negotiations." This enabled the President to proceed toward normalization "with
[congressional] assistance but with no extraneous obstruc-
tions." But lingering congressional resentment may still
complicate the administration's effort to obtain legislative
support of its new policy toward China and Taiwan.

(2) *Did the United States get the best possible terms
from the Chinese?* Some say that it did, pointing out that it
would be unrealistic to expect the Chinese to abandon any
of their three terms for normalization, or to publicly renounce the use of force in dealing with Taiwan. In the
words of Harvard University's Benjamin Schwartz, "We
could have held out, but I doubt that China would ever
openly say that it was going to assure the security of
Taiwan."

Other observers, however, raise questions concerning
the details of the normalization package. Some have asked
why the United States now "acknowledges the Chinese
position" that Taiwan is part of China, when, in the Shanghai communiqué, the United States stated only that it "does
not challenge" the Chinese view. Others have wondered
why the United States could not have maintained some
kind of official representation in Taipei, comparable to the
liaison office which existed in Peking prior to normalization. And still others have noted that the Chinese did not
repeat their preference for a peaceful solution of the
Taiwan issue in either the joint communiqué or their unilateral statement. As Senator Dale Bumpers (D–Ark.) said,
"It made me wonder how much the President left on the
negotiating table."

(3) *Even if the Carter Administration did get the best
available terms from Peking, are they terms that the United
States should have accepted?* This, of course, is the crucial
question. Did the broader national interest justify the com-

promises that the Carter Administration judged necessary to achieve normalization at this time? Is it true, as the President argued, that normalization would "enhance the stability of Asia," but would not "jeopardize the well-being of the people of Taiwan"?

Opponents of the administration's decision insist that the costs of normalization are simply too great, both for Taiwan and for the United States. Some critics say that the United States should not have agreed to normalize its relations with Peking unless it could retain its defense treaty with Taiwan, or else receive binding assurances that Peking had renounced the use of force in dealing with the island. Still others hold that the United States should have insisted on maintaining full diplomatic relations with Taiwan even after recognizing Peking. Despite the administration's insistence that it would have been impossible to normalize relations with China on such terms, these critics claim that the United States gave up too much. As one observer put it, "We forgot that we held most of the trump cards and that we could both obtain the kind of agreement needed to preserve Taiwan's security and yet proceed in a more important relationship with Peking."

Some critics also argue that the administration's decision has cast doubt on America's willingness to defend other allies, including Israel. In the words of Senator Barry Goldwater, "The President called into question this nation's treaty credibility throughout the world." Or, as John B. Oakes, former senior editor of the New York *Times,* complained, "President Carter has seriously undermined American pretensions to be the moral leader of the world and an exemplar of constancy and faithfulness to our friends."

THE ADMINISTRATION'S CASE

Supporters of the administration, in contrast, argue that the United States has obtained important benefits from normalization while fulfilling its commitments to a peaceful future for Taiwan. Peking, they say, does not have the military capability to invade Taiwan, and will not develop such capability for at least five years. As Allen S. Whiting of the University of Michigan points out, the Chinese army lacks a large amphibious or paratroop capability, while Taiwan's defenses are strong. Continuing American arms sales to Taiwan should enable the island to maintain an adequate defensive capability. Even more important, China's hostile relations with the Soviet Union to the north and with Vietnam to the south prevent it from undertaking any military action against Taiwan in the foreseeable future. China's desire for good relations with Japan, Western Europe, and the United States will also deter China from using any military means to deal with the Taiwan question. In short, in Whiting's words, "Taiwan's doom is neither inevitable nor imminent."

At the same time, the administration and its supporters point to signs indicating that China is committed to a conciliatory approach to Taiwan. Even before normalization, Vice Premier Teng Hsiao-p'ing had emphasized that China was prepared to wait for reunification of Taiwan with the rest of China. In a press conference in Japan in October 1978, Teng said that the Taiwan question "must be settled eventually. If [it] cannot be settled in ten years, or in a century, [it] will certainly be settled in a thousand years." Since normalization, there have been other signs of China's desire for a peaceful solution: Peking announced that it had halted its sporadic bombardment of the offshore islands of Quemoy and Matsu; and American officials revealed that China had moved some of its military forces away from the coastal region facing Taiwan. China has appealed to Taiwan to establish trade, air links, and direct postal service with the mainland. And, on January 1, 1979, the National People's Congress, China's legislature, said that it would "take present realities into account" when negotiating reunification and would "respect the status quo on Taiwan and the opinion of people in all walks of life" when determining its reunification policies. "In a paradoxical way," one State Department official said, "Taiwan's security is better assured under normalization than before."

Trade

We now turn to the new agenda of Sino–American issues. High on the list is trade. The normalization of Sino–American relations has come at a time when China has shown renewed interest in using foreign trade to promote its own modernization. Through the decade of the Cultural Revolution (1966–76), China's radical leaders warned that such an effort could only reflect a sense of national inferiority, would corrupt the revolutionary values of the Chinese people, and might make China politically and economically dependent on the West. After the purge of the radical Gang of Four, however, China's new leadership began to make exactly the opposite argument: that deliberate insulation from scientific and technological developments in the West reflected national arrogance and complacency, and that China could modernize only by "drawing on the advanced experience of other countries."

Once again, the door to China has been opened. But unlike the situation in the late nineteenth century, however, it is now China that is actively seeking to expand its economic relations with the West—rather than the West that is attempting to impose itself on China. And, unlike Mao's China of the 1950s, China now is clearly more interested in trading with the United States, Japan, and Western Europe than with the Soviet Union.

The results of these changes in Chinese foreign trade policy have been startling. Trade rose from $13.3 billion in 1976 to $14.6 billion in 1977 and to approximately $20 billion in 1978—more than a 50 percent increase in two years. Some transactions have been long-term commitments for the purchase of complete industrial plants. Indeed, in 1978 alone, China reportedly entered into long-term agreements having a total value of $27 billion. China's technology imports between now and 1985 are variously estimated to rise to between $40 billion and $200 billion.

Through most of the 1970s, the United States represented a relatively small share of China's trade. Because

Washington and Peking had not yet established formal diplomatic relations, Sino–American trade was often subjected to political pressures, and the United States was considered, in some respects, to be a "supplier of last resort." Trade between the two countries fell sharply in 1975 and 1976, partially as a result of Peking's dissatisfaction with the pace of normalization. Chinese grain purchases, a major part of Chinese imports from the United States in the early 1970s, were completely halted for four years.

In early 1978, China decided to resume and accelerate its purchases of American grain and technology even in the absence of normalization. U.S.–China trade exceeded $1 billion in 1978—an all-time record. The normalization of relations, together with China's interest in importing advanced technology, should stimulate further increases. Estimates of two-way trade for 1979 range as high as $2.5 billion.

Despite China's clear interest in trade with the United States, and despite the beneficial effect of normalization on Sino–American trade, there are still some important unresolved economic issues in U.S.–China relations.

The administration's supporters argue that normalization will promote greater trade and cultural ties with the PRC. It will consolidate our relationship with Peking, reinforce our two countries' parallel interests, and thus contribute to peace and stability in Asia. Moreover, they also suggest that normalization will encourage China to take an active and constructive role in regional and global affairs. They fully endorse, in other words, President Carter's claim that normalization "will be of great long-term benefit to the peoples of both our country and China and, I believe, for all the peoples of the world." . . .

The most serious constraint on American exports to China, however, will be China's limited ability to pay for them. While the expansion of both tourism and exports will bring more foreign exchange to China, Peking's program of importing technology from abroad will still have to be financed largely through various kinds of loans and credits. China's credit rating is excellent. Still, according to Seth

Lipsky of the *Asian Wall Street Journal,* there is a growing concern in Hong Kong that "foreign banks and suppliers are offering—and Peking might inadvertently take on—more credit than the nation's backward economy will be able to repay in the medium term." In other words a "China bubble" may be emerging, which, if it bursts, could have drastic effects on China's foreign trade. Should Chinese development projects fall behind schedule, or Chinese exports fail to find responsive markets, there is the possibility that China would be forced to reschedule its payments of foreign loans, or even to cancel import contracts.

CHINA: SECOND THOUGHTS?

Finally, it is important to remember that policies of seeking trade and technology from the West have been controversial issues in China, not only since the establishment of the PRC in 1949, but ever since China's first major contacts with the West in the early 1800s. The Chinese, for more than a century, have been caught in a serious dilemma. On the one hand, they have recognized the desirability of strengthening their country by learning from the West. On the other, they have also suspected that China could not import Western technology without being corrupted by Western cultural and political values. Recent admonitions to "learn American technology but not American culture" are only a current manifestation of one historical response to this dilemma. They echo the call of late nineteenth-century reformers to retain traditional Chinese culture but to adopt modern Western technology. Yet, there have always been Chinese who have insisted that technology and culture will come wrapped in the same package. The Gang of Four's suspicion of foreign trade was but the most recent example of a viewpoint that long predated both Mao and the Chinese revolution, and might surface again.

In the years ahead, therefore, growing numbers of Chinese may begin to have second thoughts about their Western-oriented development program. They may have difficulty absorbing advanced Western technology. They may begin to doubt its quality, or its compatibility with Chinese cultural conditions. They may suspect that it breeds a privileged technological elite, divorced from the Chinese peasant masses. Or they may worry that their national independence has been compromised by their new economic relations with foreigners.

All these considerations suggest that the "new China trade" may not grow as smoothly or as rapidly as the most optimistic observers have predicted. And disappointment with trade may become an important source of tension between China and the United States. To quote A. Doak Barnett once again: "In the period ahead, one can expect that, if and when major problems or disputes regarding economic and technological relations arise—as they surely will—frustrated or disillusioned businessmen will turn to their governments for help in dealing with the Chinese." Conversely, Barnett and other observers speculate that the Chinese may well hold Western governments responsible for their own problems in dealing with foreign businessmen, or for the unpleasant social and political consequences that may arise from importing foreign technology.

Scientific and Educational Exchanges

In human terms, one of the most significant consequences of normalization will be the increasing exchange of students and scholars between China and the United States. The hostile relations between the two countries during the 1949–71 period almost completely terminated direct contact between the Chinese and American peoples. Since President Nixon's visit to Peking in February 1972, however, travel between the two countries has increased greatly. Now, the development of scientific and educational exchanges will add a whole new dimension to Sino–American relations.

The Chinese have decided that modernization will require more than importing advanced technology from the West. Some observers estimate that there will be as many as 10,000 Chinese students and scholars abroad by 1980, and as many as 30,000 by 1983. This would far exceed the number of Chinese scientists and engineers sent to the Soviet Union and Eastern Europe for training in the 1950s.

Whatever the total, a significant proportion will be sent to the United States. An advance guard of more than 50 Chinese scholars, most of them mid-career scientists, arrived in the United States in late 1978 to conduct research and receive advanced training. Some 500 to 600 more are expected to arrive in 1979. At the same time, a smaller number of American scholars and graduate students, mainly in the humanities and social sciences, will visit China for research and language training. According to preliminary estimates, the Chinese would like to send upwards of 5,000 students and scholars to the United States over the next several years. . . .

There is the problem of designing an exchange program that will be truly reciprocal. Absolute equality and exact reciprocity will be impossible in the Sino–American exchanges. For one thing, the United States has reached a much higher level of scientific and technological development than China. Although there are some areas, such as seismology, in which we can learn much from China, the relationship on balance is one in which the Chinese will probably benefit more than Americans. Nor will there necessarily be equality in numbers of participants, for the Chinese would probably like to send more students and scholars to the United States than they themselves could receive, or than the United States would want to send. Costs will also be unequal. Assuming that each side pays its own expenses, the Chinese, by sending more people to a country with a higher cost of living, will have to pay out much more than the United States. Nor can reciprocity mean that the two sides will exchange scholars in the same areas—a doctor for a doctor, or an economist for an economist. China will probably send mainly scientists and engineers to the United States, while most Americans studying in China are likely to be social scientists and humanists. Given these differences, the exchange program will always be vulnerable to charges from both sides that the other country is somehow "getting the better deal." . . .

At present, scholarly exchange between the United States and China operates on at least three levels. Some exchanges have been arranged on a direct, personal basis by individual Chinese and American scholars. Others are based on agreements and understandings between American universities, professional organizations, and corporations, on the one hand, and Chinese universities and research institutes, on the other. Still a third exchange program is conducted on a national scale by the Chinese and American governments. On the American side, specialized organizations, principally the Committee on Scholarly Communication with the People's Republic of China and the National Committee on U.S.–China Relations, were established some years ago to help manage the exchange process.

Some Americans defend this multiplicity of arrangements as being conducive to experimentation and innovation, as meeting individual and institutional needs, and as being the only kind of exchange compatible with the pluralism of American society. As Albert H. Bowker, chancellor of the University of California at Berkeley, has put it: "Higher education in this country is very decentralized, and I don't see any reason why each institution should not be able to do what it wants." Others, in contrast, call for greater centralization and coordination of the exchange process. Says J. W. Peltason, president of the American Council on Education: "If each institution makes its own arrangements with the Chinese without informing others, we will lose the opportunity to develop some common policies, and we may well lose the chance for adequate reciprocal exchange privileges." These critics charge that the present decentralized arrangements hamper coordination of tuition and admissions policies, and may make it easier for the Chinese to play one university off against another. They also question the desirability of maintaining separate organizations to manage exchanges with China, and propose integrating them with the current exchange programs with other countries. . . .

Military and Strategic Relations

One of the most potentially dangerous developments in international politics in the last fifteen years has been the increase in military forces along the Sino–Soviet frontier. Beginning in the mid-1960s, the Soviet Union transferred large numbers of army and air force units to Siberia and Outer Mongolia for a possible military confrontation with China. Over the last several years, the number of Soviet troops along the border has remained relatively constant, but Moscow has made an impressive effort to reequip them with more modern weapons and to provide them with a more effective logistical base. During the same period, the Chinese also redeployed a large part of their own army from south to north to reinforce their units on the border.

As a result of these redeployments, one-fourth of all Soviet ground forces, approximately one-fifth of the Soviet tactical air force, and large numbers of Russian intermediate-range ballistic missiles are now arrayed against China. On the Chinese side, Peking has now placed about two-thirds of its main-force army divisions in the military regions facing the Soviet Union.

In technological terms, the Chinese forces are far inferior to their Soviet counterparts. Western analysts agree that the People's Liberation Army (PLA), long designed to fight a "people's war," seriously lacks advanced antiaircraft systems, antitank weapons, antisubmarine-warfare capability, armor, fighter aircraft, and artillery. Chinese military technology is, on the average, ten to twenty years behind that of the Soviet Union.

Given the backwardness of China's armed forces, it is hardly surprising that China seeks to develop a more modern military establishment over the next 20 years. And this poses an important policy decision for the United States. Through trade and exchanges with China, the West is helping to develop China's civilian economy and its scientific and technological base, and thereby making an indirect contribution to China's military modernization. Should the United States do more than this? Should it deliberately and

directly contribute to the modernization of the PLA
through the transfer of military-related technology to
China? And should the United States, through its participation in COCOM, encourage or discourage comparable efforts by its Western European and Japanese allies?

CHINA SHOPS ABROAD

. . . The Chinese have expressed an active interest in
purchasing various kinds of military related technology from
the West, including not only advanced weapons systems
but the production processes as well. At various times, the
Chinese have explored the possibility of purchasing such
items as engines for jet fighters, antitank missiles, military
helicopters, tanks, surface-to-air missiles, radar, communications equipment, and, in one of the most widely publicized negotiations, a large number of British Harrier
fighter aircraft. With the tacit approval of the United States,
the Chinese actually purchased $200 million worth of Rolls-
Royce Spey jet engines in December 1975, for use in a new
fighter plane of Chinese design. At the same time, the Chinese also acquired the technology that would enable them
to manufacture Spey engines on their own. In 1978, Peking
also purchased British diesel engines for use in Chinese
naval vessels. . . .

A CLOSER MILITARY RELATIONSHIP?

The question of the military and strategic relationship
between the United States and China began to arouse public attention and controversy in 1975. Proponents of a closer
military relationship with China have usually begun by
pointing to the "parallel interests" of China and the United
States in resisting Soviet expansion and in preventing a
Sino–Soviet war. A stronger PLA, they argue, would continue to tie down a substantial part of Moscow's armed
forces along the Sino–Soviet frontier, would reduce Soviet
military pressure against Western Europe, and would decrease the Soviet Union's ability to undertake military adventures in Africa or the Middle East.

At the same time, military cooperation between the

United States and China would help prevent a Sino–Soviet war, both by increasing China's own defensive capability and by warning the Soviet Union that the United States might not remain neutral in the event of such a conflict. Thus, as early as 1976, Jerome Alan Cohen of Harvard University proposed that the United States should sell equipment to China that would reduce the technological gap between it and the Soviet Union and should permit its allies to sell "plainly defensive military equipment" to China. He even suggested that the U.S. might also "reserve the option to make direct sales of defensive military items to China if Soviet–American relations or Sino–Soviet relations deteriorate."

Opponents of such a military relationship between the United States and China have usually relied on two sets of arguments. First, they point to the competitive interests of China and the United States—and of China and Japan—in some parts of Asia, notably Korea, Southeast Asia, and the territorial seas off the Asian coast. Given such a potential for conflict, they consider it unwise for the West to increase China's military capability. These critics also warn that, at a time when the United States is trying to discourage the PRC from using force to gain control over Taiwan, it would be inconsistent for the United States simultaneously to strengthen China's own military establishment. O. Edmund Clubb, a former foreign service officer with extensive experience in China, cautions that "guns bear no allegiance," and that a stronger China might not necessarily use its military forces merely to deter Soviet attack. Instead, he sees the possibility that "China will undertake first to overcome lesser antagonists, some of whom might be America's friends —even allies." In a similar vein, the *Christian Science Monitor* editorialized in late June 1978 that "the West is well advised to think twice about helping arm a nuclear power, and an authoritarian, Communist one at that."

BAITING THE RUSSIAN BEAR

Critics of military cooperation between the United States and China raise, as a second point, the possibility of a hostile reaction from the Soviet Union. They note that the Soviet Union has repeatedly warned Japan, Western Europe, and the United States against selling arms to China, or engaging in any other form of overt military cooperation with Peking. A Soviet Politburo statement in August 1978, for example, warned that such a relationship might have serious consequences for the SALT negotiations. And Georgi A. Arbatov, the Kremlin's chief "America-watcher," declared in November that extensive military cooperation between China and the United States would mean that "there is no place for détente, even in a narrow sense," between Washington and Moscow. . . .

THE CASE FOR CAUTION

On one point, however, proponents and opponents of military cooperation agree. If the United States decides to begin any program of military assistance to China, it should do so slowly and cautiously, taking into full account the evolution of Sino–American, Sino–Soviet, and Soviet–American relations. They also agree that there is a wide range of options available to the United States should Washington decide to begin military cooperation with Peking. Some would clearly be more provocative in Soviet eyes than others. Providing China with military information about Soviet deployments and force postures, for example, would probably be less intolerable to the Russians than transferring military technology. Selling purely defensive weapons to China would be less provocative than selling weapons that could be used offensively against the Soviets. And, most observers believe, Moscow would object less if China purchased military technology from Western Europe or Japan than if it bought it directly from the United States. Obviously, Moscow would be most concerned by any kind of formal military alliance between Washington and Peking.

The Fundamental Issue

The best way to summarize this discussion of U.S.–China relations is to reconsider the fundamental issue in our China policy: how to define our overall relationship with Peking for the 1980s. In essence, there are four possibilities. We could maintain a dispassionate and somewhat distant relationship with China. We could try to forge an economic partnership with Peking. We could see China as an important counterpart in international and regional negotiations. Or, we could go further and view China as a military and strategic ally. These options are not mutually exclusive. The task ahead, therefore, is not necessarily to choose one over the others, but to find the proper balance among them. . . .

TAIWAN[2]

History

Taiwan is a mountainous island 100 miles off the southeast coast of the China mainland. Portuguese explorers called it Isla Formosa—beautiful island. Taiwan was originally inhabited by people of Malay stock, but Chinese began to migrate there in the fifteenth century. The Dutch established a trading post in the early seventeenth century. Chinese forces soon drove them out, and the imperial government ruled Taiwan, first as a frontier area and later as a province. Following the Sino–Japanese War of 1894–95, China ceded Taiwan to the victorious Japanese. For the next fifty years, Japanese colonial administrators ran the island and developed its economy.

Taiwan returned to Chinese jurisdiction at the close of World War II. Harsh occupation by Nationalist forces provoked a native Taiwanese uprising which was brutally suppressed in February 1947. When the Communists won the mainland in 1949, Chiang Kai-shek fled to Taiwan with over one million supporters. The Nationalist government has been there ever since: it claims to be the legitimate government of all China, located temporarily on the island until recovery of the mainland becomes possible.

[2] Excerpt from book entitled *Asia: Half the Human Race*, by Terry E. Lautz, ed. p 94–6. Published by the Council on International and Public Affairs in cooperation with the China Council of the Asia Society. Copyright 1979 by the Asia Society Inc. Reprinted by permission.

Initially, Taiwan was in danger of capture by the Chinese Communists. But following the outbreak of the Korean War in June 1950, President Harry Truman ordered the Seventh Fleet to patrol the strait between Taiwan and the mainland. The United States continued to recognize the ROC (Republic of China) as the government of China, and in 1954, the two countries concluded a mutual defense treaty.

Thanks to a land reform program, pragmatic leadership, and American aid and protection, Taiwan has become an "economic miracle." Although the government remains authoritarian, political participation has been expanded at lower levels and martial law has been eased.

Chiang Kai-shek died in 1975. His son, Chiang Ching-kuo, had already become the Nationalists' de facto leader, and he was made chairman of the party and then president of the republic in March 1978. On January 1, 1979, the U.S. de-recognized Taipei in favor of Peking and gave the one-year notice required by treaty to terminate the 1954 mutual defense pact with Taiwan.

Taiwan Today

Taiwan is an island in search of an identity. Both the Nationalists and the People's Republic of China (PRC) agree that it is a province of China. But Taiwan is controlled by the Nationalists, who claim to be China's legitimate government. In 1979, the United States has formally recognized the PRC, and only twenty countries continue to have diplomatic relations with the Nationalist regime. Even so, Taiwan maintains close economic and cultural ties with many nations, including the United States.

Washington's recognition of the PRC had been expected ever since President Richard Nixon's trip to Peking in 1972. Yet when President Carter announced the normalization of Sino–American relations, Taiwan reacted with shock and anger. Anti-American demonstrations erupted in Taipei. President Chiang indefinitely suspended scheduled elections for the legislative council and the National Assembly, and the Nationalist army was put on full alert. When a U.S. delegation led by Deputy Secretary of State Warren Christopher arrived to discuss the nature of U.S.–Taiwan ties following the severance of diplomatic relations, a mob pelted the motorcade with eggs and rocks.

In announcing the opening of U.S.–China relations, President Carter stated that the United States "will continue to have an interest in the peaceful resolution of the Taiwan issue. I have paid special attention to insuring that normalization . . . will not jeopardize the well-being of the people of Taiwan." Moreover, the U.S. announced that it would continue to sell defensive arms to Taiwan even after the termination of the mutual defense treaty at the end of 1979. In February 1979, the United States and Taiwan reached agreement concerning the conduct of unofficial relations between the two countries. The American Institute, a non-governmental but government-funded agency, replaces the American embassy. It performs virtually all the functions of an embassy. The Taiwan equivalent in Washington is the Coordination Council for North American Affairs.

The PRC has refused to rule out the use of force in reunifying Taiwan with the mainland. But Peking has also indicated that it hopes to reach agreement peacefully. PRC spokesmen have proposed unification talks and the establishment of postal, air, and trade links between the PRC and Taiwan. Meeting in January 1979 with U.S. senators, Chinese Deputy Prime Minister Teng Hsiao-p'ing declared that if Taiwan recognized PRC sovereignty, it could retain its own government, its own security forces, and its own economic and social system. Taiwan responded negatively to Peking's overtures. Indeed, President Chiang asserted in his 1979 New Year speech that "Our anti-Communist struggle will never cease until the Chinese Communist regime has been destroyed."

The Nationalists remain in firm control of the Taiwan government. To defuse dissent among native Taiwanese, who make up 85 percent of the island's population, the Nationalists have allowed Taiwanese to hold more, and more important, government posts. Even so, the number of influential Taiwanese remains small, and government security agencies keep dissent firmly under control.

For the foreseeable future, the Nationalists will clearly be able to defend themselves. Taiwan's armed forces number nearly 500,000 well-trained men, backed up by a large reserve force. The air force is equipped with nearly 400 combat and transport planes, including F-5E jets. Western military analysts say that the PRC is incapable of mounting a successful invasion of Taiwan.

Taiwan's strongest asset, however, is its economy. Intensive development of agriculture and industry has raised the gross national product to an annual $24 billion. The economy grew at 13 percent in 1978. Annual trade of $23 billion makes Taiwan a leading commercial power. To make Taiwan more self-sufficient, an ambitious building program is under way which includes nuclear power plants, steel mills, and a new rail line.

Taiwan's future is a major question mark. To counter Peking, Taiwan could conceivably ally itself with the Soviet Union or develop nuclear weapons. But either of those moves would clearly antagonize the PRC. The evolution of Taiwan's domestic politics is difficult to predict, especially since Chiang Ching-kuo has yet to designate a successor. A further complicating factor is that some native Taiwanese favor the establishment of an independent Taiwan. As one long-term possibility, some Western experts theorize that Taiwan may recognize Peking's jurisdiction but manage to retain complete autonomy. But how the Taiwan puzzle will finally be solved, only time will tell.

IS IT WORTH THE PRICE WE PAID?[3]

In mid-December the inevitable finally occurred. Anti-American demonstrators hooted in Taipei, capital of what

[3] From article entitled "The Break With Taiwan: Is It Worth the Price We Paid?" by Robert Elegant, author of *Dynasty* and other books on China. *National Review*. 31:348–50. Mr. 16, '79. Reprinted by permission of National Review, 150 East 35th Street, New York, NY 10016.

had been an American ally since the Second World War. At the same moment, Americans were applauded in Peking, capital of what had been an enemy of the United States from the intervention of "Chinese People's Volunteers" in the Korean War in 1950 until Henry Kissinger's secret visit in 1971.

Public attitudes in the "two cities" were radically altered by an action that had impended since Peking and Washington realized that their joint interest in curtailing Soviet imperialism far outweighed the conflicts that divided them. The United States and the People's Republic therefore agreed in mid-December to raise their liaison offices to the rank of embassies. That formal agreement required the United States to close its embassy in Taipei: it could hardly maintain full diplomatic relations with two nations that both claimed to rule all China, including Taiwan.

The break with the Nationalists was highly regrettable from the American point of view; even more lamentable was the abrogation of the mutual defense treaty, since the U.S. could hardly afford still another public abandonment of an ally. But for Peking, establishing full diplomatic relations with the U.S.—"normalization," in the current jargon—had been a matter of some urgency since the fall of South Vietnam in 1975. Communist Peking was at least as badly shaken as Washington by the sudden collapse of the anti-Communist government in Saigon. Vietnam's subsequent conversion into a vociferous Soviet ally—and military base—on China's southern flank made it imperative for Peking to draw as close as it possibly could to the only force in the world capable of stemming the rising Muscovite tide.

If the Chinese got what they wanted, they did not get what they do not (yet) want. The People's Republic does not yearn to assume responsibility for the exuberant capitalist territory of Taiwan, whose people live in extravagant comfort compared to their Mainland cousins. Taiwan *irredenta* is in Teng Hsiao-ping's eyes a minor problem beside the transcendent Soviet threat. Peking therefore settled for the minimum it could accept: withdrawal of the vestigial

American military presence in Taiwan and abrogation of the mutual defense treaty. Hua Kuo-feng, Vice Premier Teng's highly nominal superior, accepted with only perfunctory protest the stated American intention of continuing to sell arms to Taiwan; he furthermore linked Taiwan with Hong Kong, which he most certainly does *not* now wish to liberate from "British imperialism." Hua thus told the world—and the Chinese people—that he had no intention of altering the status quo for some time to come.

In the realm of *Realpolitik* it is vain to brood over the fact that Taipei is less corrupt, less dissension-ridden, more intelligent, more liberal, and far more successful in promoting the well-being of its people than Peking, which in plain truth does, after a fashion, rule China. Full diplomatic recognition was inevitable in the long run, and let us not object too harshly to its timing.

Still, the American gesture was, I feel, premature. Such haste was unnecessary to the protection of America's interest —and harmful to the world's perception of American reliability. Even the pro-American and anti-Soviet *Sunday Telegraph* of London noted: "The Bamboo Curtain was broken over the head of Taiwan. . . . For the world at large, and not excluding America's NATO partners, it [the repudiation of Taiwan] is a grim reminder that no alliance can last forever and that, ultimately, there is no substitute for self-reliance to ensure one's own security." Too true, but the damage done by "normalization" has already occurred. Now the question is what the United States has gotten for it.

The immediate payoff is presumably economic. Both Coca-Cola and Pan-American Airways, supremely non-ideological like most corporations, are crowing over their direct access to the fabled China market. That market is assumed to be so vast that, as Lord Elgin told the English merchants of Shanghai in 1861, "all the mills of Lancashire could not make stocking-stuff sufficient for one of its provinces."

In reality, however, the China market has proved limited both in the more remote and the recent past. Neither stockings nor any other consumer goods are high on China's shopping list. Statistically, of course, Sino–American trade is bound to show a marked increase—presumably as a result of the exchange of ambassadors. Many American technical products, now bought through third countries, will be purchased directly from American companies. In time American weapons will be sold directly to China. But Sino–American trade expanded dramatically after the establishment of the liaison offices in 1972—and then declined. Both proportionally and absolutely, that trade is all but certain to decline again after the first careful raptures. Were I so fortunate as to receive a royalty of (say) half a cent on every bottle of Coca-Cola sold in China, I should not anticipate its making me wealthy.

The other payoffs are at once less certain and less definable. They depend on how the new relationship is managed by both sides. The Sino–American quasi-alliance, which has already functioned (albeit feebly) since Richard Nixon's visit to Peking in 1972, could rapidly become an effective alliance, even without a formal mutual defense treaty.

But on the whole I feel that the sudden step of formal recognition—with its inescapable repudiation of solemn obligations to Taiwan—was at this moment supererogatory. It was like drawing for a full house with a pair of aces showing and a pair of kings in the hole, while no other player shows either a picture card or a pair. The hyper-Machiavellian treatment of Taiwan has rent again our threadbare credibility—not least among the men of Peking, who will not regard us more highly for the ease with which they won major concessions without making major concessions in return. Contrary to Washington's belief, Hua conceded nothing substantive in his implicit toleration of Taiwan's independence. The Chinese knew they could not possibly insist that we formally stop arms sales to Taipei, and a frontal attack on the island would destroy the impression of sweet reasonableness they wish to convey. An unsuccessful invasion would be more damaging still. For all of these reasons, "normalization" could have waited, and should have.

But Americans should nonetheless avoid recriminations. The *fait accompli* stands. Perhaps, as its advocates insist, delay would have actually allowed public opinion to harden against a gesture that had to come sooner or later.

The Chinese leadership faced a public relations problem of their own—more complex, no doubt, though outsiders can now descry its outline while remaining ignorant of its nuances. The dissension is no less important for the fact that debate is confined to the hundred or so men and women whose voices resound within the councils of the Chinese Communist Party.

China's highly ideological "hawks" argue (a) that the fierce antagonism between Moscow and Peking should be ameliorated; and (b) that it is shameful to postpone Taiwan's return to the Motherland. China's "doves" contend (a) that the hostility is forced on China by a Russia that has for 150 years sought to extend its sway over Chinese territory, and now seeks to strangle China by encirclement on land and sea; and (b) that Taiwan's inevitable reversion to Peking's control should not be immediately forced if that would mean sacrificing more vital factors in terms of China's security and territorial integrity. Shortly before the Sino–American announcement of "normalization," senior party members and cadres were elaborately instructed that Taiwan's return might take "several generations"—and that the waiting game was completely justified. Like the American rationale for immediate "normalization," the Chinese explanation insisted that "normalization" had to be undertaken when it was possible on Chinese terms, lest it become impossible in the future.

Now, all this microscopic dissection would be superfluous, and the American verdict would have to be that "normalization" is quite unnecessary now, if the issue were simply Sino–American relations *in vacuo*. But it is as obvious as it can be that the United States needs China almost as badly as China needs the United States, for one overriding reason: to help counter Soviet expansion. Because of that need, Americans should neither agonize over the immorality (whatever that may mean in the amoral arena of the international power struggle) of partially abandoning Taiwan, nor keen over our inordinate haste in making the change.

The Chinese view of the fundamental problem, as recently re-stated by Vice Premier Teng, is stark. The Soviet Union, Peking believes, is determined to bring the entire world under its sway. Moscow's strategy is to acquire preponderant influence in areas that possess either great natural resources or vital strategic locations—or both. To the Chinese, the expansion of Soviet naval power, merchant shipping, and military bases throughout the world is one with the extension of decisive Soviet influence to Vietnam, Afghanistan, and Africa. (Perhaps Iran tomorrow?) The Chinese know the Russians have diligently studied Admiral Alfred Thayer Mahan's theses on the decisive influence of sea power. Peking believes, as does Moscow, that the Russians can attain effective domination over the world by seizing control of the seas. The Chinese have warned us most sincerely, with a paraphrase of an old Chinese adage: "The Russians are feinting to the East [China] in order to strike in the West [Europe]." Peking does not primarily fear a direct Soviet attack but, rather, slow strangulation through the success of that Soviet strategy.

Two decisive questions therefore obtrude: Will the burgeoning Sino–American alliance be effective in checking Soviet imperialism? And is the likelihood of its being effective worth the risk of assisting China's progress toward the state of a superpower that could, at some time in the future, threaten the U.S., Western Europe, and Japan? The questions are so interrelated that they can be answered with reference to the same considerations.

A combination of China, rich in manpower and natural resources, and Japan, rich in technical skill, industry, and commercial acumen, could in time become a third center of world power that could challenge the two existing superpowers and their respective allies. There is, however, no need for such an exclusive alliance between two basically antipathetic nations, largely because the United States is the vital factor in the individual development of each, as well as in the development of their relationship. If the United States remains a major force in Pacific and world affairs, an exclusive Sino–Japanese grouping is most unlikely. Indeed, it can be most convincingly argued that "normalization" seeks, among other goals, to prevent such a grouping. But there is one stern condition: the United States must be seen to be powerful and active abroad.

Moreover, China's power remains largely potential. The People's Republic possesses great natural resources, not the least of which is an intelligent and adaptable population of great size. But its resources cannot be exploited effectively without foreign—preferably American—assistance on the broadest scale. Otherwise, all those resources—like the enormous population, which requires immense food supplies—could become great disadvantages, attracting the covetous Russian barbarians to the north.

For one thing, the People's Republic has vast petroleum resources. Estimates range from ten to twenty billion (that's *billion*) tons, equaling—perhaps exceeding—the reserves of Saudi Arabia. Intelligent exploitation of that heavy counterweight to Middle Eastern oil could sharply tilt the world balance of power. But those reserves, the greater part lying under the seabed, cannot be exploited effectively without advanced American technology and, almost certainly, American technicians. So anxious are the Chinese to tap their oil reserves fully that some participation by American companies in both financing and rewards—which, even in a veiled form, would have been unthinkable 18 months ago—is now possible. Joint exploitation would, of course, increase Sino–American interdependence, thus cementing the alliance.

I would further propose that all the advanced weapons and weapons systems that the Chinese can usefully employ to deter or counter the Russians should be made available to them. Even with such weapons, the People's Republic cannot possibly become a serious threat to anyone before the turn of the century. My own crystal ball dims into opacity beyond a span of twenty-odd years, and I hold with Sir Winston Churchill that "it is a mistake to look too far ahead. Only one link in the chain of destiny can be handled at a time." The reasons for my confidence in China's essential harmlessness during the next two decades are, however, quite simple.

Somewhere between twenty and fifty thousand of the most intelligent, diligent, and highly educated men and women in the world manage the People's Republic—quite well, in truth, when they are not harassed by idiotic ideological campaigns like the Great Leap Forward and the Great Proletarian Cultural Revolution. Below that elite are between 850 million and one billion largely uneducated and unskilled persons, whose native talents require intensive cultivation. China must concentrate on the education of the "great masses" for at least a generation, just as it must concentrate on basic mechanization/modernization of its agriculture—both, preferably, with much outside assistance.

China is today still "poor and blank," as the late Chairman Mao Tse-tung was wont to point out. The economic and social infrastructure is attenuated and feeble. Show communes no more than 25 miles from Peking are approached on packed-earth roads, and their inhabitants still lack running water. The Chinese would be delighted to possess roads half so good as the rudimentary road network of the west of Ireland.

China's internal evolution is properly the matter for a separate article, since it is also hazy with dubieties and perplexities. I shall, therefore, conclude by pointing out certain dangers which the Mainland Chinese do not have the power to ward off, whatever their influence on the resolution of those perplexities.

The Nationalists of Taiwan have been warning for several years that they might decide to play the Russian Card if the U.S. played the China Card. It would be most naïve to assume that diverging ideologies would deter the Nationalists—any more than conflicting ideologies prevented the American move. Besides, Russia would be delighted to complete the arc of bases enclosing the Chinese littoral from Siberia to Vietnam and would pay handsomely to acquire the former American protégé, Taiwan. But although the Nationalists will be greatly tempted to strike a deal with the Soviets, ingrained Chinese suspicion of the Russians will, to a certain extent, discourage them. Besides, the move could be unnecessary—unless the United States behaves with surpassing stupidity.

A PRICE FOR TAIWAN[4]

At issue in the dispute about President Carter's China transaction is not whether the United States should have a wide range of relations with China. It should, and does. Indeed, relations have been expanding so fast that defenders of the transaction are hard put to explain why it was necessary. Neither is the issue whether full diplomatic relations are desirable. They are.

Rather, the issue is the price Carter paid. The price makes the transaction seem dictated more by the administration's political needs, and the ideology of the State Department's seventh floor, than by any larger imperatives. . . .

If today's leaders of China (no one knows who tomorrow's leaders will be) are indeed pragmatic, the administration paid too high a price. Pragmatic leaders would not allow the Taiwan question to impede cooperation important to China's development and defense. If China's leaders are not pragmatic, then it is to dangerous men that the United States has consigned Taiwan. . . .

Carter acceded to three demands: severance of diplomatic relations with Taiwan, unilateral termination of the defense treaty, and removal of U.S. forces. In return, the

4 From article by George Will, Pulitzer prize winner for "distinguished commentary" in 1977, and former editor, National Review and Newsweek. Washington Post. p A15. D. 21, '78. © 1978, The Washington Post Company. Reprinted by permission.

United States is allowed: to delay for one year termination of the treaty; to say that it wants the Taiwan question resolved peacefully; and to sell arms to Taiwan. The first "right" is trivial, the second vacuous, the third nugatory.

The "Taiwan question" is like the *Judenfrage* (Jewish question) in the 1930s. It is one of those antiseptic abstractions by which politicians disguise (sometimes from themselves) the nature of what they're doing. The "Taiwan question," like the *Judenfrage,* is only a "question" for one side. Just as European Jews had no "question" (they only wanted to be left alone), the "Taiwan question" is not Taiwan's. Plainly put, the "question" is: How shall Taiwan's liberty be extinguished?

On "Meet the Press," Cyrus Vance, the secretary of state, said that China had not "contradicted" the United States when the United States expressed its "expectations" that the question would be answered peacefully. Asked if the United States had even asked for a Chinese commitment, he said: "The Chinese have made it very clear all along that they will not state that the resolution of this problem is a problem for anybody else to determine, other than them." In other words: NO. As in SALT, the adversary's intransigence determined the scope and thus shaped the result of negotiations.

Regarding arms sales to Taiwan, the administration's eagerness to comply with Peking's wishes means that there probably will not be sales that might offend Peking.

In an unintended way, Carter's China transaction was timely. The administration has become Egypt's partner in pressuring Israel to rest its security on a treaty that is increasingly honeycombed with problems. But Taiwan's fate reminds Israel that parchment is a thin shield for a small nation. Furthermore, as often occurs when Israel's security anxieties become inconvenient for an American administration, there is talk of assuaging those anxieties with a U.S.-Israel defense treaty. Surely this administration will not have the impudence to suggest such a thing.

In his broadcast announcement on China, Carter did

not see fit to mention to Americans that what he was doing involved disavowing a treaty obligation. He left that troubling detail to television commentators. Why? Having recently made a speech reminding Americans that, at last, they have a president virtuous enough to care about human rights, perhaps he did not want to dwell on the fact that he was doing more to jeopardize the rights of the Taiwanese than he has done to enhance the rights of any other people.

OUR CHINA "TILT"[5]

After a lifetime of criticizing a United States policy which shunted China aside, this reporter is in the awkward position, at least for the moment, of disliking the current U.S. infatuation with the People's Republic. While normalization was proper, sane and decades overdue, U.S. policymakers have, in a sense, overdone it. Most visibly and tragically, this is apparent in the U.S. reaction to the Vietnam-Cambodia and Vietnam-China wars. Instead of maintaining an evenhanded approach in these "Communist wars," the Carter Administration has tilted toward China. Perhaps without even meaning to do it, the U.S. has erred.

Nevertheless, one main result has been to somewhat aggravate tensions in Southeast Asia. In battles which Sen. Patrick Moynihan (D—N.Y.), among others, has called the "possible beginnings of World War III," the U.S. has tended to act as a partisan rather than a neutral force which would mediate. While it would be pure thoughtless anti-Americanism to blame the fighting on U.S. decisions, still the U.S. has not used its considerable influence to help bring peace.

This is not to say that U.S. policy has been gung ho Chinese. At times the U.S. attitude seems to be that there is really nothing disastrous if one Communist country fights another. Even though the State Department has called for

[5] Article entitled "Our China 'Tilt': How About Peace Now?" by Peter Kovler, writer, legislative assistant and speech writer for Washington political figures. Commonweal. p 133+. Mr. 16, 1979. Copyright © 1979 Commonweal Publishing Co., Inc. Reprinted by permission.

both China and Vietnam to stop their fighting, there has been neither action nor the threat of action to support the rhetoric. The administration's attitude is often reminiscent of the view toward Mafia wars where there is a platitudinous pronouncement to stop the killing but where, in truth, there is indifference: Let "them " kill "them"—as long as they don't come near "us." But this attitude has mostly given way to a pro-China position.

U.S. Reaction to Vietnam Invasion

When Teng Hsiao-ping visited here in January, the warnings of an imminent Chinese invasion were so blatant that even a casual newspaper reader could have picked them up. Indeed, there have even been reports, although unconfirmed, that the U.S. was told there would be an invasion which would last from ten to twenty days. As the Vice-Premier made his way West, his verbal attacks on Vietnamese "hegemonism" became increasingly ominous. Everyone knew that Teng wanted to "punish" Vietnam. By the time he departed from Japan, few doubted that war was close.

In response, President Carter is supposed to have told Teng that he disapproved of any "incursion." Since the invasion the administration has, again, expressed its disapproval while reiterating the call for Vietnamese forces to leave Cambodia. In fact, our State Department has expressed so much disapproval that they are almost believable. But, in truth, such words are as meaningful as when the State Department in another era in Southeast Asia "disapproved" of Thieu's harsh regime.

If the U.S. were really sincere, it would have used real pressure on the Chinese. For years I have looked forward to U.S.-China trade but the stalling of trade could have been used as a lever to slow down the war and make the Chinese get out of Vietnam. Instead, the U.S. eagerly sends Treasury Secretary Blumenthal to Peking for economic talks with his hosts. Admittedly, Blumenthal has criticized his hosts for their "transgression.' But to quote Washington *Star* reporter Lee Cohn who is in Peking, "Chinese leaders . . .

refuse to take offense at the criticism." For all the emphasis that has been put on how the Chinese value formalities and courtesies, the U.S. government has managed to be publicly critical without in any way upsetting China. The only possible interpretation of this event is that from the Chinese viewpoint, Blumenthal is even less than a paper tiger; he is a paper tiger critic.

Perhaps the most perspicacious comments on Secretary Blumenthal's trip came from Sen. Charles Mathias (R—Maryland) : "The Soviets may believe the U.S. gave the Vice-Premier a 'green light' for his attack on Vietnam, and China may feel it can do anything and not risk our criticism. The Secretary," he continued, "has become part of the administration's misplayed 'China card.' The administration's decision to go ahead with (his) trip to China is a serious mistake. Dispatching a senior U.S. official to Peking seems only to send another warning signal to a dangerously troubled region."

U.S.-Vietnamese Relations

A second policy which indicates the China tilt by the U.S. has been the way we have acted toward Vietnam. By treating their country during the war as a Soviet satellite, the U.S. has misunderstood (for a change) the Vietnamese and has invited them to oppose the U.S. directly. If the U.S. had relations with Vietnam, there would at least be a chance that—as in the Mideast—the U.S. could bring the parties together. But because the U.S. has snubbed Vietnam, it has meant that they have had to go to the only ones offering assistance, the Russians. In turn, this has meant that they have become part of the Sino-Soviet fight. Indeed, if one of the most strategic bases in Asia, Cam Ranh Bay, becomes a port for the Soviets, the U.S. will have only itself to blame.

But even before the China invasion, U.S.-Vietnam policy had taken a terrible turn for the worse. Whereas six months ago we were close to normalizing relations with Hanoi, in the intervening period an anti-Vietnam mood prevailed in the administration. As a result, normalization was dispensed with. The real reason for this may be something for historians to discover. But at present there are two theories. Either normalizing relations with Vietnam just "fell through the cracks" when China normalization began. Or, perhaps, it was made part of the U.S.-China normalization deal. Even though the evidence is now somewhat sketchy and circumstantial, one has to wonder at the coincidence of the U.S. effectively breaking off talks with Vietnam while, simultaneously, opening up relations with China. But whatever the reason, one thing is clear: With Vietnam, the U.S. continues to impose a trade embargo and will not normalize. With China, however, trade and diplomatic relations obviously could not be better.

In considering the issue of withdrawal, the U.S. has again portrayed itself as disinterested and evenhanded. Territorial boundaries should unquestionably be observed, goes the administration's thinking. But one must hope that the administration is not entirely serious on this matter when one considers what the results would probably be. That is, if Vietnam were to go along with the U.S. position and withdraw from Cambodia, doubtless the group returning to power would be Pol Pot's. Does the U.S. really want to see those bloodthirsty tyrants back in charge?

Finally, the Carter Administration has failed to give credit where it is deserved—to the Russians. While the USSR has acted brutally in Eastern Europe and while it has been trying to expand its power in parts of Africa, in Southeast Asia, so far, it has acted with great restraint. As everyone tries to "save face," it is a pleasant surprise that the Russians have not come to the aid of Hanoi by attacking China. If the administration were really evenhanded (instead of still trying to seem tough toward the Russians for the sake of not appearing too dovish as it prepares to sell the SALT treaty), the congratulations would be in order.

I do not mean to suggest that the Vietnamese are pacifistic angels, the "victims" of "imperialistic" China and that, as a consequence, the U.S. should support them. On human rights, for example, Amnesty International reports that "there is still grave concern at the continued detention of tens of thousands of people who, so far as is known, have not been charged with any offense . . . (they are still in camps) more than three years since the change of government in what was formerly South Vietnam." It's a mistake to believe that in East Asia there are "good guys" and "bad guys."

But what is most crucial is that, to borrow a phrase from another Vietnam war, there should be "peace now." Unquestionably, in some small ways the U.S. has pushed for this. For instance, leading the attempts to make the UN consider the war has been a good decision. More, the administration has pledged not to get militarily involved. Even if this seems like an empty gesture (after all, there isn't one person in the world who has publicly suggested otherwise), given the way our Presidents have acted in Southeast Asia, it is somewhat reassuring. But on the whole our moves have not been so sound.

If the U.S. continues to tilt toward China it can only make Southeast Asia look like even more of a tinderbox. As it is now, to most of the world it appears that the two superpowers have each taken one side. With that development, a local conflict takes on the possibility of becoming a worldwide one. But the U.S. could work meaningfully for peace if it would relinquish partisanship for true evenhandedness: We should be friends with China but we should also be friends with Vietnam. Sadly, however, that is not the way the administration views the Vietnam war.

CHINA TIES AND THE U.S.-SOVIET BALANCE[6]

Teng Hsaio-ping's visit and the "normalization" of our relations with the People's Republic of China bid fair to create the same lack of understanding between the admin-

[6] Article by John A. Armitage, former deputy Assistant Secretary of State for European Affairs, now diplomat-in-residence, University of Virginia. Washington Post. Op. ed. p 15. F. 11, '79. © 1979, The Washington Post Company. Reprinted by permission.

istration and the American people as did the Nixon visit to the Soviet Union and the policy of "détente."

People understood in 1972 that what had been set in motion was (1) a process for progress in reducing the danger of nuclear war and (2) a political settlement in Europe that laid a basis for moving away from confrontation in that area of prime interest to our security. But they did not understand that, for the Third World, all that had been done was to reduce the prospect of nuclear confrontation there. Expectations that contention in the developing areas would sharply diminish received a rude shock in Angola. President Ford then disavowed "détente" and refused to grasp the nettle of SALT II.

Is it too much to ask that the administration now try to make it clear what the new relationship with Peking does and does not do?

The problem is that the administration does little to make its policy intelligible. The president's adviser, Zbigniew Brzezinski, goes to Peking, chortles with his hosts over the threat of the "polar bear to the North" and speaks of the "common interests" of Washington and Peking. Peking wants territory in Soviet Siberia and plans to build up its nuclear power to press its claims. To Moscow, this Peking position is a matter affecting Soviet national security. Is this an interest of Peking that the administration shares?

President Carter explains that we wish equally good relations with Communist China and the Soviet Union, that our relations with one are not directed against the other. But then Teng's visit is arranged so that he has a most unusual private dinner with Brzezinski on his first night and, after announcing that there would be no communiqué following the visit, Teng and Carter issue a joint statement affirming their opposition to any nation seeking world "hegemony." This seems to add nothing new; we are opposed to any one nation or group of nations dominating the world. But Moscow knows and Washington knows that "hegemony" is Peking's buzzword for its own undiluted confrontation with the Soviets.

It should be no surprise that Soviet President Leonid Brezhnev immediately asked for an explanation. One hopes that his demand will not make it more difficult for the administration to clarify its position.

A starting point may be to look at the fundamental political underpinning of our Soviet policy and see how it is affected by our Chinese connection. The powerful, though limited, shared interest that brought the Soviet Union and the United States together was the danger of a nuclear war. But it required a deeper political agreement on at least two essentials to give negotiations any chance of success. First was the understanding that each accepted for the foreseeable future the authority of the governing structure in the other and would not, as a matter of policy and active conduct, seek to change it. Second was the understanding that each accepted the existence of a rough balance of power between the two countries.

The Carter Administration demonstrated its poor grasp of the first element in its early handling of the human-rights issue. It failed to see that in Soviet eyes the president's extension of support, personally *and publicly,* to specific imprisoned dissidents went beyond general advocacy of civil rights. The Soviet leadership construed it as a possible U.S. commitment actively to encourage Soviet citizens to oppose the regime. The attendant uncertainty left U.S.-Soviet relations dead in the water for most of 1977 while the administration backed and failed to clarify its position on that first underlying understanding.

The administration's handling of "normalization" with China has called into question its grasp of the second understanding—the balance of power between the two countries. This understanding is tentative and only partially defined in any case. Its acceptance, indeed its acceptability, is called into question by powerful groups on both sides. Its definition is the substance of the upcoming debate on SALT II. But without mutual allegiance to the basic proposition that the military power of the two countries should be essentially equal, the whole framework of the negotiations begins to unravel. So do efforts to stabilize the military balance in regional theaters: in Europe, where Brezhnev has now accepted the crucial Western position that there be common ceilings (a regional balance) for the NATO and Warsaw Pact forces; in the Indian Ocean, where the fate of the stalled negotiations will bear significantly on stability in Africa; in the Middle East, where U.S.-Soviet agreement on limiting arms shipments to the area would add measurably to the stability of the hoped-for political settlements.

The goal of establishing ever wider areas of stabilized military relations will not come easily. Our determination to sustain the military balances will remain an essential precondition to negotiating arrangements to stabilize them.

But it is not just Brezhnev, but also the American people who must know how we relate "normalization" with China to the basic understanding of a balance of power between the United States and the Soviet Union. In the SALT II negotiations, the Soviet side initially insisted on an allowance of nuclear weapons greater than ours on grounds that they were needed to counter a hostile, neighboring China. It was a major concession, requiring Brezhnev and Politburo intercession, when this demand was dropped—one, incidentally, given surprisingly little weight in our debates. The Soviet leadership apparently decided that the question of Chinese nuclear power and its relevance to the U.S.-Soviet balance could be addressed at a later date. The state of the Chinese economy put limits on the speed of a nuclear buildup; Maoist doctrine did not stress high-technology weaponry; and the prospect of some Soviet-Chinese reconciliation in the post-Mao period was not discounted.

Now that situation has markedly changed. Teng's China is bent on invigorating the economy with its own and Western technology and on building modern military forces, including modern nuclear armaments. The enshrinement of the Soviet Union as "enemy No. 1" becomes ever more unequivocal.

In this context, we cannot dodge the question of how we view the emerging Chinese power. Even if it is more prospective than in hand, it counts. Do we see Chinese power, including nuclear power, added to our own, tilting the balance in our favor, invalidating our understanding on balanced U.S. and Soviet power? The temptation to convey intimations to that effect will be strong when SALT II is debated. But if we do so, will SALT II not be the last SALT, taking with it our hope of reducing the nuclear-arms level and the prospect of force reductions in Europe? And what of Soviet actions toward China itself? Would we expect the Soviet Union passively to await the day when Chinese claims on current Soviet territory could be pressed with superior U.S.-Chinese nuclear power behind them? Or do we accept the increased risk of a Soviet preemptive attack on China, where our choice could be involvement in nuclear war or passive acceptance of Soviet destruction of China's counter-weight—and a demonstration of our impotence and lack of wisdom?

Or, rather, are we conscious of the importance of the balance of U.S.-Soviet power? Do we envisage drawing China into the arms-limitation process and the process of negotiated accommodations? And trading on equivalent terms with China and the Soviet Union?

Teng's visit and "normalization" has given a new dimension to U.S. foreign policy. But without clarification of how the Chinese connection affects the basic understanding on the military balance between the United States and the Soviet Union, we cannot know where we are going. And, without clarification, the administration will encounter fundamental misunderstandings in this country that can frustrate and complicate the conduct of any effective foreign policy.

III. IN PURSUIT OF MODERNIZATION

EDITOR'S INTRODUCTION

China has embarked on an ambitious ten-year plan of industrial and agricultural modernization in order to achieve its goal of rising to the status of a superpower by 2,000. In a report entitled "New Economic Policies," Central Intelligence Agency sources detail the range of China's economic aims, including the efforts to develop oil and to import foreign technology.

Trade with the United States is high on China's list of priorities and in the second article, reprinted from the *Far Eastern Economic Review,* Melinda Liu details the economic provisions of the U.S.-China Trade Accord and China's bid for international credit and most-favored nation status. The next two articles, both from *Business Week,* suggest that China might not go through with its so-called "Four Modernizations"—of agriculture, science and technology, industry, and defense; the enormous plan is not only too costly, but also requires a relaxation of socialist tenets that Chinese Communist ideology could not stand.

Fox Butterfield, China correspondent of the New York *Times,* reports ample evidence of private enterprise, in the quiet revival of small businesses in Peking. In the final selection, Louis Kraar, writing in *Asia,* comments on the fact that overseas Chinese businessmen have been invited back to the mainland to bring the knowledge and experience gained in business ventures around the world.

NEW ECONOMIC POLICIES[1]

Modernization and the 10-Year Plan

Peking has yet to specify what is meant by its announced goal of achieving "front rank" economic power by the year 2000. This obviously requires a major breakthrough in the lagging agricultural sector, greatly expanded industrial capacity, and the development of a strong capability in science and technology, especially of an applied nature. Progress along these lines should lead to substantially improved living standards and real incomes. But this could hardly create, in a single generation, anything resembling an affluent society. For example, were China able to sustain its historical growth rate of about 6 percent annually, by the year 2000 its GNP would still be 15 percent below what U.S. GNP was in 1975. And with a population that is likely to approach 1.5 billion by the end of the century, China's per capita GNP would be less than $1,000, about equal to that of Brazil at present. Even remarkable Chinese success in implementing birth control programs would not alter this judgment. Actual possibilities for the economy over the next two decades, of course, fan out considerably depending on how much progress is made during the next eight years, the first phase of the modernization program.

Agricultural Goals

Peking's target of producing 400 million tons of grain in 1985 implies average annual growth of 4.3 percent in 1978–85, compared with a 3.6-percent average during the previous eight years and no increase at all in 1976 and 1977. Attainment of this goal would mean grain production of more than 350 kilograms per capita, well above the 300-kilogram level achieved in the late 1950s and regained in recent years. China's planners clearly are banking on early

[1] Excerpt from U.S. Government document entitled *China: In Pursuit of Economic Modernization*. A research paper prepared for the use of U.S. government officials, by the Central Intelligence Agency. National Foreign Assessment Center. D. '78.

payoffs from expanded mechanization and land improvement programs, as well as improved seeds and rapidly increasing output from imported chemical fertilizer plants now coming on stream.

Since other agricultural subsectors, such as livestock and subsidiary production, have consistently grown more rapidly than grain output, the goal of 4 to 5 percent annual growth in the total value of agricultural production should not be too difficult to achieve *if* the grain production target is attained. Realistically, output is likely to fall somewhat short of these goals.

Industrial Targets

The planned annual increase of more than 10 percent in total industrial output seems within reach, given the 9-percent average annual growth of the past decade—which occurred in spite of periodic, politically caused disruptions. Still, the Chinese will have to make an enormous effort in energy—especially oil and coal—and steel, and increase their purchases of foreign-made plants and equipment. The planned change in the pattern of growth, favoring light industry, may also cause unforeseen difficulties.

Investment Priorities

AGRICULTURE

Peking's 10-year plan places heavy demands on agriculture for foodstuffs and industrial raw materials, both for domestic consumption and export. The stagnation of grain production since 1975—following a decade and a half of heavy investment in agriculture—has once again demonstrated the vulnerability of the economy to agricultural setbacks. Earlier this year, party Chairman Hua Kuo-feng spelled out the implications of continued slow growth in agriculture:

. . . Agriculture is the foundation of the national economy. If agriculture does not develop faster, there will be no upswing in our industry and economy as a whole; and even if there is a temporary upswing, a decline will follow. There will be really serious trouble in the event of major natural calamities. . . .

To accelerate output growth—or, perhaps more realistically, to guard against the possibility that a series of poor harvests will undercut the 10-year plan and stall the drive for modernization—Peking has stepped up its investment in agriculture.

Current agricultural policy emphasizes increased mechanization along with a push for farmland improvement. As a result of steel shortages in 1976–77, the mechanization program is behind schedule, but the leadership intends to make up for lost time and fulfill the original targets. These targets call for the "basic" mechanization of agriculture by 1980. Goals for major items, apparently stated in terms of inventory (except for fertilizer), include:

—A 70-percent increase in large and medium-sized tractors.
—A 110-percent increase in machine-drawn farm implements.
—A 86-percent increase in hand-guided tractors.
—A 32-percent increase in drainage and irrigation machinery.
—A 58-percent increase in chemical fertilizer production.

To achieve these goals, state-supplied steel for the manufacture and repair of farm machines during 1978–80 will be raised by a total of 50 percent over the previous three-year period; and the share of locally produced steel used on the farm and in machinery production will be upped from the current 30 percent or so to more than 40 percent.

Perhaps because these objectives are so ambitious, and the sector so backward, Peking has selected the farm machinery industry as one of the first industries to be reorganized under a plan that may eventually encompass all of industry. Underlying this action is the familiar proposition that production, quality of output, and productivity can be substantially improved by setting up large, highly specialized production facilities [they are now all-inclusive]. Although small, locally managed plants will continue to be important sources of simple machinery and equipment for the farm sector, they will no longer be the primary agent for mechanization. Many of these plants instead will be absorbed into local or regional networks featuring large-scale, specialized production and assembly facilities. One of the reports delivered at the Third National Conference on Agricultural Mechanization, held in January, told how authorities in one municipality had doubled the output of tractor gears in only six months by pooling the gearmaking equipment from seven different tractor plants and adopting more up-to-date production techniques.

Increased mechanization is designed first of all to relieve seasonal labor shortages, the most immediate and direct effect of which will be to permit an increase in multiple cropping and raise grain yields. Larger supplies of irrigation and drainage equipment will improve Chinese capacity to deal with drought and flooding and will aid in the expansion of areas of "high and stable yields."

Mechanization will also help compensate for the loss of agricultural labor to nonfarm activities—a problem that appears to have been significant during recent years. Since the early 1970s, as a result of the rapid development of rural industry, demand for rural labor has greatly increased. Large numbers of peasants have been drawn away from collective agricultural activities, resulting in a shortage of farm labor and, in some areas, a decline in farm output. Increased mechanization will help solve these problems and will also encourage more rapid industrialization in those areas where industrial development has been retarded by labor shortages.

The growth in use of machines envisaged by Peking will encounter difficulties, many of which relate to or affect the demand for farm machinery. Poor machine quality, the lack of standardization, and the limited range of equipment and accessories available have been cited as major reasons for the reorganization of the farm machinery industry. Without substantial improvements in these areas, rural communes and production brigades may be reluctant to make major investment purchases. An additional factor in this investment decision is the scarcity of trained manpower to operate and repair farm machinery. Peking anticipates considerable improvement in these areas (the number of technicians is to be doubled by 1980) ; and to further attract purchasers, it plans to cut costs—and presumably prices—20 percent by 1980.

The goal of 85 percent mechanization set for 1985 means that investment in machinery will continue to absorb a large share of agricultural investment during the Sixth Five-Year Plan (1981–85), but there will be a shift of emphasis away from simple machinery and tractors to heavier, more sophisticated items. Farmland capital construction, particularly those programs other than irrigation and drainage, will receive relatively greater emphasis during 1981–85 (compared with 1976–80) in order to meet the 1985 target of providing one *mou* (one-fifteenth of a hectare) of stable, high-yield farmland per rural resident. Peking also plans during the next plan period to invest more heavily in land reclamation, much of it in border areas where state farms are predominant; more than 13 million hectares of land are to be reclaimed during the next eight years, expanding farmland by some 12 percent. The chemical fertilizer industry should continue to receive a large share of investment during the Sixth Plan period; although the last of the 13 large imported urea complexes will be in full production by that time, the rate of application of chemical fertilizers still will be low compared with usage in Japan and Taiwan.

The above discussion highlights the more important components of agricultural investment scheduled for 1976–85. Peking is aware of the complexities of rural development and that the above programs are only part of the matrix of inputs and practices that are associated with the modernization of agriculture. Current programs do not ignore, for example, the investments that must be made to improve seed varieties, to develop better methods of plant protection, and to adapt cultivation techniques to new crops and cropping patterns. For the moment, however, the emphasis is on machinery, land improvement, and chemical fertilizer production—which apparently are thought to offer quick payoffs in terms of sharp increases in labor productivity and output growth.

INDUSTRY

Hua Kuo-feng has sketched out the investment program that will be required to generate an overall industrial growth rate of more than 10 percent annually during the next eight years. According to Hua:

> . . . the state plans to build or complete 120 large-scale projects, including 10 iron and steel complexes, nine nonferrous metal complexes, eight coal mines, 10 oil and gas fields, 30 power stations, six new trunk railways, and five key harbors.

The cost of the program, in terms of funds budgeted for capital construction in industry during 1978–85, will approximately equal the total of the previous 28 years.

Metals. The 10 projects in the steel industry apparently include the construction of three entirely new complexes and the renovation and expansion of seven existing facilities. Peking is seeking the latest technology from Japan and possibly West Germany for these projects, and the cost will be enormous. The foreign exchange bill for one new plant alone could easily exceed the combined cost of all of China's whole plant purchases in the early 1970s. Because of the high cost and China's limited experience in constructing huge integrated plants, the steel modernization program almost certainly will be stretched out, perhaps even into the 1990s.

Little is known about the nine nonferrous metal complexes cited by Hua, although Peking has approached both Japan and Italy regarding facilities for processing aluminum and copper. China's capabilities in these industries are badly dated, and Peking will probably seek out foreign suppliers of complete plants as the quickest means of expanding capacity and updating technology.

Energy. Plans for 1985 indicate an attempt to rectify the longstanding imbalance in investment allocations that have grossly favored the oil industry and neglected coal. (Coal accounts for 66 percent of primary energy production, petroleum 23 percent, natural gas 10 percent, and hydroelectric power one percent.)

During 1978–87, Peking plans to double coal production to reach an output rate of more than one billion tons per year. This will prove difficult: the implicit average annual growth rate would be 7.2 percent, compared with the actual 6.3 percent average growth in coal production since 1970. The industry is technologically backward and its labor productivity notoriously low; over one-third of total output is produced at small mines and pits. To accomplish its goal, Peking plans to increase mechanization at existing mines and open eight new large mines.

Oil production probably is planned to grow at rates comparable to those of recent years—around 13 percent annually—rather than at the rates of earlier years—over 20 percent. Nonetheless, the share of investment allocated to the petroleum industry shows no signs of declining. The costs of finding and producing oil are steadily rising. Most of China's readily accessible deposits—shallow deposits in the north and northeast—have already been tapped and in some cases are showing initial signs of depletion. For example, Ta-ch'ing, which produces one-half of China's oil, is yielding an increasingly large water cut (the field is water injected) and its shallow reservoirs have come within sight of depletion. The shallow deposits at Sheng-li and Ta-kang, which together produce another 30 percent of total production, have some potential for expansion, but from their beginnings these fields—because of complex geological conditions that have resulted in a multiplicity of scattered, small reservoirs with widely differing characteristics—have taxed Chinese technical capabilities. Outside of a few fields with shallow deposits of unknown potential, additional production gains will have to come from deposits that are deeper, offshore, or located in the far west—and which therefore require large investments in infrastructure and more advanced technology.

Primarily as a result of coal shortages, domestic oil consumption has grown at an average annual rate of more than 15 percent since 1970—a rate that Peking considers excessive, since it has eaten into the surplus available for export. Petroleum now supplies a little over 20 percent of China's energy needs, up from 13 percent in 1970. This shift toward greater use of oil is bound to continue, despite efforts to spur the growth of coal production.

An examination of energy consumption trends indicates that it will be very difficult to slow the growth of demand for oil; indeed it will probably grow more rapidly as modernization gets under way. Mechanization will greatly add to petroleum consumption in the agricultural sector, where energy use has nearly tripled since 1970. And the expanded use of diesel locomotives and motor vehicles, together with agricultural mechanization, probably will more than offset any successful efforts by industry to reduce its per unit consumption of petroleum. With crude oil output rising at an average rate of 11 percent annually since 1974 and the future demand for oil—for domestic use and export—likely to exceed 15 percent annually, it is not hard to understand why Peking has moved so quickly to initiate talks with U.S. and Japanese oil companies about possible cooperative development of China's offshore oil resources. As a result of domestic consumption trends and the importance of crude oil exports in foreign trade plans, the petroleum industry will continue to command a large share of state investment and in addition will receive a substantial infusion of foreign capital.

The 30 new power plants, together with capacity increases at small plants and the expansion of existing facilities, should enable the Chinese to maintain high rates of growth in electricity output through 1985. Nevertheless, capacity will expand at best by 6 to 8 million kilowatts per year (compared with an average of about 5 million kilowatts annually in recent years), and production will have difficulty keeping pace with demand. Local shortages will continue to occur. The severity of those shortages will depend upon the effectiveness of conservation measures and the degree to which transmission and distribution facilities are improved.

TRANSPORTATION

The six new trunk railroads and five new harbors mentioned by Hua are only the more visible parts of a comprehensive program for modernizing the transport sector.

Plans for the railroads, the backbone of China's transport sector, call for:

—Widespread use of diesel and electric locomotives, lightweight passenger cars, greater capacity freight cars, and the most modern high-speed passenger trains.

—Extensive adoption of heavy-duty rails, automatically controlled crossings, and increased capacity bridges.

—Introduction of computer services throughout the system.

—Mechanization of cargo handling, track maintenance, construction, and locomotive repair.

To increase traffic on other transport modes—trucks, ships, and aircraft—China can be expected to introduce such intermodal services as containerization and piggyback operations.

In nearly all aspects, the Chinese must look abroad for both equipment and technological know-how. Although no major new contracts have been signed, substantial orders from Japan, West Germany, and France are in prospect. In addition to diesel locomotives, jet transports, and motor vehicles, the shopping list includes technology related to centralized traffic control systems and other computer applications.

New Quest for Efficiency

The above list of projects will greatly expand productive capacity. To realize its modernization goals, however, the Chinese leadership is counting on substantial payoffs from new and improved systems of economic management.

It is in the realm of planning and management that recent initiatives contrast most sharply with the practices of the past 10 years. Current economic policies in many ways resemble, in their demonstration of flexibility and pragmatism, policies that were discussed and experimented with during the early 1960s, before the Cultural Revolution.

Then, as now, a leadership headed by economic moderates faced the problems of rebuilding a weakened economy and establishing new organizational and incentive structures more supportive of future growth. In recent months Peking has taken measures to restore peak levels of productivity and to improve the efficiency of resource use. New initiatives are most apparent in the areas of wages and incentives, factory management, planning and organization, and in policy toward science and technology. The political and ideological relaxation that has followed the purge of the Gang also extends to economic discussion, and prominent economists are again playing a role in public affairs.

WAGE REFORM

Peking's success in bolstering economic growth during the remainder of the Fifth Plan period depends heavily on its ability to improve work incentives and boost labor productivity. When the present government took office in October 1976, it faced a disgruntled work force which since 1974 had increasingly resorted to slowdowns, absenteeism, and strikes to protest low wages and eroding living standards. One year later, with low morale and low productivity still serious problems, the new leadership announced pay increases for three-fifths of the urban labor force, stressing that the improved economic situation made it possible to raise wages. Nonetheless, everyone realized that the move was intended to buy time until a more thorough consideration of wage policy was possible.

The pay hike probably has had a beneficial impact on work discipline and, therefore, on productivity. However, the wage increase—amounting to some 10 to 15 percent for the lowest paid workers and around 10 percent overall—is probably regarded by many as inadequate. The abolition of production bonuses in the late 1960s (which cut personal incomes of industrial workers by approximately 10 percent), followed by a period of essentially unchanging wages and larger-than-normal price increases, resulted in serious losses of purchasing power which the wage increase leaves largely unrestored. In view of the magnitude of discontent over wages and living conditions, any substantial improvement in work incentives—and productivity—will require further concessions by Peking.

The current leadership recognizes the need for a comprehensive wage reform which in addition to raising pay rates and sanctioning the use of production bonuses and piece rates, would, *inter alia,* establish rules governing eligibility for and regularity of promotions. This may involve no more than enforcing existing regulations—regulations that have been widely ignored during the past decade.

The basic problem, however, is in deciding just how much wages should be raised; or, whether bonus and piece rate systems—or some combination of the three—may be more effective in raising labor productivity. And these decisions must be coordinated with plans for consumer goods production and imports. The apparent inaction on wage reform may signify that Peking is hoping that the small wage increase granted in 1977, along with the introduction of bonuses and piece rates and some improvements in living conditions, will reduce worker dissatisfaction (that is, raise labor productivity) to an acceptable level.

Hua Kuo-feng's remarks at the National People's Congress last February ended any doubts that the leadership plans to make greater use of material incentives. Hua said that the staff and workers of state enterprises should be paid "primarily on a time-rate basis with piecework playing a secondary role, and with additional bonuses." He also indicated that preparations for a reform of the wage system were under way.

The length of Hua's comments on wages and living conditions is revealing. Past references to these topics by members of the leadership have been brief and for the most part noncommittal statements to the effect that, as production increased, consumption and living standards would increase accordingly. Hua's remarks are further confirmation of the pressures being exerted by Chinese consumers and of the leadership's recognition that these demands can no longer be ignored or turned aside by ideological condemnation of material incentives and appeals to patriotism. The 12-percent annual rate of growth planned for light industry during 1976–85—2 percentage points higher than for industry as a whole—and the apparent decision to import consumer goods when excess demand becomes a problem are examples of the type of policy that can be expected from Peking.

Strengthening Enterprise Management

With the elimination of revolutionary committees in production units, Peking has mounted a concerted attempt to restore the systems needed for effective management, for example, financial and quality controls, material consumption norms, and the like. The most recent, important development in this area has been the issuance in April of the Central Committee document, the 30-Point Decision on Industry. The *People's Daily* editorial announcing the action called the document the "fundamental law" for industrial and communications enterprises, which, it said,

provides a basis to eliminate chaos, restore order, and set things straight from the bottom up. . . . It specifically defines a series of principles and policies on tasks and basic regulations for enterprises, methods and work styles, and ways of improving industrial management and quickening the pace of industrial development.

The 30 Points represents a major accomplishment in the lengthy attempt to bring order to the economy. In recounting the history of this struggle, and of the document, *People's Daily* pointed out that it retains "many" good points from the 70-Point Decision on Industry promulgated in the early 1960s, the 10 Points of 1972, and the 1975 document referred to as the 20 Points.

The appearance of the 30 Points, bearing the imprimatur of the Central Committee, should help dispel the misgivings of managers and middle- and lower-level functionaries who thus far have been reluctant—for fear of a sudden change in policy that would make them targets for leftists—to implement the policies of the new government. Indicating that not even this action is expected to completely allay the fears of lower level officials, *People's Daily* cautioned that, "Due to the longtime ideological confusion caused by the Gang of Four, we may encounter some ideological obstacles during this trial implementation."

The 30-Point Decision on Industry is mainly concerned with immediate productivity increases and the reestablishment of familiar institutions and practices which can be expected to have a positive impact on efficiency. Perhaps more significant over the long run is Peking's curiosity and questioning about managerial techniques used in other countries with vastly different economic systems—implying that China's leaders are considering further, perhaps major, changes in the economic system. In the most publicized instance, they have shown considerable interest in the Yugoslav system; but the list of countries where official Chinese visitors have displayed more than a passing interest in management extends to Japan, several countries in Western Europe, and Romania. There is nothing to suggest what changes Peking may have in mind, but the flexibility that such a search implies is remarkable when one considers the ideological rigidity that has constrained public discussion and policy during much of the past 10 years. . . .

REAPPEARANCE OF PROMINENT ECONOMIC OFFICIALS

Among the signs of a budding economic liberalism are the rehabilitation of once-disgraced economic officials and the promise of a return to more substantive economic discourse.

Perhaps most symbolic of Peking's about face in economic policies is the reappearance of economist Sun Yeh-fang. During the Cultural Revolution, Sun—a former director of the State Statistical Bureau and once head of the Economic Research Institute of the Academy of Sciences—was denounced as "China's Liberman" for advocating study of Yugoslavia's use of profits as a management tool. The vehemence of the attacks on Sun made his rehabilitation in 1977 as remarkable as Vice Premier Teng Hsiao-p'ing's reappearance in 1973.

Sun since April has been an adviser to the Economic Research Institute where he shares responsibility for restoring and planning China's economic research effort. In May, he, along with another prominent rehabilitee, Hsu Ti-hsin (now head of ERI), and a third economist, Kuang Jih-an, presided over a series of regional economic planning forums. In addition to holding discussions of current economic conditions and the 10-year plan, forum participants also discussed ongoing research and proposed topics for future work. The proposed topics, as reported by New China News Agency, presage a movement away from the "quote Mao, quote Marx" economics that had become standard fare in recent years. This change is beginning to be seen in the journal *Economic Research* which resumed publication this year after a decade-long hiatus.

Hsueh Mu-ch'iao is another rehabilitee of note. He once headed the State Statistical Bureau, was a deputy on the State Planning Commission, and was head of the National Price Commission. Hsueh's current role is unknown; he has been noted in attendance at important functions, and some of his writings from the 1950s have been republished—for no apparent reason except perhaps to notify the bureaucracy of his return.

Widening Role for Foreign Technology

Just as China is looking abroad for models of managerial efficiency, so are its planners turning to the foreign sector for acquisitions of modern plants and technology. With investment priorities now generally established, extensive negotiations are under way with Japanese and Western firms for a new wave of technology imports that should continue for the next several years.

Complete industrial plants top the shopping list. Major interest centers on facilities for the steel, electric power, petrochemicals, and fertilizer industries. Inquiries also have been made for plants producing nonferrous metals, locomotives, trucks, and electronic components. In addition to whole plants, the Chinese have shown great interest in purchasing specialized machinery and equipment, particularly items needed by the fuel industries. Computers and telecommunications equipment also are high on the list.

Despite Peking's new overtures, however, technical and financial constraints restrict the scope of any drive to expand technology imports. While a sizable army of middle-level factory technicians has been spawned by China's "learning by doing" approach to industrial training, there is a serious shortage of experienced design and production engineers and other highly trained technicians essential in setting up and operating a modern factory. Even with the new emphasis on expertise, a resolution of this problem is bound to take a very long time.

A major financial constraint is China's limited capacity to earn foreign exchange. Credits and other forms of import financing can smooth the repayment obligations, but ultimately higher levels of exports are needed. Many traditional exports depend directly on the backward agricultural sector, and the past failure to invest in mining and processing of metals and minerals forces China to import many of the goods that it should be able to export. Technical problems and rapidly increasing domestic demand will constrain exports of petroleum. Nevertheless, as Peking progresses with its modernization plans, China is likely to evolve new methods of financing foreign purchases. These methods may take the form of greater acceptance of foreign debt and widening interest in generating new sources of export earnings.

In recent months, for example, Chinese officials have been considering trade and financing arrangements that they would not even discuss previously: (a) long-term credits and the financing of capital imports through foreign bank deposits with the Bank of China; (b) barter and compensation deals for plant purchases; (c) the importing of materials to reprocess for export; (d) designation of certain factories to produce goods for specific foreign markets; and (e) fuller compliance with international standards on patents, trademarks, and copyrights. There has also been some talk of cooperative ventures with foreign oil firms to develop China's offshore oil resources. How far Peking is willing to pursue these more adventurous trade and finance practices is unclear. Stated policy still precludes direct loans, joint ventures, and foreign investment. The leadership likely will introduce these more flexible practices on a selective basis, redefining self-reliance to justify their actions, but not abandoning the basic principle.

Competing Needs and Policy Choices

Productivity gains play such an integral role in the 10-year plan that the deftness with which Peking handles related topics like wage reform, bonus schemes, and consumer goods markets will have a major impact on the success of the plan. The sensitivity of the wage issue and the possibility that by responding to worker demands the leadership may be contributing to an incipient consumerism have wide-ranging implications that will be discussed at length by the Politburo. The very fact that these problems are by and large unfamiliar to the leadership makes unlikely their quick *and efficient* resolution. And it increases the possibility that misjudgments will further jeopardize plan goals.

In earlier years, Peking could concentrate on maximizing the rate of investment and output growth, while avoiding bottlenecks and inflationary pressures. Consumer needs were not ignored; but the consumer was made to understand that, at least for the time being, growth in personal real incomes had to remain small. Because the price level generally was kept under control, a small annual increase in wages was acceptable to the work force. Open complaints were very infrequent and work slowdowns, absenteeism, and strikes were practically unheard of. This is no longer the case.

Workers learned during the Cultural Revolution that they could express their economic grievances with a degree of impunity and effectiveness that was previously unsuspected. The abolition of production bonuses in the late 1960s (which cut personal incomes of industrial workers by approximately 10 percent) followed by a period of essentially unchanging wages and larger-than-normal price increases turned minor grievances into serious labor problems. Government inaction resulted in a variety of job actions and a sharp decline in labor productivity.

Peking not only has to face up to the problems of lost purchasing power and wage reform, but it must also convince the worker that this government is fair and can be trusted. First and most important, however, it must come up with a package of wage increases and bonuses that significantly increases incomes, and it must ensure the availability of goods at prices that leave the worker with real gains.

In the next year or two, consumption increases can be achieved by tapping unused capacity in light industry and restoring order to markets, especially those for nonstaple foods. Productivity growth in response to the wage increase in late 1977 and in anticipation of further wage adjustments will also provide for some increases in consumption.

Beyond 1980 and until the current investment program is completed, more than moderate gains in consumption seem unlikely. Investments in agriculture are being substantially increased. Since foodstuffs account for about one-half of consumer expenditures, increases in agricultural investment imply gains in consumption. And because a large share of the raw materials used in light industry also comes from the agricultural sector, growth in industrial consumer goods output should also improve. Agriculture, however, is fickle; without favorable weather, investment may not yield the anticipated growth—particularly if one is looking for a payoff within the relatively short period of five to 10 years. When discounted for variation in weather and the complexities of agricultural development, the agricultural component of investment can be expected to yield only moderate gains in output and consumption growth.

Light industrial output is to grow by 150 percent during 1978–85, an average annual rate of slightly more than 12 percent. Comments by the head of the State Planning Commission and by officials in the Ministry of Light Industry indicate, however, that these gains are intended to come largely from fuller utilization of capacity and more efficient use of inputs, not from investments in new capacity. Our estimate of growth in consumer goods production shows an average annual rate of growth of 7 to 8 percent since 1957. This falls so far short of the planned 12 percent that one has to be skeptical of Peking's ability to achieve its goal without massive additions to capacity.

The growth of per capita consumption will also be constrained by yearly population increases of 1 to 2 percent and by exports of consumer goods. Foodstuffs and light industrial products account for over 50 percent of total exports. Raw materials, particularly crude oil and coal, are to become an increasing share of exports, but until the mid-1980s when current investments in those sectors really begin to pay off, foodstuffs and light industrial goods will continue to be important export items.

All of this suggests that Peking may find itself still faced with labor problems and lagging productivity throughout the 10-year plan. If it turns out that moderate consumption gains will not induce the productivity gains implicit in plan goals, then Peking may be forced to cut back on its investment in heavy industry, something that would be done only reluctantly.

The defense budget cannot be regarded as a significant source of transferable funds. Cuts in defense spending in the early 1970s (with no evidence of substantially larger expenditures since) and the real need for a costly program to modernize conventional forces have probably been cited in arguments for an increase in military budgets. However, in the debate last year on military spending, the Hua regime argued that a strong defense requires a modern industrial base. The debate apparently ended with a consensus (1) to hold military spending at a level which allows for the most essential aspects of defense modernization and (2) to make underutilized resources controlled by the military partially available for civilian industry. The impression is that much of the resources which are transferable to civilian use has already been—or soon will be—tapped, lessening the possibility for significant resource transfers during 1981–85.

Peking is showing less reluctance to rely on the foreign sector, and it conceivably could invite additional foreign investment in its consumer goods industries; but such arrangements could hardly provide a significant share of the needed increase in consumer goods production. Similarly, further efforts to improve efficiency, if successful, would seem to offer the hope of only marginal gains in the output of consumer goods.

When one considers the political as well as the economic difficulties that China's modernizers are likely to encounter, the undertaking they have embarked upon is even more impressive. Considerable controversy appears inevitable—not only over basic policy changes certainly but also over the nuts-and-bolts issues of inplementation that affect the political and economic status of bureaucrats and bureaucracies. Nevertheless, Peking seems capable of resolving these difficulties in ways that will allow satisfactory gains in per capita consumption and, at the same time, permit rates of investment and industrial growth that are reasonably close to plan goals. In short, the 10-year plan is likely to be a successful first step toward the modernization of China's economy.

U.S.–CHINA TRADE AGREEMENT[2]

Canton

On top of the old wing of the Dong Fang Hotel, a motley gathering of foreign businessmen, journalists and diplomats watched curiously as two harassed Americans rushed in waving a sheaf of papers which will move the normalization of Sino–U.S. commercial relations into gear: the U.S.–China trade accord.

After more than 10 days of intense negotiation—during which 75–80 percent of the original text which left Washington was redrafted—a bilateral trade accord was initialled on May 14 by Chinese Foreign Trade Minister Li Qiang in

[2] Article entitled "U.S. and Peking Find a Way," by Melinda Liu, business editor. *Far Eastern Economic Review.* p 73–4. My. 25, '79. Copyright 1979. Reprinted by permission.

Peking and by U.S. Commerce Secretary Juanita Kreps in Canton. The initialling paves the way for U.S. granting of most favored nation status and official credits to China, as well as for a significant increase in commercial contact on all levels.

Earlier in Peking, Kreps also signed the frozen assets agreement initialled by U.S. Treasury Secretary Michael Blumenthal during his trip to Peking at the beginning of the year [1979]. Under the agreement, China is to pay U.S. $80.5 million to U.S. claimants, while the U.S. will unfreeze some U.S. $80 million in Chinese assets.

Resolution of the long-standing frozen assets issue, which has blocked normal bilateral commercial and financial relations for nearly three decades, was a precondition to the forging of the trade accord. In turn, the trade agreement initialled here establishes the framework for normal commercial relations, perhaps the most important of which is U.S. granting of most favored nation status. This will reduce tariffs on Chinese exports to the U.S. by up to 75 percent.

The existence of a bilateral trade accord is also a principle prerequisite for granting China U.S. Export-Import Bank credits, in which Chinese officials have expressed open interest. Members of the Kreps delegation said that at current exim rates and with the kinds of projects they have seen in China, the potential for exim credits to China would probably be in billions of U.S. dollars.

They also pointed out, however, that the exim bank is tightly constrained by budgetary considerations, and that as a banking organization wanting an assurance of China's ability to repay, the exim bank would need information on economic conditions, prospects and policies before it could offer credits. "Whether difficulties arise here depends on what exim asks for," said one U.S. representative. Moreover, the question of government and exim bank claims (as opposed to private claims) —involving about U.S. $26 million in principal and an equal amount in interest—must be resolved before China can take exim credits.

In the past, Chinese reluctance to disclose key economic indicators was seen as a major stumbling block to its membership in such organizations as the International Monetary Fund and the World Bank.

During the trade accord talks in Peking, the exim question exemplified the type of compromise which both sides reached. A U.S. spokesman said: "The Chinese did not want anything in the trade pact on supplying information, and the Americans did not want anything on granting exim credits. And that's the way it came out."

The accord had undergone arduous discussion in Peking before it was initialled ad referendum the evening before Kreps left China. The Chinese had wanted more of a general statement in principle and the U.S. had wanted more detail. When the two sides finally arrived at the 15-page text (in English, double-spaced) it was the longest and most complicated trade accord China had concluded with any country.

The accord includes provisions for reciprocal most favored nation status; non-discriminatory customs procedures and conditions for sale in internal markets; a framework for financial transactions (including use of convertible currency) ; the prompt resolution of commercial disputes which might arise between private parties; resolving trade problems between the two governments; and the protection of patents, trademarks and copyrights.

Before Kreps left Peking, five other agreements (apart from the claims/assets agreement) were signed. One dealt with the exchange of commercial exhibitions and four dealt with cooperation in science and technology—weather research, oceanography, weights and measures, and the exchange of information. In addition, a number of protocols were reached on lower-level matters, and the two sides held maritime and aviation discussions which will lead to future negotiation.

Several elements must fall into place before the trade accord can be implemented. After formal signing it will be submitted to the U.S. Congress for approval.

Separate Sino-U.S. textile negotiations are scheduled to

resume on May 21, and Assistant Secretary of State for Economic Affairs Dick Cooper, a member of the Kreps group, says: "The trade accord is not likely to pass Congress unless a textile agreement is signed. We envisage a signing of the textile agreement in late May or June."

In addition, there is still the Jackson-Vanik amendment to the U.S. Trade Act of 1974 which has been applied to China and the Soviet Union. The amendment prohibits the granting of most favored nation status or official credits to a socialist country which denies or prohibits the right or opportunity of its citizens to migrate.

The U.S. president could waive the amendment in China's case if he decides it will encourage more liberal emigration policies and if Peking has assured him of its intention to permit freer immigration in the future. There is also talk in Congress that Senators Jackson and Vanik might amend or withdraw their own amendment, or attach a rider to the trade accord. Moreover, the administration has expressed a desire to grant most favored nation status "even handedly" to both China and the Soviet Union, and ensuing legislation may thus include a package involving both countries.

U.S. spokesmen have not ruled out the possibility that the Sino-U.S. trade accord might run into some last-minute snags—as the claims/assets agreement did—before the formal signing. One such hitch was the Chinese request for a list of holders of assets seized by China. The impasse was resolved when the U.S. agreed to provide a list of holders of assets whose claimants are government agencies or Chinese banks. The main U.S. concern had been to keep confidential the list of holders who are private citizens.

THE LONG ROAD TO LARGE-SCALE TRADE[3]

Western businessmen's expectations of large-scale trade with China are not going to be fulfilled for a long time, if

[3] From article entitled "China's Long Road to Large-Scale Trade," by Lewis H. Young, editor. *Business Week*, p 132–3. My. 28, '79. By special permission, © 1979 by McGraw-Hill, Inc., New York, N.Y. 10020. All rights reserved.

ever. The Chinese cannot afford the ambitious economic expansion program, including 120 major projects costing more than $250 billion, that they announced in February 1978. China's leaders now see that their country's administrative systems will have to be modified drastically to allow rapid growth of foreign trade, particularly with the industrialized West. And a germ of allegiance to Chairman Mao's longtime policy of economic self-reliance is still alive.

In Japan, whose businessmen have been building up trade with China since 1972, many China experts doubt that the Chinese now have the managers and technicians needed for the giant economic development program they have started. During most of the Cultural Revolution, from 1966 to 1976, universities were closed, and no new scientists, engineers, or managers were trained. And as many as half of the managers appointed to high posts in ministries and factories were chosen for their political reliability rather than their management expertise. They are still in those jobs.

Reassessment

There is now a marked pause in the "Four Modernizations"—of agriculture, science and technology, industry, and defense. Chinese officials call it a "reassessment" or "readjustment." But the fact is that, after a veritable blizzard of signings last October and November, almost no new contracts, except for very small ones, have been signed with U.S., German, or Japanese companies during the past three months.

The big question, though, is whether the current reassessment represents another dramatic change in China's domestic and foreign policy. At the U.S. embassy in Peking, economic and political officers are accepting the Chinese view that it does not. When Commerce Secretary Juanita M. Kreps visited Vice-Premier Deng Xiaoping [Teng Hsiaoping] in Peking on May 9, he told her that the Four Modernizations remain China's basic policy.

After Mao's death, as China began to allow individual ministries and plants to make big economic decisions on their own, a lot of projects were started without anyone considering whether there was enough money to pay for them or an infrastructure in place to accommodate them. Through an interpreter, Deng explained the problem to U.S. journalists who accompanied Secretary Kreps to Peking. "For a number of years the factors in our economy have been in imbalance," he said. "We don't have enough electric power, for example. If you want to build more factories, how are you going to operate them without power? If we don't improve our transportation, how can we expand?" He added: "Through this readjustment, we are trying to speed up the pace of our development, not slow it down."

Certainly the priorities have shifted. Instead of concentrating on building up heavy industries such as iron and steel, chemicals, and petrochemicals, the Chinese now say they will emphasize:
—Development of electric power, particularly hydroelectric plants on the Yangtze River.
—Mining to produce coal for power plants and nonferrous metals for export (in order to earn foreign exchange).
—Transportation.
—Light industry such as textiles, dinnerware, sporting goods, and hardware, also in order to earn foreign exchange.

Building up light industry has other advantages: It can be carried out more quickly, will contribute to an improved standard of living, and will increase the volume of products that China is already producing, without requiring new technology. Big contracts for projects in these areas will begin flowing by September, one U.S. embassy official is betting, because the Chinese seem so positive about these new plans.

By that time the normalization of economic relations with the U.S. will be nearly completed. The process started on March 2, [1979] when Treasury Secretary W. Michael Blumenthal initialed an agreement during his visit to Peking to settle claims on blocked assets. Secretary Kreps signed that agreement during her visit, after negotiators from both sides had argued for nearly two months over how the agreement was to be implemented and how much help the U.S. would give in finding Chinese assets that are scattered in U.S. banks. Without this accord, Chinese goods or ships that arrived in the U.S. would be subject to seizure to satisfy claims by U.S. citizens against the Chinese government.

The next step is the trade agreement that Kreps initialed on May 14 in Canton. Required by the U.S. Trade Act of 1974, this agreement sets up a framework for trade between the two countries. Among other things, it assures patent protection for U.S. products, establishes procedures for preventing disruption of the U.S. market by exports from China, and provides for offices for private U.S. companies in Peking, where office space is scarce. Japanese trading companies have been able to negotiate extraordinary facilities for themselves, including very large meeting rooms in the Peking Hotel, the city's best, while U.S. companies have had to scurry to get small, bug-infested rooms at the Minzu Hotel, the lesser of the two in which foreigners are billeted.

Ticklish Textile Questions

It may take many weeks for negotiators to work out the meaning of each section and methods of implementing the agreement before it can be formally signed. Congress will then have to approve it. But before sending the pact to Capitol Hill, the Carter Administration faces the ticklish job of negotiating an agreement to limit Chinese textile exports to the U.S., thus allaying U.S. textile makers' fears. The Chinese are balking at restrictions they consider too tight, because they see textile exports as one of their best means of earning foreign exchange. But once the trade and textile accords are approved, the President will ask Congress to authorize Export-Import Bank credits for China and grant most-favored-nation tariff treatment to Chinese goods. The Chinese want MFN badly, not only as a stimulus to their exports but also as a symbol of equal status with other countries.

After that, only minor steps will remain to complete normalization. A maritime agreement will facilitate ocean shipping. And the Ex-Im Bank still has a claim against China for repayment of a $26 million loan, plus $24 million interest, that was made during the 1940s to finance railroad equipment. As a final step, the U.S. would like to see China draw up an investment code that would spell out how U.S. companies could invest in China and what protections they would have. The Chinese have proposed setting up joint ventures with Western companies, but Secretary Kreps told Vice-Premier Deng that a code was essential in order to interest American business in such schemes. The Chinese are taking the suggestion seriously, and they expect to publish a code by early 1980.

The Carter Administration's efforts to speed up the process of normalization explain why so many Cabinet officers have gone to China during the past nine months. Energy Secretary James R. Schlesinger and Agriculture Secretary Bob Bergland went to China last year, and visits by Special Trade Representative Robert S. Strauss and Health, Education and Welfare Secretary Joseph A. Califano Jr. are scheduled in late May and June. "Each Cabinet officer brings expertise to a certain area which has to be developed in our relationship," says Richard N. Cooper, Under Secretary of State for economics. "President Carter wants to get each of these things moving, and a way to do so is to send out his top officials." Kreps's visit is a good example of how the process can work. Her presence broke the deadlock over claims and assets, because the Chinese wanted to accomplish something tangible while she was there. And by focusing Chinese attention on the trade agreement, her trip resulted in initialing of the pact, even though this had not been expected when she left Washington.

An important reason for the U.S. interest in speeding up normalization, of course, is Peking's role as a balancing element in a triangular relationship with the Soviet Union, the U.S., and China. But "even if the Soviet Union did not exist," Cooper insists, "it would be desirable to normalize relations with China, given its size and importance as a country and an economy."

That is why U.S. China watchers insist there will be a

long-term payout for U.S. companies that have the persever-
ance and patience. Christopher H. Phillips, president of the
National Council for U.S.-China Trade, a quasi-governmen-
tal organization, estimates that despite the current reassessment, China's trade with the West will grow 18 percent to
20 percent a year (from 1978's estimated $21 billion) in
each of the next six years to between $63 billion and $65
billion by 1985. Last year, U.S. companies accounted for
only about 6 percent of China's worldwide trade. By 1985,
Phillips believes, the U.S. share will roughly double that
figure to between 10 percent and 12 percent.

Intellectual Property

As Chinese leaders attempt to reorder their priorities,
they will have to devise ways of adapting their centralized
decision-making to the requirements of foreign trade. China
conducts all its trade through just 20 state corporations,
while thousands of U.S. companies import and export. As
Kreps explained to Deng, the U.S. government will merely
establish a framework within which trade takes place; individual companies will carry it out. China will also have
to recognize intellectual property, a concept it does not have
now. No one will sell China advanced technology until it
has set up a system of patents and copyrights to protect
ideas on paper and in products.

Beyond that, if China is to set up joint ventures to draw
on the management, marketing, and technical expertise of
foreign business, it will have to accept the idea of private
equity ownership by the foreign partners. At present, only
personal items such as bicycles, cameras, and clothes can be
owned by individuals in China; not even automobiles can
be privately owned.

But one of the most frustrating disparities between
Americans and Chinese in doing business, Secretary Cooper
believes, is attitude. "Americans want to write everything
down; we are a very legal-minded society," he says. "The
Chinese operate on the word of the two parties." The Chinese believed that the trade agreement was too long and

involved; U.S. negotiators had to explain that Congress mandated many of its clauses.

So far, China's new leaders have not been afraid to look at some ideas that diverge radically from the precepts of Chairman Mao, who preached egalitarianism. Bonuses and incentives are being introduced gingerly in factories to try to boost production and productivity.

At the Capital Steel Works in Peking, where the average monthly wage is 63 yuan (about $44), most of the workers are receiving monthly bonuses of 12 percent to 15 percent of their base pay. And 200 employees of the plant divided up a 2,000-yuan incentive payment for devising a new process to increase the concentration of iron in the blast furnace feed, while reducing the cost. At the Peking Glassware Factory, an incentive award of 7 yuan is given to the worker who wins recognition as the best employee of the month.

Some of the political excesses imposed on workers during the Cultural Revolution are also being eased. Employees who used to have to attend four evening political education classes a week now attend only one. Instead, some take training courses one night a week to help them in their jobs.

Broad Consensus?

Because no foreigners really understand how the Communist Central Committee, which runs China, makes its decisions, or what the power relations between its members are, some businessmen still fear that Chinese policy could take yet another lurch and wipe out the relaxation that is now under way. One current rumor in Peking is that Vice-Premier Deng was sharply criticized at an April conference of leaders by members who adhere to Mao's thinking. In this view, the current reassessment of policy is the result of such opposition.

Deng insists that such stories are untrue. He told Secretary Kreps that he is not personally in charge in China, as he is represented in the foreign press, but that there is a broad concensus among China's leadership and people in favor of the Four Modernizations.

If that is true, then there is hope that Western trade with China will indeed be on a big scale.

WHAT WENT WRONG WITH THE MODERNIZATION PLAN?[4]

Surprisingly frank revelations voiced at China's recent National People's Congress finally made apparent the real reasons for Peking's cooling of its vast modernization program. Prior to the congress, which provided the first public review of China's economy in 20 years, China-watchers attributed the slowdown to two factors: lack of money and fear that the ideology could not stand the strain.

Delegates to the congress heard a different story from such officials as Finance Minister Zhang Jingfu [Chang Ching-fu] and Planning Minister Yu Qiuli [Yu Chiu-li], who worried about their lack of control over foreign technology deals and about such capitalist problems as rapid inflation, high unemployment, and a crisis in the budget. Zhang then headed for the U.S., where he has been talking credit and trade with the Export-Import Bank, the Treasury Dept., private bankers (China may borrow $2.6 billion from abroad this year), and with potential suppliers in Texas.

Formidable Task

The Chinese government's current trouble springs from a series of substantial wage increases it granted last year. In October, 1978, Peking gave 15 percent to 20 percent raises to 60 percent of the country's 95 million industrial workers. Then in December it promised peasants 20 percent more for this summer's grain harvest than it paid last year, with a bonus for grain produced above the quota, and a 25 percent increase in payments on 18 other farm products.

The impact of these gestures fell resoundingly on the 1979 budget. The wage increase and other "gifts," such as

⁴ From article entitled "China: What Went Wrong With the Modernization Plan." *Business Week.* p 42+. Ag. 6, '79. By special permission, © 1979 by McGraw-Hill, Inc., New York, N.Y. 10020. All rights reserved.

a reduction in taxes for poorer communes, will cost the state more than $10.5 billion this year. When budget makers saw this they tried to hold expenditures even with last year's $70 billion. At that, finance chief Zhang noted at the time, "fulfilling the budget would be a formidable task."

Zhang also says that China's extremely high rate of spending for capital construction will be lowered from 40.7 percent of overall outlay to 34.8 percent. The central government will spend about $25 billion on capital construction in 1979.

Western businessmen who were expecting a huge rise in Chinese imports of complete industrial plants and technology now learn that only $3 billion is being allocated for that purpose this year and that renegotiation of contracts will provide for more deferred payments than cash. Most of the money China spends will go to raw and semi-finished materials for its textile and light industries. But Westerners can take some hope in a joint-ventures law that has just been rushed through the Peking congress. Under this new legislation, foreigners may completely repatriate profits—after payment of a yet-to-be-decided tax. Foreigners may not take less than a 25 percent interest in joint-venture companies, and the chairmen of such enterprises must be Chinese. The law specifically authorizes joint ventures to borrow from foreign banks.

Restive Population

Energy is high on Peking's agenda. It hopes to turn its oil reserves into foreign exchange quickly. But its enormous coal reserves and hydro potential are slated to be developed for domestic use. Coal already supplies 70 percent of China's energy needs, but hydro power has barely been tapped. One major problem: Because of the vast distances between most power sources and principal industrial consumers, an extensive, and expensive, transmission system will be required.

Besides its strictly economic problems, the Peking government faces an increasingly restive population. The Chinese people are no longer willing to be ideologically pure, if all purity brings them is a poor standard of living. Hundreds of thousands of youths, sent down to the farm under Maoist decrees "to learn from the peasants," have returned to the cities demanding jobs, consumer goods, and a politically freer society. Estimates of the jobless run to 20 million, or 4.5 percent of the total work force. The percentage is not high by Western standards, but worrying for Marxist planners. The government is trying to create 7 million jobs this year, mostly in urban service industries, such as restaurants, repair shops, and beauty parlors. And the state will push production of such consumer items as TV sets, bicycles, sewing machines, and cameras. Even the congress' revelatory speeches had a primarily political motive. The Chinese leadership—not unlike the Carter Administration—was attempting to reunite the nation by sharing these confidences of state.

CHINA RESTORES SMALL BUSINESSES TO PROVIDE JOBS[5]

The entrance to the Balizhuang Hotel is an unobtrusive flight of concrete steps leading down into the ground. It may be the world's only hotel built in a subterranean bomb shelter.

The hotel was put together by 10 unemployed young men and women from the Balizhuang neighborhood in Peking. They made its 104 iron bedsteads by hand and installed the hotel's plumbing and ventilation in part of the capital's enormous underground civil defense works. They now operate the hotel.

A few miles away, on the Great Wall of China, foreign tourists have recently been besieged by another new sight for Communist China: peddlers touting everything from cold drinks to "antique" coins.

[5] Article by Fox Butterfield, China correspondent. New York *Times*. p A1 and A5. O. 8, '79. © 1979 by The New York Times Company. Reprinted by permission.

Revival of Individual Enterprise

The underground hostelry and the hawkers are part of an attempt by the government to revive small trades and services run by local initiative, what are known as collective enterprises. In the United States, they might be called individual enterprise, though under Communist law they are not owned by individuals.

The employees of the collectives, which are locally managed, are paid salaries, but the profits are diverted to the state. And there have been press reports of instances of funds saved for new equipment being confiscated by the state. Recently economists have urged the government to be more generous with the collectives.

The collectives, as opposed to big state-owned factories, have long been the poor cousins of China's Communist system. They have been regarded as "a tail of capitalism," a vestige of the bad old days before the Communists came to power in 1949, and work in them has been viewed as degrading.

Workers in the collectives have been paid about a third less than their counterparts in state factories. They seldom get free medical care or pensions, as the others do. And they do not have the lifetime job security provided by the big factories that is now regarded by many Chinese as a major accomplishment of communism in China.

As a result, the number of private enterprises as well as the small traders and vendors, from knife-sharpeners, cobblers, house painters, and barbers to sidewalk restaurants and handicraft factories, has shrunk by two-thirds since the 1950s, according to a recent report by the New China News Agency. At the same time, the population has grown by more than 400 million.

Peking's rediscovery of the collectives has two purposes. The government hopes that they can reduce the vast number of unemployed young people in the cities, who have created a major headache for the regime. At the same time, Peking sees expanding the collectives as a way to provide the many services that have become almost impossible to find.

Unemployment Figures Unclear

For example, it is literally impossible for a person to get a snack in the middle of the morning or after 2 P.M., since restaurants are open only at fixed hours for breakfast, lunch or dinner. Similarly, if your bicycle has a flat tire, unless you are one of the lucky few to have your own pump, it may take hours, or days, to find a shop that will fix it in some parts of the country.

Exactly how many people are unemployed is unclear, since the figures released by the government are somewhat contradictory. One senior official has spoken of a total of 20 million people. At the National People's Congress last June, it was said jobs had to be found for 7.5 million city people this year. Over each of the next five years, the *People's Daily* has estimated, more than three million students will finish school in the cities and need jobs. Only 4 percent will be able to go to college.

Peking has also compounded the problem by its system of assigning jobs to school graduates rather than letting them find work on their own. In fact, the Chinese term for unemployment is *dai yeh,* or "waiting for work," meaning that a person has not yet received his or her assignment.

In Peking, out of an urban population of 4.7 million, 400,000 are waiting, according to recent articles in Peking.

Eggshell Factory Earns $200,000

The government has also contributed to the situation by a decision last year to stop its old system of avoiding unemployment by automatically assigning jobs to large numbers of young people and then dumping them on already overstaffed factories.

Deng Meilian, a 19-year-old woman who graduated from high school last spring, said that she knew no one from her class who yet had a job.

The collectives offer a relatively cheap and flexible alternative, requiring much less state investment than the big factories. Some have proved successful, like a handicrafts shop on 2 Dragon Street in western Peking that produces painted eggshells for export. The *People's Daily* said that the small factory, in an old brick building, earned $200,000 in foreign exchange last year.

Some of the other new enterprises have no monetary motive. Near the Xinjiang Restaurant, a young man was helping run a bicycle parking lot big enough for only about 30 bikes.

His wage is the equivalent of 53 cents a day, paid him by his neighborhood street committee, which set up the tiny business. He does not get free medical care or other welfare benefits. But the young man, who says he was asked to quit high school by his teacher because he is an epileptic, commented, "It's better than sitting home."

A middle-aged woman with short salt-and-pepper hair who runs the bicycle lot said only two of the six people in her own family have jobs. A 28-year-old daughter who spent 10 years working in a village in the northeast cannot get an assignment because she is considered too old. And although she passed the university entrance exam this year, she is also too old to be accepted for college.

The woman's married daughter and son-in-law, with their infant child, live with her at home. Neither of them has a job.

Near Democracy Wall on Changan Boulevard, a young man was hawking a single-sheet newspaper put out to give the results of China's current national games. "Don't buy it," he told a customer. "It's got nothing in it."

But the man bought the paper anyway. "You should yell, 'New world record broken!' " he advised. "That would get people to buy more."

The young man said he earned half a Chinese cent for each paper sold, about one-third of an American cent. Yesterday he sold 200 papers. But next week, when the games end, his job will too.

OVERSEAS CHINESE CONNECTION[6]

Henry Lee, a Hong Kong business executive, went to his family's hometown of Guangzhou (Canton) on a mission that made world headlines early this year. As managing director of Harpers International, he signed an agreement for the first foreign automotive assembly plant in the People's Republic of China. But for Lee the event also held a deeper, more personal meaning that escaped public attention, even though his feelings are widely shared around Asia these days.

As he told Chinese government officials that day, "We come from a completely different society, a capitalistic one, and we're here to make profits. But being Chinese, I also feel very proud of the opportunity to participate in 'the four modernizations.'" Lee's remarks brought cheers from his Communist business partners. Ideology seemed less important than the fact that two groups of Chinese, speaking the same language, had come together for a venture that served their common interests.

China is rediscovering a special treasure-trove of talent and capital for its modernization drive—the overseas Chinese. They are widely known as *huaqiao* (*hua ch'iao*), or literally, "Chinese at a resting place or inn on a journey." But the 22 million sojourners have settled down in Hong Kong, in Singapore, and throughout Southeast Asia, where they dominate—and stimulate—much of the trade, finance, and industry.

Though scattered among many countries, Chinese entrepreneurs are a potent regional force. They are linked together by a loose network of family bonds, clan associations, and personal contacts that is easily able to move goods, capital, and economic intelligence across national frontiers. As Wong Nang Jang, an executive vice president of the Oversea-Chinese Banking Corporation (OCBC) in

[6] Article entitled "Beijing's Overseas Chinese Connection," by Louis Kraar, member of board of editors, *Fortune. Asia.* 2:4–7+. Jl./Ag. '79. Reprinted by permission of *Asia* and the author. Copyright 1979 The Asia Society.

Singapore, says, "The Chinese are the common denominator of Asian business."

Lively and astute, Wong perfectly fits his own characterization of overseas Chinese—"enterprising people who possess a great sense of individualism in business endeavors." Educated in his native Singapore, he first rose swiftly through the ranks of Citibank. He comfortably operates in most Asian nations, where he knows the business leaders. Recently, Wong decided that he would center his career on the OCBC, Singapore's largest local bank, which has branches in China. And his latest vacation took him to Shanghai, where his family originated, and Guangzhou, the home of his wife's family. Wong had no trouble getting around because he speaks the dialects used in both those Chinese cities.

The overseas Chinese tend to be among the most modern and adaptable people in Asia. They share many common values that encourage achievement—a devotion to thrift, a Mandarin respect for education, and family ties that extend to adopting as cousins anyone who comes from the same village in China. Wee Mong Cheng, who is now Singapore's ambassador to Japan, once explained why he brought over relatives to run his thriving businesses: "I both fulfilled obligations to my ancestors and assured myself of trusted successors."

The huaqiao originally left home in hopes of amassing fortunes and then retiring in China. The drive for self-improvement and the peasant poverty of south China sent millions on a tide of immigration more than a century ago. Despite their penchant for hard work and frugality, most of the Chinese could never afford to return. A hardy few accumulated enough capital to get into trading, which laid the foundation for their present economic primacy and enabled many at least to visit their mother country.

Though the overseas Chinese have long embraced their adopted nations, they have also continued to take pride in China. From 1949 to 1967, some 500,000 Chinese did return —some eager to help build a new China, others fleeing inhospitable conditions elsewhere. But the Cultural Revolution and hard working conditions sent many of them out again in 1971. Until recently, China's Communist regime had no real place for them. Many overseas Chinese regularly sent money to their relatives in the People's Republic, but during the political turmoil of the past decade, those relatives became the targets of suspicion and mistreatment because of their foreign ties.

Now Beijing's (Peking's) more pragmatic leaders are realizing the value of the overseas Chinese. As an editorial in the *People's Daily* proclaimed last year, the overseas Chinese "are still our kinfolk and friends." The mistreatment of their relatives in China was blamed on the Gang of Four, and overseas Chinese were hailed as "an important link" in China's development efforts.

China's new attitude is encouraging many overseas Chinese to make visits, donations, and investments in their cultural homeland. They are also being invited to buy retirement homes in China, which has restored property and funds (with interest) that were previously seized by the government.

The response of some overseas Chinese is dramatically visible in Hong Kong. Customers at the Beijing-controlled China Products Emporium are lining up to buy television sets for their relatives in China. As one Chinese resident of the British colony says, "We're getting letters from relatives who even tell us what brand and model they want." The purchasers pay as much as $500 for a color set, plus a 50 percent customs tax that helps supply Beijing with much-needed foreign exchange. This new shopping service is, of course, an extension of the old tradition of remitting money to relatives in China, and provides the People's Republic with foreign exchange totaling an estimated $1.5 billion annually.

A few wealthy overseas Chinese are making contributions directly to China, rather than to relatives. Their donations include used equipment from a power station in Hong Kong and six chicken farms that are being established near Guangzhou with the advice of an American expert on poultry. John Kamm, the Hong Kong representative of the National Council for U.S.-China Trade, explains: "It's an expression of loyalty to the homeland by people who definitely have a bourgeois life style and prefer to stay outside China."

Sometimes, of course, such donors may be looking for something tangible in return. One overseas Chinese entrepreneur in Indonesia, for example, gave 200 television sets to a hotel in his hometown of Fuzhou (Foochow), the capital of Fujian (Fukien) Province. The hotel then was able to raise the rates for rooms with television. Shortly thereafter, the merchant gained exclusive rights to distribute a popular herbal medicine made in that province.

Increasingly, Beijing is using overseas Chinese as both unofficial envoys and contacts with the outside world. Before visiting the United States, even Vice Premier Deng Xiaoping [Teng Hsiao-ping] tapped an overseas Chinese connection to help prepare him. Deng quietly asked an old Chinese friend in America to come to China and brief him. The friend, who was ill, had to decline but sent his son instead. This enabled Deng to get a more intimate preview of the U.S.—through Chinese eyes—than diplomats could provide.

At less lofty levels, overseas Chinese visitors from Asian countries play a vital psychological role in China's attempt to transform its economy. One Chinese observer notes that seeing dock workers from Singapore, bankers from Thailand, and loggers from the Philippines "provides the Chinese people with evidence that they can succeed in any occupation. It's an important kind of moral encouragement for the modernization program."

Philip H. Liu

Overseas Chinese are often the best introducers of foreign know-how in China, as some American corporations have learned. Initially, Pullman Kellogg of Houston had difficulty finding an opportunity to describe its chemical fertilizer plants to the Chinese. In 1972 a Chinese-American executive, Philip H. Liu, made a private visit to Beijing for the October 1 celebration, and managed to use the occasion to tell Chinese officials a little about the company's technology, which had helped increase agricultural productivity in many nations. Liu opened the door for a business relationship that has brought the U.S. company more than $200 million in contracts and has given China a means to increase its output of food.

Henry C. K. Liu

Lately, the Chinese government itself has recruited loyal friends among the overseas Chinese to bring in expertise from the West. China's official agency for developing tourism, for instance, first solicited proposals for building hotels through Henry C. K. Liu, an architect and professor at Virginia Polytechnic Institute who went on to help Intercontinental Hotels sign a tentative agreement. His unusual role as a middleman for China can perhaps be best accounted for by a family connection: Liu's father has long helped the People's Republic from Hong Kong, and his sister, Liu Yiu-chu, is a legal adviser to several Beijing organizations there, including the Bank of China.

At her law office in the colony, Ms. Liu, an intense young woman, explained how she came to spend her career "working for China." In 1955, as a student at Hong Kong University, she accompanied a group of professors to China and met the late Premier Zhou Enlai (Chou En-lai). "Somehow I drew his attention, perhaps because he was always very kind and encouraging to young people. By no effort or credit to myself, I got pushed into the limelight. That gave me direction."

She joined the New China News Agency, Beijing's official news service, as a member of its English language news section in Hong Kong. Teaching English to its senior staff members from China, she says, "made me unique. I got to know the older people there, for the Chinese have a way of being very respectful to their teachers—even young English teachers." Later she studied at Oxford but retured to the colony to practice law and serve clients from Beijing.

During the Cultural Revolution, however, Ms. Liu was

brought to "a turning point" by the death of two children in Communist-led riots in Hong Kong. "I knew something was wrong," she now asserts. "Revolutions shouldn't kill children, and Beijing couldn't have possibly wanted this to happen." Appalled by the incident, which China has since blamed on its discredited radicals, she left Hong Kong in 1969 to live in the U.S. While her husband studied design at Harvard, she did legal research. Ms. Liu resumed her law practice in Hong Kong in 1975, when she "saw an indication that things were going to change in China."

Becoming instrumental in those changes herself, she has helped draft preliminary agreements for several joint ventures between China and foreign companies. By studying Western legal institutions, she believes she has developed a sharper understanding of Chinese law: "China has the longest history of resolving disputes by negotiation and reconciliation. I wish people would keep an open mind about its legal system."

Most overseas Chinese have not been as close to the People's Republic as Ms. Liu. Their attitudes about China are part of the broader mosaic of their lives. And in a few illustrious cases, they have been caught up in the sweep of their country's turbulent modern history.

Lien Ying Chow

Consider Lien Ying Chow, a self-made millionaire in Singapore. He is exploring the prospects for building a hotel in China, a venture that is only natural nowadays for a banker and the founder of one of Singapore's leading hotels, the Mandarin. But his interest represents a full turn in Lien's life. He left the poverty of south China more than 60 years ago to better himself in Nanyang (the South Seas), as the Chinese call Southeast Asia. Now he is 73 and senses opportunity in the People's Republic.

Few have kept such an uncanny eye on China. Lien demonstrated his prescience in 1963, when he played host to an American lawyer representing Pepsi-Cola. Bottling the soft drink in Singapore is one of Lien's far-flung business interests, so he had much to talk about with the visitor —including China. He has recalled telling the American, "You're mistaken about Mao, who wants to clean up a corrupt China. Mao is like water, bringing together sand and cement to make China one house." At the time the attorney—Richard Nixon—was not convinced.

Recounting the incident in December 1970, when Nixon was in the White House and seemed far from approaching Beijing, Lien told me, "One day, I'm sure, you'll see Nixon and Mao shaking hands. China is coming out of isolation." Lien knew nothing about secret negotiations, but he had an intuitive feeling about where China was heading.

Lien's foresight is complemented by a thorough knowledge of history, one gained largely through self-education. Most of his formal schooling was in the village of Taipoo in China's Guangdong (Kwangtung) Province. Lien's father, a textile merchant with a scholarly bent, died when the boy was only 9 years old. Since his mother had passed away earlier, Lien went to live with relatives in Hong Kong and began a long struggle to better himself.

At 12 Lien was brought to Singapore by a dutiful uncle, who helped him find a job and then left for Thailand to seek his own opportunities. The boy worked for a small Singapore trading firm with a zest that would have shamed even Horatio Alger. "Anything they asked me to do, I did, even cleaning up the office," he recalls. As a teenager Lien was already an assistant officer manager who supervised 40 people by day and worked each night to improve both his English and his Chinese. The company that gave him that first break was run by a man from his home village in China, the sort of link that customarily encourages overseas Chinese, as he puts it, "to help each other come up." By the time Lien was 21, he had saved enough money to start his own little trading house.

Once his business flourished, Lien realized the dream of many huaqiao. He took his wife and sons on a visit to his old home village in China. There, he says, "they saw us as people who dared to go away from the homeland to make something." Before leaving again, Lien bought some land so that his cousins who still lived in the village would have an income.

Back in Singapore Lien's success as a trader gradually boosted his standing among his own commercially-minded community, which elected him president of the Chinese Chamber of Commerce in a crucial year—1941. Two days before the Japanese army arrived, Lien (with permission from the British colonial governor) left Singapore. On Friday the 13th, which happened to be during the Chinese New Year, he boarded one of 20 vessels leaving for Indonesia. Half of them were sunk by Japanese forces, but his small cargo boat made it. Lien moved on to Australia for several months, then India, and finally returned to China.

In its wartime capital of Chongqing (Chungking), he helped organize relief efforts and encouraged overseas Chinese to support the British in their eventual liberation of Malaya and Singapore. Lien also seized another business opportunity. Bankers from all over China had fled from the fighting and streamed into Chongqing, and he enlisted them to establish a new bank there for overseas Chinese. After the war its executives became the nucleus for his Overseas Union Bank in Singapore.

The British banking establishment raised skeptical eyebrows when Lien set up his headquarters in what had been their exclusive preserve, Raffles Place in downtown Singapore. But Lien could call on a wide network of contacts. "I got in touch with people from Thailand, Hong Kong, and Vietnam, bringing Chinese together as both stockholders and depositors," he says. Still, he had to overcome a general distrust of banks among many overseas Chinese, who in those days tended to stash their savings under mattresses. Lien appealed to the thrifty nature of his compatriots by explaining to small traders the value of a bank's help and handing out piggy banks to their children. His bank became one of the largest in Singapore.

Lien's personal roots, as well as his business interests, are firmly fixed in Singapore. He was among the first overseas Chinese residents to become a Singapore citizen.

Demonstrating the traditional overseas Chinese concern for education, he helped start two colleges in Singapore. He felt an especially strong obligation because of his own sparse opportunities for formal schooling. "Society is my university," he says, "and Chinese education has taught me that you're never too old to learn."

While his total political loyalty goes to Singapore, Lien also personifies the transnational character of many overseas Chinese. He has teamed up with Thai bankers who originally came from his home district in China, Shantou (Swatow). His relations with Sino-Thai businessmen have helped promote Thailand's maize trade with Singapore, an enterprise that won Lien an official decoration (the Third Class Order of the Crown of Thailand) in 1965. And after Singapore was expelled from the Federation of Malaysia, Lien was pressed into diplomatic service by his own government because of his close business associations in Malaysia. As high commissioner, the equivalent to ambassador in British Commonwealth nations, Lien worked to make sure that the political split would not rupture economic relations with Malaysia.

The changing policies of Beijing have undoubtedly reminded him of some unanswered letters. Lien once mentioned them to me, saying: "When I was working in China during World War II, I knew Zhou Enlai [Chou En-lai], who enjoyed champagne and other capitalist pleasures. For about 10 years after the war, he wrote to get me back. I never replied." Now, finally, Lien can comfortably look homeward again for business.

Y. H. Kwong

One of Lien's friends in Hong Kong has just made a full turn in his life, too. Y. H. Kwong, a resilient entrepreneur, recently returned to Shanghai for the first time in more than 40 years. An American-trained civil engineer, he began his career building roads in China. Now, at 70, he is chairman of a newly acquired trading concern, William Hunt & Co., that has old ties to China. In between these two activities, Kwong has overcome setbacks—amid wars and revolution—that would have demoralized most people.

Y. H., as he calls himself, epitomizes the adventuresome spirit and adaptability of many overseas Chinese. At an age when most men with his wealth are ready to enjoy retirement, he sits in his Hong Kong office as alert and energetic as a 50-year-old. A few months ago I found him poring over the history of his latest company, which was started in 1925 by William Hunt, a former American consul in north China, and operated there until the Communist revolution made it impossible. "Just think," he says with delight, "of all this outfit has gone through." But his own past is even more impressive.

The son of a Guangzhou merchant, Kwong studied at Stanford and Cornell universities, and thus had the luxury of choosing among many jobs in China. At 28 he joined the public works department in Gianxi (Kiangsi) Province because he "wanted to go some place where most people didn't want to go." Later Kwong managed a plant that produced automotive components until the Japanese started bombing it and forced him to leave in 1937.

Soon Kwong was recruited by the Chinese government for an intriguing assignment in Southeast Asia. The Sino-Japanese war threatened to block China's supplies from the outside world, and he went to work with the engineering corps that carved out a backdoor route—the famed Burma Road. Early in 1941 Kwong resigned to take advantage of a war boom in trucking goods up the road to Kunming in south China. "It was the golden era of the Burma Road," he recalls. "You could make a 100 percent profit every four weeks." The Japanese invasion of Burma ended the "era" in less than a year. Kwong and his family fled to India, where he spent World War II waiting and planning for a more permanent future in Burma.

Kwong envisioned himself as a purveyor of the tools of modernization. "I felt that with its huge agricultural areas, Burma could become a very rich country," he says. After the war Kwong took the first available plane to New York and arranged to sell International Harvester vehicles in Rangoon. As it turned out, he became the leading dealer in the country for all kinds of trucks, cars, and earth-moving equipment. He expanded his activities to include construction, handling such projects as the present Rangoon airport.

Like many overseas Chinese at that time, the Kwong family settled into Burmese society and felt a sense of belonging. Y. H. was friendly with Prime Minister U Nu and other government officials. He also enjoyed attending horse races on weekends with General Ne Win. "Sure, I made profits," Kwong says. "Business is supposed to compensate an individual for his work, and I also helped build up the country." But after spending 12 years in Burma, Kwong suddenly lost everything that he owned there.

When Ne Win initially took control of the government in 1958, Kwong returned home from work to find four officials bearing a military order for his immediate expulsion. Stunned, he invited them to sit down for dinner and phoned friends around Rangoon to find out why he was being forced to leave. Later it became clear that the Ne Win regime wanted to remove what it considered undue foreign influences, including overseas Chinese. "I figured that I'd better go," Kwong recalls. En route to the airport that night, he stopped by his office for an address book "because that is the record of my contacts, where one always has to begin."

Kwong rebuilt his life in Hong Kong by applying the lessons he had learned in Burma—above all, Y. H. stresses, "the inherent dangers of operating in only one country, particularly for a Chinese." Like many thrifty compatriots, he had already invested some savings in the United States. Kwong put them into an ailing Hong Kong company, The China Engineers, which he turned into a flourishing business by launching projects throughout Southeast Asia. As he explains, "A loss in one place would not then wipe us out."

While he relishes business challenges, Y. H. is also motivated by a desire to serve his family in a traditional Chinese manner. Beginning in 1960, he planned the career of one son known as C.C., who studied engineering and industrial management at the Massachusetts Institute of Technology, went to Columbia for a master's in business administration, and worked several years for an American bank. Y. H. says, "Then I told him that he should come back and prepare himself to take over the business."

While fathers' attempts to bring sons into family businesses often prove to be frustrating in the West, Kwong believes that Chinese parents are aided by some enduring values. "Obedience to your father and mother is one of the first things you learn. Filial piety is a great virtue in Chinese philosophy. These traditions still have a great influence, so Chinese youth don't rebel as often as Western youth do. I think the age of our culture has something to do with it."

Old customs work well for Kwong partly because he uses them in modern ways. Y. H., for example, genuinely welcomes "the imagination and new ideas" of his son. Not long ago Kwong sold his holdings in The China Engineers, but C.C. continued working there as a senior executive. Among other things, he helped to plan the entry of Harpers International, which is part of China Engineers, into automotive manufacturing in the People's Republic. The younger Kwong believes that one reason the deal was successful is that it was negotiated exclusively by Chinese on both sides.

Now C.C. is joining his father's new company, William Hunt, which the elder Kwong describes not merely as a business but as "something for my children." He wants them to provide leadership for the family's future prosperity. "We have got to work hard and get ahead because there's no other place to go," Y. H. says.

With China's keen interest in economic development, it is no wonder that Beijing is turning to the resourceful overseas Chinese. For the first time perhaps, the huaqiao can help the People's Republic without giving up their lifestyle or their loyalty to adopted countries.

IV. INSIDE CHINA

EDITOR'S INTRODUCTION

This section attempts to give the reader some idea of what life is like inside China; how people think and behave in a society that is very different from our own.

First, Fox Butterfield, writing in the New York *Times*, describes the elderly as content with the Communist "munificent retirement plan." Next, in an article reprinted from *Art In America*, Ann-Marie Rousseau shows how far Chinese women have come from the days of footbinding to Mao Tse-tung's "genuine equality between the sexes. . . ."

A government family-planning drive expects women in China today to have no more than one child. In the third article, reprinted from the *Far Eastern Economic Review*, Stewart Fraser takes note of the government's system of conferences, rewards, and sanctions that is intended to drastically reduce population growth in the interest of modernization.

In the fourth article, from *Human Behavior*, Dr. Alfred Messer, a clinical psychologist, tells us that suppression and repression of individual impulse have been effective in reducing crime, drug addiction, prostitution, and other forms of antisocial behavior. Dr. Messer suggests that we may have something to learn from the Chinese, as does Arthur Kleinman, the author of the next article, in which he suggests that Western-style medicine could benefit from the more humanistic approach of native healers in Taiwan.

The next two selections—by Alexander Taffel, writing in *Outlook,* and James Aronson, writing in the *Nation*—comment on the new freedom of expression in the classroom and in literature, the arts, and theater.

As Frank Ching indicated in his article in Section I, religious tolerance seems to be on the increase. The next article, a *Time* report, describes a new recognition of Christianity in China and a renewed emphasis on Article 46 of the Chinese constitution, which guarantees freedom of religion. Next, Jerome Alan Cohen, a Harvard law professor writing in *Asia,* suggests that a new legal system may be on the way in which the concept of individual rights will have greater importance than ever before.

In the final selection, Michel Oksenberg in an article for the Foreign Policy Association's Headline Series, analyzes the five systems of belief—frequently in conflict—that form the Chinese mentality and that seek the path toward resolution and balance, the Chinese philosopher's "middle way."

THE GOOD LIFE IN RETIREMENT[1]

Every morning at 6:30, several hundred elderly men and women gather in a park near the ornate Nationalities Palace to perform China's ancient form of calisthenics, *tai ji.* They glide through the movements as if in slow motion, stopping now and then to chat with a neighbor or a new acquaintance.

It looks almost like an advertisement for a retirement colony. But the appearance is deceiving because the elderly in China, unlike their American counterparts, may be better off than any other segment of society. They are the beneficiaries of both the traditional Chinese chivalry toward old age, which is still honored, and a munificent Communist retirement plan.

Elderly Remain With Families

In a city family with a retiree and four workers, a common proportion, the retired person's income usually accounts for half of the total. This is the conclusion of

[1] Article entitled "China's Elderly Find Good Life In Retirement," by Fox Butterfield, China correspondent. New York *Times.* p 1 and 13. Jl. 29, '79. © 1979 by The New York Times Company. Reprinted by permission.

Deborah Davis-Friedmann, an assistant professor of sociology at Yale University, who has been studying the care of the elderly in China this summer.

The financial status of the elderly, along with the respect for them, has helped insure that they remain with their families and are not sent off to old-age homes. "The old three-generation family of grandparents, parents and children is still alive and well in China," Professor Davis-Friedmann said in an interview.

She also found that most elderly people were deeply grateful to the Communists for their treatment. "They are the ones who remember how hard life was before 1949, when you could die of starvation or disease," Professor Davis-Friedmann said.

But the advantageous position of the elderly is in part a result of the severe problems faced by the young people. Because of the shortage of housing, because 20 million are said to be unemployed, and because young people are paid low salaries, many urban Chinese depend heavily on their families up to the age of 35.

They can earn enough to support themselves only by living with their parents and grandparents. Even if they could afford their own apartments, they would find them difficult to obtain. In Peking, the State Housing Office allots a maximum of three square yards of housing space per person. If you have more than that, you cannot apply for new housing.

These shortages grew out of the baby boom in the 1950s and 1960s, when Communist rule brought peace and a sharp reduction in the mortality rate. In 1949, China's population was 540 million; today it is 958 million.

Many Early Retirements

The effects of the population explosion have been compounded by the disruptions of the Cultural Revolution, which started as the surge in young people began to come of age.

As one measure to cope with the paucity of jobs, Peking

has sought to make use of its unique system of permitting a retiring worker to bring in one of his or her children as a replacement. This year in Peking alone, according to the New China News Agency, 50,000 people, half the retirees in the capital, have taken advantage of this plan. Many chose to retire early. Professor Davis-Friedmann found that up to 80 percent of the workers in some factories she visited obtained their jobs from their parents.

The policy may tend to dampen worker motivation, as China's lifetime job-security policy already does. But if a man and woman comply with the Communists' provisions for delaying marriage until they are nearly 30 and then limit themselves to having one or two children, they are assured of finding jobs for their children.

Those retiring now are the first generation to get full benefits under the system set up by the Communists, since a worker must have 20 years of service to be eligible for a pension of 75 percent of his preretirement salary. "They are the ones who got in on the golden ground floor in the 1950s when there were jobs and housing available and wages were still going up," Professor Davis-Friedmann said. Mao Zedong [Mao Tse-tung] froze most wages in 1959.

Men, who can retire at the age of 60, often find second jobs, particularly if they are technicians or skilled workers and are willing to move to the countryside where factories are desperate for their talent. Between their pensions and a second income, their earnings may surpass their pre-retirement salary, Professor Davis-Friedmann has found.

Women can retire at 50 but are less likely to take another job. Many prefer to stay home and take care of their grandchildren, Professor Davis-Friedmann said. "American women would see it as a putdown," she added, "but most Chinese women, except former cadres accustomed to authority, enjoy it."

After their hour of morning exercise, retirees spend a lot of time shopping, especially for items like chickens and fruit, which are beyond the average person's means. This tends to add further to their power in the family.

As another benefit, if retired people agree to move back to the countryside, where many of them came from, they receive $195 each, or $390 for a married couple, to help them build a new house. In China, it is usually adequate.

WOMEN IN CHINA[2]

Mao Tse-tung wrote, "Genuine equality between the sexes can only be realized in the process of the socialist transformation of society as a whole." This transformation must be brought about with the full support and equal participation of women in all aspects of family, community and work life. Women "hold up half the Heavens."

The Revolution and the passing in 1950 of the marriage laws, which allow both sexes to choose whom they marry and opened up the possibilities of divorce, have meant great changes for women in China. The low status, economic dependence, social isolation and virtual slavery of pre-revolutionary Chinese women is legendary.

How have conditions changed for women of China? On this trip we met women students, women doctors, women workers. Out the bus window we saw them on the streets of Peking, Sian, Soochow, Loyang and Shanghai. Rushing by on bicycles, pulling heavy carts, carrying baskets and holding babies, selling fruits in the markets and walking arm in arm, they appeared as ruddy and smiling as in the paintings by the Husian peasant painters shown in New York. How to come to any real understanding of these women in just 18 short days?

Our principal opportunities to talk with anyone were in formal discussions through interpreters. After a tour of each site, we met with the revolutionary committee of the school, factory, hospital or museum to drink tea served in covered teacups, patterned in beautiful designs different for each location. We asked our questions, and received an-

[2] Article from "Report from China" entitled " 'Holding Up Half the Heavens': Women in China," by Ann-Marie Rousseau, writer, photographer and artist. *Art In America.* 67:16+. Mr. '79. By permission of the publisher and author.

swers repetitiously similar to the latest pronouncements in
Peking Review, yet seemingly heartfelt and sincere.

One night after a freezing afternoon trip to the Great
Wall, Yang, an International Travel Service guide, is
assigned to take me to the Peking emergency room because
I have come down with severe flu. This affords me a rare
chance to relate to someone outside formal sessions. My
relationship with Yang is cordial, friendly and official.
Since becoming ill, I find her constantly at my side in our
outings. Would I like to sit down? Can she carry my bag?
Would I like a cup of tea? I enjoy talking with her, although much of what she says seems straight out of Mao's
Little Red Book.

She dresses in a dark blue suit with baggy trousers that
is almost identical to those worn by the male guides, and
like the other Chinese women we saw, wears no makeup or
jewelry. Her square plain face is set off by black horn-
rimmed glasses and her straight hair is blunt cut at chin
level. Only a tiny hint of self-expression is reflected in
the triangle of bright pink sweater that peeks from under
the plain, warm clothing.

It is late at night as we speed in a taxi to the hospital.
On the streets of China I feel a security and freedom from
harm that I have not felt anywhere else—so unlike the
streets of New York. I ask Yang if it would be dangerous
for a woman to be out alone at this hour. She replies that
it would not be wise. "While generally there would be
nothing to fear, there are still counter-revolutionary elements in the society that must be rooted out." This does
not prevent her from going out alone at night when it is
necessary, but she cautions me against wandering around
late by myself.

At the entrance to the Peking emergency room we are
met by a receptionist and led down a long dark hallway
to a room filled to the ceiling with files and records. Yang
speaks to the girl at the desk who appears to be about 17
and is very beautiful with a bright smile and long shiny
braids to her waist. To my amazement she pulls out a file
with my name on it. I am on record in the Peking

emergency room because a doctor visited me at the hotel the night before.

After forms have been filled out and Yang has shown me how to write my name phonetically in Chinese, we sit down to wait for the doctor. Our conversation turns to the long braids and flowered jacket of the girl at the desk. Yang says with some emphasis that she dislikes long hair. The flowered jackets are usually worn by women from the countryside, and she refers with obvious pride to the practicality and style of her own blue suit and boots of real leather.

Yang asks me if I have a boyfriend. Am I engaged? Why am I not married? She is shocked to find that it is typical for American women to have several relationships before marriage. She is incredulous and fascinated, and questions me about the living arrangements of unmarried couples in our group. "Do they really *live* together?" she asks. "Don't American women mind? Why don't they get married if they are living as though they are married?"

I explain as best as I can and ask her about her relationships with men. I am surprised to see her behavior—normally so direct—transformed into that of a shy teen-ager. She reveals with some embarrassment that she does not have a boyfriend and indeed at 28 has never had one. One day she would like to marry, but so far there have been no possibilities. Meanwhile she is patient, and "Life in the women's dormitory of the International Travel Service provides meaningful friendships and a sense of community."

We are told throughout China that 25 is the average age for women to marry, and Yang says this is true. Chinese women normally meet men at their place of work or are introduced by family and friends. But Yang's family lives in the countryside and none of her co-workers has ever thought to introduce her to anyone. She says, "Most likely they are unaware that I might be interested and probably feel it is more valuable for me to devote myself fully to my work at this time." With a trace of sadness she adds that her work is very important and she takes great pride in her job.

Her life, she says, is radically different from her mother's, whose feet were bound and who had no opportunity for an education. For me, the unimaginable suffering and past oppression of women in China is symbolized most powerfully by foot-binding. Soaking the feet in hot water and bending the toes under the foot, they began the process which was excruciatingly painful and ended in permanent crippling, when the girl was four or five. I saw old women in the Peking streets hobbling on tiny feet; they scurried behind doorways and around corners the moment I lifted my camera. Yang shares with me a horror at this practice, outlawed since the Revolution.

She states that life is now vastly improved for women. Men and women are free to choose their own partners, and while divorce is legal, very few request it. I ask about mistakes—the inevitable poor decisions—few though they may be. "In these cases," Yang tells me, "the couple would go before the revolutionary committee at their place of work. They would bring their problem before their comrades and discuss it openly." I find this difficult to envision in a country of people so reserved and careful to hide their emotions in public, and I ask Yang if she has ever personally known of a couple going before a revolutionary committee with their problems. She acknowledges that she does not know of any specific cases. Does she know anyone who ever got a divorce? No, she does not.

Because of my continued illness I spend time with Yang and other female guides in the waiting rooms of hospitals and doctors' offices in the cities we visit. Only in small glimpses did I see any signs of conflict or doubt— Yang's sadness at not having a boyfriend, another guide's uneasy acceptance of the separate living arrangements which would be necessary when she married, because her fiance worked in another city, a hotel worker's avid interest in relationships among young Americans. In all my talks with these women it was clear that while conditions have radically changed for the women of China, the changes have been tailor-made to fit the needs of socialism, and individual women are attempting to fit themselves into this new reality as best they can. Sometimes it is a difficult fit.

ONE IS FINE . . .[3]

We must conscientiously carry out ideological, educational and technical work as well as child care and health work throughout the country so that people can practise family planning willingly, safely and effectively. Practical measures should be taken to reward couples who limit themselves to a single child and gradually to institute social insurance for aged people who are childless . . . This year, we must do everything we can to lower the country's population growth rate to about 10 per thousand and we must continue to lower it year by year in the future. By 1985, it should drop to 5 per thousand.
—Premier Hua Guofeng [Hua Kuo-feng]: *Report on the Work of the Government,* Peking, June 25, 1979.

China's population today is fast approaching the billion mark and new birth-control measures have been introduced throughout 1979 in a drastic attempt to curb the nation's growth rate. Considerable publicity has been given to promoting as the ideal model the one-child-family. Specifically to encourage the strict limitation of family size, a massive educational campaign, involving a unique series of incentives and disincentives, is also being introduced throughout China. The viewpoint that one is wonderful and two is more than adequate will be underpinned officially with coercive warnings that three is too many and four will certainly merit political, social and economic penalties.

The growth rate of China's population has been gradually pushed down during the past decade from more than 2 percent to nearly 1 percent per annum. Premier Hua Guofeng first revealed the government's increasing anxiety on the subject in February 1978, by declaring that "the

[3] Article entitled "One Is Fine, Two Is More Than Adequate," by Stewart E. Fraser, Melbourne correspondent. *Far Eastern Economic Review.* p 61–2. O. 5, '79. Copyright 1979. By permission of the publisher.

goal of a 1 percent growth rate must be achieved by 1980 for all of China."

Vice-Premier Chen Muhua [Chen Mu-hua] outlined even more ambitious goals on August 11, 1979, suggesting that zero population growth (ZPG) could be realized by the end of the century if parents would strictly adhere to the new family size rules being promulgated. Today almost half China's population is under 21 with the majority of females' child-bearing years ahead of them. In addition, 80 percent of China's population are still rural dwellers whose family size has traditionally been at least double that of urban dwellers. Agricultural and industrial development have not kept sufficiently ahead of population growth. In 1949 the population was approximately 540 million, and in the 30 years since liberation nearly 600 million additional births or more people have had to be catered to—fed, clothed, housed and employed.

The inadequate provision of educational facilities has likewise been blamed on the enormous population explosion which has consumed the limited resources. It is estimated that currently at least 6 percent of children still do not attend school, 12 percent of primary school age children do not continue to lower middle school and 50 percent are unable to secure a place in high school. Less than 5 percent of high school graduates are able to proceed to university.

The direct costs of raising children to the age of 16 has been calculated as varying from Rmb 1,600 (US $1,046) in rural areas to as much as Rmb 6,000 in major cities. A university education is estimated to require a further Rmb 7,000 for a three- or four-year program. The cost of the additional 600 million persons born since 1949 has been estimated at Rmb 1 trillion or about one third of the national income earned during the past 30 years.

This frank appraisal by Chinese leaders of the nation's burgeoning population problems is both sobering and confounding. Planned economies under socialism theoretically "should be able to regulate the reproduction of human beings so that population growth keeps in step with the growth of material production." So say China's leaders today.

Future options regarding Chinese population stabilization are somewhat limited. Migration abroad is not feasible, internal migration and settlement of virgin lands have limited prospects and long-term rustication of urban youth is unpopular. The so-called positive Malthusian checks—involving famine, malnutrition and starvation—are virtually absent today, as is warfare, while the incidence of disease has been much reduced. The only other feasible and immediate options relate to rationing births severely and changing, irrevocably if possible, family size patterns. Hence the much publicized campaign to promote as the future model for China the one-child-family launched early this year on a trial basis in several provinces.

Chinese demographers have estimated that the year 2000 could see 240 million fewer births if all newly married couples during the next two decades had only one child per family. If women would marry later (say, at 25 years of age) and bear fewer children (say, a single child), the following century might record only four generations instead of perhaps five. Unfortunately, current fertility rates and birth patterns are still not entirely conducive to such optimism. For example, some 17 million babies were born during 1978 and 30 percent were the third or more children in the family. Hence the present urgent campaign to minimize births with two as the upper limit and preferably one as the ideal.

To force the present growth rate down from 1 percent to 0.5 percent by 1985 and to ZPG by the year 2000, China has launched a uniquely ambitious program of social and economic incentives and disincentives. These have already been widely publicized and are already undergoing trial in a variety of provinces notably Sichuan, Yunnan, Guangdong [Kwangtung] and Anhui [Anwei].

Family Planning Law

In June at the National People's Congress in Peking a draft law was proposed concerning a new family planning and birth control law. When the topic has been more thoroughly discussed and revised, it will be submitted to the standing committee of the National People's Congress for approval. The draft law in brief stipulates that married couples with only one child are to receive child health subsidies, bonus work points, higher pensions and priority in the allocation of housing in cities and private plots in the countryside.

Full details of the law are still to be determined. However, various provincial regulations already have been widely promulgated and, though still provisional, do provide some indication as to the scope and nature of the final birth control law which is expected to be enforced throughout China in the 1980s. The Anhui provincial regulations noted below are typical and certainly reflect the current official viewpoint in Peking.

Rewards: For those having a single child and ensuring that they will not have a second

—Issue of a "planned parenthood glory coupon" providing priority for entrance to nursery and kindergarten as well as free medical treatment and hospitalization.

—Between the ages of 4 and 14, a son receives a subsidy of Rmb 5 per month and a daughter Rmb 6 per month.

—In urban areas living floor space will be allocated as if there were two children in the family.

—In rural areas an only child will receive an adult's ration of grain.

—Households with only one son or two daughters will receive priority in labor recruitment.

Sanctions: For those having a second child after being rewarded for only having one, and for those who have three or more children

—The planned parenthood glory coupon will be withdrawn and all the child's health expenses or supplementary work points recovered.

—5 percent of total family wages or income will be deducted from welfare expenses, 6 percent deducted for a fourth child and 7 percent for a fifth child.

—For third and additional children, confinement medical

expenses must be paid by parents and children will be
unable to participate in comprehensive medical schemes.
—No coupons for commodities or subsidiary foodstuffs will
be available for third or fourth children before age 14.
No extra housing space in urban areas or additional land
for private garden plots in rural areas will be provided.
—Couples who undergo sterilization (and medical workers
performing such operations) will receive economic rewards and public recognition.
—Planned parenthood is to be considered one of the criteria
for issuing rewards. Couples who have a third or additional child may not be assessed progressive producers or
workers for a year after the birth of such a child.
—Women who are already pregnant for a third time or
more can take measures to retrieve the situation as early
as possible, such as by having an abortion. Those who
have not yet taken sterilization measures should do so as
rapidly as possible.

Family Planning Conferences

During the last quarter of 1978, a series of family planning conferences were held at the provincial level in many
parts of China. These were but a prelude to the initiation
of a major national conference in Peking, which brought
specialists from all over China to discuss ways of solving
the population problem.

The first National Conference on Population Theory
was held in Peking from November 24 to December 5, 1978,
sponsored by the Population Research Institute of the recently founded People's University of China. It was followed by the National Family Planning Conference, also
held in Peking, from January 4–10, 1979, and chaired by
Vice-Premier Chen Muhua, one of China's foremost women
leaders who is also head of the Family Planning Leading
Group of the State Council.

Chen Muhua emerged during 1979, as one of the more
articulate and forceful speakers calling attention to the
potentially explosive problems in population futures and

proposing radical solutions to overcome prevailing attitudes and half hearted solutions of the past decade.

Rewards and Sanctions

In January 1979, Guangdong province promulgated a comprehensive set of stringent regulations for encouraging family limitation through an incentive and disincentive scheme. These were the first of several provincial attempts to bring economic sanctions to play on family size conditions and were followed by a series of further provincial conferences held throughout February in other provinces such as Xinjiang [Sinkiang], Shaanxi [Shensi], Qinghai [Tsinghai], Guizhou [Kweichow], Yunnan and Henan [Honan], among others.

In March, Sichuan [Szechwan] released its own provincial guidelines for birth control incentives and in April Anhui province promulgated its own detailed system of rewards and sanctions. In July, academic societies for population studies were founded in both Peking and Shanghai. Equally important in the academic and research policy field was the rehabilitation in July of Ma Yinchu, the well-known economist and former president of Peking University. He had initiated a series of controversial debates in the late 1950s concerning the drastic need for population stabilization and for family size limitation. Ma had been labelled as neo-Malthusian and his population control theories were discredited for nearly two decades.

It is perhaps no minor coincidence that the 98-year-old radical thinker in the field of population dynamics has been rehabilitated with much public discussion. If Ma's controversial but farsighted ideas had been translated vigorously into government policy in the 1950s and 1960s, China could have contemplated a steady population state and ZPG approaching in the 1980s and 1990s with a population perhaps approximating 800 to 900 million. Instead, China can only hope to achieve a ZPG figure of perhaps 1,200 million by the year 2000 if it accedes to what are undoubtedly the most draconian family planning guidelines to have appeared in modern times.

It is perhaps pertinent to draw attention to China's unique and perhaps unintentional contribution to celebrating the International Year of the Child, namely by proclaiming the importance of *the* in the definitive singular case. China is perhaps the first country to endorse vigorously as national policy the promotion of the single-child family and has taken a great social leap forward in proclaiming the national and personal value of the single child totally bereft of family siblings. The economic consequences are clearly spelled out and those with larger families will in future directly subsidize parents who have only one child. The implications are likewise enormous in terms of the quantity and quality of educational resources which have to be planned for and allocated to schools and the teaching force.

The Four Modernizations now being undertaken need to be underpinned by, and are predicated on, an immediate and drastic drop in population growth rates. The long-term consequences of adequately satisfying educational and welfare needs should be seen against the most optimistic scenario of a projected population increase to 1,200 million persons by the year 2000 of whom at least 400 million will be under the age of 15.

In view of the best or lowest case population projections made for China today, one can appreciate the urgent and forceful need of far-sighted Chinese officials at all levels —whether educators, population specialists or economic planners—to introduce the single-child concept to the masses as an immediate, drastic, political and social expedient.

The more globally accepted norm of a two-child family, leading to a replacement society in the long run, is unacceptable to China's planners. Hence the enormous gamble in trying to change family size patterns overnight. It remains to be seen if the scheme is feasible and if the system of rewards and sanctions is sufficiently strong to change totally a nation's attitude towards one of its most popular products—babies.

CURBING THE URGE[4]

To a Westerner accustomed to violence in the streets, sex on television and drug addiction among too many of his fellow citizens, mainland China was both refreshing and surprising. The Chinese seem to have conquered many social ills with minimal, if any, feelings of oppression or deprivation among the populace.

Prostitution, perhaps the world's oldest social problem, was eradicated in three years. Drug addiction had plagued China for centuries; it was eliminated in five years. Within six years the Chinese Communists had screened some 800 million people for venereal disease and rid themselves of that problem, too. Violent crimes and vandalism are almost unheard of in the People's Republic.

These sweeping changes required great self-discipline by the Chinese, but they have not created a totally inflexible social structure. Western cultural and technological remnants were brutally purged by Mao Tse-tung and his youthful "Red Guards" during the 1950s; by 1978, Chinese leaders had a change of attitude and now seek trade, tourism and industrial know-how from the West and from Japan.

My travels in the People's Republic recently convinced me, furthermore, that the Chinese society was overhauled so thoroughly and quickly not because of the Communists' armed strength, but because of the intense self-discipline cultivated by most Chinese. This discipline, which I shall call "impulse control," is oriented toward societal goals and an individual's duties to that social system, rather than toward individual achievement. Mao Tse-tung and other leaders of the 1949 revolution are primarily responsible for creating this loyalty to the state. The methods they used to

[4] From article entitled "Curbing the Urge in Red China," by Alfred Messer, MD, formerly with Columbia University Psychoanalytic Clinic; now a family specialist. *Human Behavior*. p 18–23. Ap. '79. Copyright © 1979 *Human Behavior* Magazine. Reprinted by permission.

create it were simple and, from a psychiatric perspective, brilliant.

When Mao battled Chiang Kai-shek off the mainland in 1949, he had a firm foundation on which to build a state-centered society. Confucianism and Taoism, China's oldest and most widely practiced religions, stressed unselfish devotion to family and friends. Duty and sensitivity to others were set forth at great length and in very intellectual style in books such as the *Confucian Analects,* and Mao made no attempt to change this sentiment.

Rather, he expanded upon it. Using day-care centers and schools for children, and self-criticism groups for the adults—along with "political reeducation" camps or banishment for "reactionary" adherents to pre-Revolution traditions—the Communists gave their citizens a political education that stressed devotion to the state even above devotion to the family, since the state was seen as a superfamily.

The Chinese exercise conscious control over the most basic impulses, including sex and aggressiveness. Premarital sex is discouraged. Two students at the University of Shanghai found making love in the bushes were publicly chastized and received little sympathy from their classmates. "They let themselves go while others have to hold themselves in," was the reaction. Most Chinese men and women seem to follow the government's suggestion that they "take a cold bath" or divert their minds to other, more constructive, thoughts when the sex urge arises. Even husbands and wives make no public display of affection. Government "edicts" tell men not to marry before 28 and women not before 25. Moreover, they are encouraged to have no more than two children.

Western children are reared by one or two authoritarian parents. When American children misbehave, they are likely to receive a slap on the wrist and a curt admonition, "Don't ever do that again." Asian children are raised in a more permissive atmosphere—they are allowed to nurse for a longer time than American children and are not expected to be toilet trained as early. Chinese children usually are tended by a great many surrogates. A high percentage of them are placed in day-care centers for five days a week when they reach eight weeks of age and their mothers return to their jobs. When Chinese children misbehave, parents or attendants are likely to call their attention to social consequences of their acts. At one day-care center I visited, a two-year-old stopped crying after a nurse gave him a cloth to dry his eyes and said, "You don't want everyone to think you're a backward child, do you?"

These differences in upbringing result in psychological contrasts between Western and Asian adults. Americans tend to internalize codes of behavior that are acquired from authority-figure parents. When these codes of behavior (conscience) are violated, we feel guilt and seek to atone for the transgressions.

Chinese are more likely to feel ashamed. They grow up viewing acceptance by elders and peers as the chief index to social conduct. When they think they have failed to meet the expectations of those around them, they feel they have lost "face," or "lien." Shame is much more intellectual and volitional. Persons socialized using shame tend to be very sensitive to their environments and to consciously restrict thoughts and impulses they know are not acceptable to their colleagues.

Suppression and Repression

We must also distinguish two principal mental mechanisms for dealing with conflict, *suppression* and *repression*. Suppression, closely related to shame, allows people to deal more harmoniously with conflict than do repression and guilt. With suppression, unacceptable impulses are voluntarily inhibited and those who suppress them, having nobly fulfilled their duty, themselves feel more fulfilled; with repression, the impulses are automatically excluded from conscious awareness or are symbolically distorted. There is no compensation for those in whom unacceptable impulses are repressed; they may even feel guilty for having the impulses, without even realizing they exist as a force in their subconscious minds. Repression tends to create a storehouse of psychic energy that can explode at any time, for any reason. In common parlance, we often refer to overcontrolled, cautious, serious individuals as "repressed persons"; but watch out, they're easily provoked into "blowing their tops."

Shame has another characteristic of great benefit to the Chinese Communists: it is very malleable. Guilt and repression, based on internalized conduct codes, tend to be indelibly fixed within each individual—and to be passed on more or less intact from one generation to the next. It may take four generations to radically alter subconscious codes in a Western individual. In China, such a change was wrought in less than one generation. All the leadership needed to do was to set the appropriate social tone, and most of its citizenry easily and willingly adapted itself to the new conditions, even de-Maoification.

Mao and his followers established several levels of "tone-setting" social organizations; all of them focus on politics. In day-care centers and elementary schools, children "are educated for the revolution," as one attendant said. They play games similar to our cops and robbers, but the cops are Chairman Hua Kuo-feng and the robbers are the Gang of Four, his banished political opposition.

Whenever there is "blaming behavior"—whether in families or societies—psychiatric study shows that scapegoating is one mechanism that can be utilized to reduce interpersonal tension and conflict. At every briefing I attended during my journey in China, the party member who briefed us always had a scapegoat ready on whom he or she could blame any deficiencies.

In adult life, all Chinese belong to self-criticism groups organized at workplaces, social centers and educational institutions. The groups meet weekly, and every member is expected to rise and tell his or her five to seven colleagues about any transgressions he or she may have committed against revolutionary doctrine. Each member also is responsible for educating other group members about their failures, and it is not unusual for a low-level worker to question the actions or motives of a factory manager. These sessions strongly reinforce the shame mechanism. Acting in concert with broader social conditions—such as encouraging women to dress in plain shirts and baggy pants, or emphasizing nonaggressive sports (gymnastics, Ping-Pong with aggression against the ball, etc.) —the groups have the power to change society by changing each of its members, a notion frequently found in Christian thought.

Mao also devised a scheme to counteract entrenched bureaucracy. White-collar workers, be they chiefs or clerks, spend a month each year "serving the people" by doing manual labor on a commune. When we had dinner with the head of the China Travel Service in Peking, he had just returned from his stint as the lowest worker on a rural commune, raising pigs. (It would be equivalent in the United States to the head of the General Services Administration fixing flat tires at a government motor pool four weeks each year.)

The Chinese have several means of dealing with less-than-perfect behavior. Rapists and murderers may be publicly executed, as were two during my stay. China has surprisingly few jails for so large a country in which violent criminals are incarcerated. Confirmed "political deviants" who repeatedly disagree with the party line may be shipped to remote communities, demoted in their jobs and salaries or sent to "political education" centers where they are expected to achieve a greater appreciation of party doctrine. They may be forced to publicly shame themselves once or twice a year by wearing dunce caps and confessing their wrongs to hordes of people gathered to celebrate the anniversary of the revolution.

Crime and political nonconformism are not the only expression of deviance. For example, a psychiatrist sees deviant behavior reflected in the symptoms of mental illness. Again, it is up to the small group to provide the "initial diagnosis and treatment." These sessions not only help individuals maintain control of their behavior, but also prevent many forms of deviance from rising to the surface. Not only do the groups instruct their members on correct behavior and reinforce conformity to group norms, but they also allow members to let out pressures before they become problems. A Chinese doctor told me that even members who do not voice their feelings of unrest or rebelliousness openly will betray them to friends and colleagues through a curl of the lip, a facial mannerism or a speech inflection.

If a problem does erupt and seems especially severe, the Chinese told me, two of the prospective patient's friends will pay the person a visit and ask him or her to be aware of his or her behavior. If this talk doesn't produce the desired results, they might suggest a visit to a health clinic. If no change in behavior is accomplished there, the deviant person may be sent to an institution—or if the deviance seems mainly "political," to a reeducation camp.

Relatively severe cases of mental illness will be referred to mental health centers such as the Chinese Mental Illness and Prevention Hospital, which I visited in Shanghai. It appeared to be similar to many large institutions in America: there are 14 wards and 1,000 beds, attended by 83 doctors, 295 nurses, 334 staff aides and 42 technical personnel staffing the pharmacy, laboratories and X-ray equipment. Each ward has a regular staff and a staff for special activities, and each mental health center is responsible for sending "revolutionary" teams to the factories, neighborhoods and farms to teach education and hygiene.

The schizophrenic in China is similar to the schizophrenic in the West. Patients withdraw into a fantasy world, describe delusions and hallucinations and become overly preoccupied with body and bodily functions. They are treated with acupuncture in the temporal area one hour each day, anti-psychotic drugs developed in the West and herbal medicine.

Group activities are important, although more rigid than those we utilize. Patients are roused at 5:00 A.M., clean up from 6:00 to 6:30 and participate in occupational

therapy from 6:30 to 9:30. No matter how simple their activity, it is deemed important to the aims of the "'revolution." Free time extends from 9:30 to 10:30, with lunch
from 10:30 to 11:30. Patients take an after-lunch nap until
1:30, then follow a similar schedule through the afternoon
until their 8 P.M. bedtime.

Case Histories

One need talk to only one or two doctors or patients,
however, to realize how different the orientation is from
that employed in America. The Chinese attribute mental
illness to an imperfect understanding of current political
doctrine. For example, psychiatrists cite Mao's essay "Where
Do Correct Ideas Come From?" as basic to psychotherapy
in the People's Republic. Mao wrote that "one's ideas will
be 'correct' if they come from three kinds of social practice:
the struggle for production, the class struggle and scientific
experiment. It is man's social being that determines his
thinking." This view is quite different from the Western
theory that the human state is determined by our thinking.
In practice, it means that Chinese psychiatrists try to
change the "social being" of their patients, not to uncover
and interpret unconscious conflict that might be at the
root of psychological problems.

Because it is assumed that all members of Chinese society
want to be perfected in their revolutionary frame of mind,
persons who treat the mentally ill look upon them as comrades in need of an education, not as sick people. Nor is
the patient held totally responsible for his or her conduct,
which is "blamed" to a surprising extent on supernatural
or superhuman causes. The notion might seem naive to
Westerners, who look for causation in psychodynamic forces,
but it does not seem to reduce the effectiveness of Chinese
therapy. In fact, lessening the shame each patient feels for
his or her failures has significant therapeutic value. Some
patient interviews illustrate these points. The interviews
were conducted through an interpreter with a doctor and
party representative present.

Liu Hua-mi, a 34-year-old single female factory worker, whose family had large landholdings, was in the hospital for the fourth time when I interviewed her. She stated: "At first, I was just weak and thought nothing about it. Then I began having hallucinations. I thought people were accusing me of being counterrevolutionary. I felt my mind was controlled by supersonic waves. I was afraid to think about anything. Then the illness became more serious because I felt people were ridiculing me when they spoke to me. When I went to the store, I felt people pushed me to the back and gave me the worst produce. When people expectorated, I thought they were spitting on me. I lost my appetite and thought of suicide.

"At the hospital," she continued, "with careful attention by the devoted staff, my true feelings came to the fore; and I began to realize the source of my illness was a misunderstanding of Chairman Mao's writings. With the correct understanding, I am now able to practice what he wrote, and what I must do is put this into social practice. From that, I will be all right."

When asked to describe her early life, the patient told of her father owning many pigs and rice fields. Did she miss her earlier life? "Oh no, things are much better since the revolution. We have rid ourselves of Fascist doctrine of the past."

Another patient, also admitted four times previously, categorized her problem, too, as "having counterrevolutionary thoughts."

"When I am alone I dance on and on and never want to stop. The world is all around me, but I don't want to be part of it. I am not in good health and have lots of things wrong with me. A man comes to visit my girlfriend, but I never think about marriage or sex. I get mad when people call me schizophrenic. I would like them to call me an ordinary worker. I have counterrevolutionary thoughts, but the doctors here are helping me straighten out my thinking. I love Chairman Mao."

These patients were typical of most that I interviewed.

Young—in their late 20s or early 30s—each had been hospitalized several times for an average of six months each visit. And, as with all other patients, they were "cured" by a political education process that papered over basic conflicts such as a desire for acquisition of property or sexual expression. These patients were reared in an environment that encouraged use of suppression of undesirable impulses. But fantasies of the past—repeating parents' lives or giving in to lustful drives—surfaced. The anxiety generated by unacceptable impulses was handled first by suppression as taught during childhood and reinforced by party discipline; then by the mechanism of simple denial, but this was inadequate; then by repression, also ineffective. As the anxiety continued to mount, the patient returned to the hospital.

A 28-year-old married woman whose husband lived in a commune miles away from her home exhibited a similar pattern. "I came to the hospital because I felt this pressure inside me. I didn't know how to control it. I would just feel more and more that something inside my head was forcing itself on me," she told the psychiatrist. Try as she might, the symptoms kept her from working.

Her mother died at an early age, leaving her to care for a younger sister. This duty forced her to forgo most of the pleasures of childhood and adolescence. How did she feel about her sister? Didn't she feel any angry thoughts toward her? Did she ever have any dreams or nightmares? "I love my sister very much and want only the best for her. Why should I feel angry toward her?" She paused. "Sometimes, I have this dream that my sister is falling from the top floor of a building, crushes her head and is killed."

The psychiatrist noted that in the dream, her sister died a violent death. The patient countered that she could not possibly understand that because she cared so deeply about her sibling and that the younger person was never a burden. She repeated that she wanted only good things for her. When the psychiatrist left, he shook hands with her and suggested that she think about rivalry having existed very naturally and normally with the sister, especially for father's attention. The patient clung to his hand. No, she insisted, she loved her sister and never thought of anything that would stand in the way of her sibling's happiness.

The need to deny any aggressive thoughts, even those evident in her dream, illustrates how hard she must work to deny unacceptable thoughts. When her anxiety reaches the point that neither suppression nor repression is effective, she seeks admission to a hospital.

At the hospital, physicians and staff members help her substitute political doctrines for the pressure of other thoughts. During each day's group activities, the patient is shown how she has deviated from revolutionary doctrine. Good thoughts and actions are reinforced, as are the patient's efforts to suppress bad ones. As the individual begins to understand where she deviated and how her weakness caused the symptoms, there is improvement. If nothing else, treatment distracts the patient from the conflict actually causing the problem and rewards her intensively for good behavior. Unfortunately, the cure seems to be only temporary. Once the patient returns to her usual life, the conflict may reemerge, and further help is needed to suppress unacceptable desires.

Still, remarkably few Chinese seem to require institutionalization. And the nation has made an amazing amount of social progress using social pressure and suppression.

The Opium Problem

Opium addiction had been a problem in China from the 1700s to 1949, thanks in large part to pressure by the British to keep the narcotic flowing into China and thereby to keep Chinese money flowing into Great Britain. Chinese laws had banned the substance as early as 1729, but the Opium Wars in the 1840s subverted these. When Mao came to power in 1949, he did not have to change laws to wipe out drug addiction. Instead, he induced sweeping and positive changes in the people. Opium traders have always depended on a supply of new users, since the old ones died, were jailed or became "clean." Mao ended this supply.

Through street committees of 100 to 200 people and through self-criticism groups, Mao's workers exerted social pressure in a full-scale antiopium campaign. To be involved in drug usage or drug trafficking was shameful. Meanwhile, national leadership promised members of the younger generation a chance to make something of their lives. They could assume lands formerly owned by landlord-barons. They could learn to read. Or study science.

If they were women, they could gain equality with men. They were presented with hope, and with a challenge to build a new world through constructive cooperation. That, plus the social pressure from the Communist governmental groups, wrought a complete change of attitude among China's youth. It meant the end of the opium trade and brought about the end of drug addiction, truly a remarkable feat.

The Chinese method of controlling deviance has its weaknesses. It might not be completely applicable to the United States, in any case, because Americans have been raised to value individualism, not duty to the larger group. But I think we could learn much from China in this regard, just as the Chinese hope to learn from our technological experts.

If it seems hard to envision the benefits of disciplined suppression on a societal scale, think in terms of individuals. Controlling unacceptable impulses by the mental mechanism of repression builds stagnant pools of psychic energy that can burst free at any moment, in a torrent of bad temper or random violence.

Consider Jim, a talented electronics engineer from Omaha, who was known for his explosive temper, which he could not control despite vows he made after reprimands from peers and superiors. He was a senior consultant in charge of reviewing projects by assistants and new recruits. If they did not perform as desired, he exploded fiercely. These outbursts could be traced to his childhood. His younger brother was born with a birth defect, and the needs of this disabled child dominated the household. Jim was constantly admonished never to show any impatience with his sibling, only acceptance. Jim repressed his anger toward his younger brother, but now as an executive he would explode whenever he had to discipline a subordinate. The current event awakened a painful repressed memory.

Consider another problem that arises in every home. As children reach adolescence, mother or father may begin to harangue them or even accuse them, for no apparent reason, of sexual involvement. This stems from the oedipal and electra complexes—attraction parents feel toward offspring of the opposite sex as they begin to blossom. The elders project their own impulses onto the adolescent. If parents can acknowledge this attraction and consciously pass it by (suppression), instead of automatically burying the impulse (repression), families would be happier and more peaceful.

Finally, consider our Chinese interpreter, a doctoral candidate in linguistics. He admitted that he sometimes felt anger and hostility, but said he dealt with these feelings by trying to think of something more pleasant. "If that doesn't work," he said, "I just go off and have a good sleep."

TAIWANESE FOLK MEDICINE[5]

. . . As a physician and an anthropologist, I am in a unique position to study folk medicine, working from a perspective that is both cultural and medical. On my three field trips to Taiwan, I have observed more than 500 patients being treated by Taiwanese shamans, or *tang-ki* (literally, "divining youth"), as well as 25 *tang-kis* going through their healing rituals. I have studied several *tang-kis* and their patients extensively over months and even years. During my study of one tang-ki, I visited his shrine on seven consecutive nights and observed his new patients, whose complaints ranged from sickness to business problems to

[5] From article entitled "The Failure of Western Medicine," by Arthur Kleinman, department of psychiatry and behavioral sciences, University of Washington School of Medicine; editor of journal, *Culture, Medicine and Psychiatry. Human Nature.* p 63–8. N. '78. Copyright © 1978 by Human Nature, Inc. Reprinted by permission of the publisher.

"bad fate." In order to determine the effectiveness of the tang-ki's treatment, for two months I followed a group of patients who were seen by the tang-ki on three consecutive evenings.

Tang-kis vary in their methods. Some spend more time talking to patients; some emphasize rituals; some specialize in prescribing medicines; and some are famous for treating certain kinds of problems and sicknesses. Despite these differences, they generally spend more time with their patients and explain more to them than either Western or traditional Chinese doctors do.

In Taiwan, encounters with Western-style doctors average just under five minutes, while those with Chinese-style physicians average seven and a half minutes. Encounters with the tang-ki last up to several hours in the shrine, but only five to 10 minutes are spent in formal consultation with the entranced tang-ki; most communication is between the patient and the tang-ki's assistants or other individuals at the shrine, who act as go-betweens. However, virtually all the time of the shaman-patient relationship is spent in explaining the disease and treatment, whereas Chinese-style doctors offer explanations to their patients for one and a half minutes and Western-style doctors for 40 seconds.

Since the tang-ki's advice is offered during a trance, it is usually either unintelligible or couched in special terms. Assistants, therefore, form a vital link between the healer and the patient. They interpret the tang-ki's instructions regarding rituals, medicine, changes in life style, and the solution of practical problems. They offer patients psychological support, calm them, and listen sympathetically to their complaints. Their function is similar to that of hospital social-service workers, paraprofessionals, and nurses.

Most patients report being satisfied with the care provided by tang-kis and believe this care to be at least partially successful. Despite this feeling, most patients who approach a tang-ki hedge their bets. Believing that full healing requires the cooperation of both god and man, they also go to a professional physician. Although tang-kis do not object to this dual treatment, they do not encourage it. Many claim they can cure all disorders, even cancer. At times, a tang-ki's claims keep his patients from seeking medical treatment for serious illnesses. In the case of a young woman suffering from acute hepatitis, a reliance on the powers of the tang-ki brought her close to death. But such effects are unusual in my experience.

One tang-ki I concentrated on lives and practices in Taipei. His explanations of sickness and healing contain a mixture of supernatural, classical Chinese medical, popular medical, and Western medical ideas.

Treatment By the Tang-Ki

During the seven nights I watched this tang-ki at work in his shrine, I counted 122 new patients. Fifty-four came seeking treatment for sickness; 33 came to have their fate foretold or their bad fortune treated; 24 came because of business or financial problems; and 11 came about personal or family problems. Most of the new patients were lower class, two thirds were female, and all were Taiwanese. At least one quarter were young children or infants.

The patients complained of a wide range of sickness: acute infections of the nose and throat, intestinal disorders (such as diarrhea), chronic disorders such as low back pain, arthritis, asthma, and emphysema. Other frequent complaints were chronic, vague symptoms that were the physiological manifestations of such psychological problems as anxiety, depression, and hysteria. Many children suffered from irritability, sleeplessness, and crying fits that were diagnosed as colic by local pediatricians, but treated by the shamans and the families of the children as "fright," a folk syndrome in Chinese culture.

Healing sessions occur every night at the shrine. The process begins after dinner and lasts until early the next morning. It can be divided into two separate parts: first, the time when the tang-ki is in his trance and consults with new patients (approximately one hour); and second, the rest of the evening, when the patients socialize with the members of the tang-ki's cult, praying, falling into trances, dancing, speaking in tongues, and engaging in activities with strong sexual overtones. Men and women massage each other, women rub the insides of their thighs, and men thrust their pelvises forward and back in imitation of the sex act. This ecstatic behavior, which is encouraged—and even expected—in the tang-ki's shrine, is unusual in Chinese culture and unsanctioned in any other public place.

After registering with one of the tang-ki's assistants, new patients burn incense and pray, asking the tang-ki's god about their problem. The patient throws divination blocks (half-moon-shaped pieces of wood) onto the floor and reads the god's reply to his prayer in their pattern; after the blocks indicate the god's consent, the patient waits for the tang-ki to go into a trance. An assistant then calls the patient, who consults with the entranced tang-ki about his problem. Occasionally the tang-ki asks a few questions, but more often he simply speaks to the patient in the name of the god believed to possess him. The tang-ki then prescribes various routine therapies for the patient's illness (ashes to drink, charms to eat or wear, brief therapeutic rituals, herbal medicines to drink, or certain foods to eat). He also gives advice to help the patient resolve practical problems and cope with personal and family distress. Then he pronounces the patient cured. The patient is instructed to return to the shrine regularly so that he will become possessed by the tang-ki's god; this possession will cast off sickness, which is frequently attributed to an attempted possession by another god. On returning to the shrine the patient is encouraged to become a regular member of the tang-ki's cult.

With each patient, the tang-ki performs two short rituals. In one he writes a charm in the air over the patient in order to transfer the god's power to him. In the other he moves his hands rapidly in front of the patient and makes a motion as if he were throwing something to the ground. This ritual cleanses the patient of bad spirits and evil influences. In the case of middle-aged or elderly people, he may massage the patients. Because of the sexual connotations, he avoids this ritual with younger patients.

After spending five minutes with the tang-ki the patient

returns to his seat. He does not consult again with the entranced tang-ki but remains in the shrine for several hours, sitting quietly, meditating, praying, or resting. He talks with other patients who regularly attend the shrine and with the tang-ki's assistants, and he may engage in such ritual activities as burning spirit money to please an angry god or spirit, or buying special foods (which are later eaten by the patient and his family) to offer as sacrifices to the gods. If he obeys the tang-ki's directions, he will attend the shrine regularly, enter trances, and become a cult member in the hope of avoiding a relapse.

Followup After Treatment

To ascertain the effectiveness of the tang-ki's treatment, I interviewed 12 of his patients in their homes two months after their first visit to the shrine. I had intended to interview 19 consecutive patients, but two gave the tang-ki's assistants wrong addresses and could not be located; three refused to be interviewed; and two had moved out of the city.

I asked each patient to evaluate the treatment and to explain why it had succeeded or failed. I asked if either their symptoms or their behavior had changed and if they thought any improvement could have resulted from the natural course of their sickness. I also asked whether they had had other health care for the problem along with the tang-ki's treatment. I gathered a brief history of each patient's sickness and assessed his or her physiological and psychological status. Because I was unable to perform standard medical tests (such as physical examinations, x-rays, blood tests, or psychological exams), my judgment of a patient's condition was limited to personal observation.

At first the tang-ki's treatment seemed outstanding; of the 12 patients, 10 claimed that the treatment was at least partially effective, and only two patients claimed that it was a failure. Six of the patients claimed to be fully healed. But all 10 patients who claimed some degree of healing suffered from one of three kinds of problems: chronic but not dangerous illnesses in which I observed symptoms that persisted after treatment; self-limiting diseases that would have cured themselves without treatment; and psychological problems with physical manifestations. In all of these disorders, managing the personal, social, and cultural problems of illness is more important than treating the medical problems of disease.

The two cases that were not cured were the only ones involving severe disorders, one physiological and the other psychological. The first was a six-year-old girl with acute kidney disease whose condition worsened while her parents were taking her to the tang-ki; she subsequently spent a month undergoing modern medical treatment. The second was a 22-year-old girl with suicidal tendencies and a serious behavioral disorder, who was taken to the shrine against her will by her mother. She reported no improvement, but psychiatric care did not help either. Her mother felt that the tang-ki would have been effective had the girl tried him longer.

The patients who claimed improvement after the tang-ki's treatment defined healing in various ways. For some, changes in symptoms were most important; a lessening or departure of pain overshadowed other aspects of the treatment. In other cases changes in general attitude were deemed most important. If a patient felt better psychologically after attending the shrine, if he came away with a better outlook on life, he considered the tang-ki to have been effective. Social changes were also important, especially for women; they were able to derive benefits from getting out of the house and away from family stresses, socializing with friends, and enjoying the exciting atmosphere of the shrine. For some, the evaluation of the therapy was based on cultural belief. The very fact that the appropriate ritual was performed and the supernatural cause of the illness confirmed, provided evidence of healing.

Five of the 10 patients who claimed that the tang-ki helped them reported positive changes in both their symptoms and their attitudes (they felt happier) ; two reported improvements in symptoms but no attitude change; one reported no change in symptoms but a positive change in attitude; one even reported a worsening in symptoms but an improvement in attitude; and one, a 10-year-old boy with disciplinary problems, was reported to have had an improvement in his behavior. (There were no changes in his symptoms, since there were no symptoms to begin with.)

Clearly the patients evaluated their care in different ways. These differences frequently carried over into particular settings outside the patients' homes. Several patients told me that they would never give a negative evaluation of the tang-ki's treatment in his shrine, since to do so might prejudice the gods against them and make their conditions worse. Others could not bring themselves to dispute the tang-ki, his assistants, and the regular shrine attenders who constantly told them that they were being healed, even if they felt no improvement. Occasionally patients credited the tang-ki with curing them even when they had taken medication prescribed by a Western-style doctor (and known to be effective) during their healing.

More important than the differences among the patients in their evaluations of treatment are the differences between the tang-ki and modern Western-style physicians in their definitions of healing. Although the tang-ki agreed with the 10 patients who said they were healed, and reinforced these feelings by encouraging the patients to think of themselves as healed, my evaluations of their conditions, based on Western medical standards, differed. Only a few of the 10 cases seemed to provide evidence that supported the effectiveness of the tang-ki, and in these natural remission and the placebo effect could not be ruled out.

When it comes to curing acute, severe, medically defined diseases, the tang-kis are ineffective. However, the tang-ki's shrine, which forms part of the patient's social network, supports him through his sickness. The "clinical reality" of the shrine reflects the culture and society of Taiwan and has more in common with popular cultural beliefs and behavior than the clinical realities of Western-style and Chinese-style doctors' offices, where patients sit quietly and perhaps apprehensively awaiting their turn with the physician and where crucial personal and social problems relating to their sicknesses generally go untreated. The shrine puts the patient at ease; it provides what Jerome Frank has called "expectant faith," an expectation of cure that prepares the patient for successful treatment—even in the case of incurable diseases. Most important, its clinical reality routinely assures treatment of illness-related problems and through their resolution may alleviate some diseases as well.

Most primary medical care is directed toward treating people with disorders similar to those the native healer treats. Both physicians and native healers treat people with minimal chronic and psychosomatic complaints. But the modern physician is likely to fail with patients because he is trained to ignore the illness and to deal only with the disease. This pattern, which is built into the training of Western doctors, fails when applied to the healing of illness, a much more common complaint. Apparently aware of the distinction, the Taiwanese go to physicians for cures of life-threatening diseases, but to native healers for illnesses.

The solution to the problem of health care may not lie with the native healer, even in developing countries. My observation of them indicates that shamans and other religious healers are too tightly bound by social and cultural constraints to be able to diagnose and treat disease systematically and effectively. Secular native healers, like Chinese-style doctors in the People's Republic of China, on the other hand, may be in a good position to integrate biomedical practices with their healing activities—although some are probably no better than Western physicians at treating illness. A more fundamental approach to health in the Third World would be to train people who already have experience in treating illnesses to recognize and manage routine diseases. The "barefoot doctors" of the People's Republic of China may already have accomplished this.

But Western physicians could broaden their own skills and knowledge, allowing them to treat both disease and illness. I am recommending not that Western physicians learn to go into trances or ask patients to burn spirit money, but that they learn to treat sickness in the context of the patient's psychology and culture. Physicians need, for example, to question patients about what they think caused their problems; how they think their illnesses should be treated; what threats, losses, and gains their sickness represents; and what conflicts they perceive between their values and the doctor's professional values.

Doctors need to be as precise in defining the life problems created by an illness as in investigating its biological basis. They should be as competent in prescribing behavioral and social management strategies for treating the illness as in prescribing technological interventions for the disease. This takes time, effort, and training. But only when physicians again treat the patient's illness, as well as his disease, and treat it with a systematic approach based on the findings of clinical social science, not with a folksy parody of shamans or old-time general practitioners, will the persistent dissatisfaction with modern medicine begin to fade. Following the example of the native healer, though not his specific methods, may be the best way to introduce humanistic medicine into the developed world.

A LOOK THROUGH THE OPEN DOOR[6]

. . . Recent changes in the political climate have thrust education to the fore as an urgent new priority. China realizes that the future depends heavily on the development of her brainpower and is paying increasing attention to her schools.

We visited three of them, two elementary schools and one post-secondary school. In Nanking we observed some elementary classes, where the children were dressed beautifully in anticipation of our visit. Their colorful blouses contrasted sharply with the plain blue and blue-gray clothes of the teachers and other adults. They were studying Chi-

6 From article entitled "China: A First Look Through the Open Door," by Alexander Taffel, director of educational programs, National Energy Foundation. Outlook. p 6–8. F. '79. By permission of the author.

nese characters. The teacher pointed to a character on the board, read it aloud, and had the class repeat it in unison. Discipline and attention were rigid by American standards but this may have been for the benefit of the visitors.

After the lesson was over, we accompanied the children to the school yard where they treated us to a delightful performance of stories, songs and dances. On our visit to the elementary school in Canton—which proved a similar experience except that the children were older—we saw what must have been the world's champion seven-year-old ping pong players shooting the ball back and forth with the speed of a bullet.

The post-secondary school in Nanning is called the Institute of National Minorities and is a training school for teachers. The word "minorities" refers to Chinese citizens not of Han ancestry who, constituting less than 10 percent of the population, nevertheless occupy a large part of the less populated areas of China. Director Kao Wu Fang explained that the school was a sort of crash program for training minority students to become teachers of English, foreign languages, the sciences, mathematics, and the Chinese language and arts. As we came into their classrooms, they rose and applauded us in greeting and we replied in kind. This manifestation of friendship for Americans was repeated many times during our trip.

The students seemed earnest, capable and eager to succeed. The English teachers-to-be, in particular, sought us out to practice and perfect their mastery in conversation with us. A request to see the science laboratories was met with the response that since the school had been closed during the cultural revolution and reopened only recently, there had not yet been an opportunity to establish science laboratories. However, I did get to visit a science class and saw a lesson on electronics. The level of the content was about that of an advanced college course in the United States. I could not tell how well the students were mastering the subject because the teaching method was mainly lecture.

The People's Republic of China leaves one with certain

deep impressions. We found it to be a nation preponderantly young, on the march towards a clear goal and having the determination to attain it as quickly as possible. That determination was dramatized by the standard uniform dress of the people that suggested an army in full mobilization. Men wear the blue Mao jacket, blue pants and blue cap while women wear blue blouses and slacks. The young women are further distinguished by the two long braids that hang over their shoulders.

In speaking with the guides, one learns that the young people regard their duty to meet the country's needs as coming before their own goals and aspirations.

Organization evidently has managed to provide food, work and the basic necessities to a billion people. While there are serious lacks and inefficiencies, the years of famine and flood definitely seem to be a thing of the past.

The new China is mindful of her cultural heritage and is taking strong action to strengthen public education. It is also assiduously reclaiming and preserving the treasures of its past: the beautiful imperial buildings, the artistic treasures and the new archeological finds are receiving expert care and are available to viewing by the general public.

While the means of communication have been under strict government control and the voices of the dissidents have been effectively muted, there has been a thaw. We saw the posters go up in Peking and were told by our guides that these were the "free" opinions of some of the people. We took it for granted that they were strictly pro-government opinions, but learned later that we were wrong. What we had seen were the first of the comments critical of Chairman Mao and of the government to go up in the sudden new atmosphere of free expression. Whether this atmosphere will endure, only time will tell.

There is almost no interest in religion to be noticed in the parts of China that we visited, and we wondered if that fact accentuated the need for the people to deify their leadership. In Peking, they have built Chairman Mao a vastly more impressive mausoleum than that of Lenin in

Moscow. Mao lies there in state to be viewed by the millions of people who file silently by his bier each year.

Though the vagaries of recent politics have cast a shadow on some of his ideas and deeds, it is highly likely that Mao will continue to be revered as the father of a regenerated China.

THE THRIVING CULTURAL SCENE[7]

Some visitors complain that there's no night life in Peking. That's not quite so: it's just that the Chinese have not got around to telling about it in English. Lights-out certainly is earlier than in New York, but everything is moved up accordingly—performances begin at 6:30 or 7 P.M. In one week recently, in five consecutive evenings, I was at the theater, an acrobatic/magic variety show, two films and the China-U.S. basketball game. I never did that in New York. Couldn't afford it. Prices here for most entertainment are 3 to 4 *mao* (20 to 27 cents). There's plenty going on.

There's even more going on behind the scenes of the performing and creative arts, a ferment and an excitement unparalleled since the first years of the People's Republic. In book and magazine publishing, in the fine arts and the theater, in music, opera and the dance, cultural life has been coming alive again since the fall of Mao Zedong's [Mao Tse-tung] wife, Jiang Qing, and her associates in the Communist Party and governmental hierarchy. In some places the tender shoots are tentative; in others they are breaking through boldly. Everywhere people are meeting and talking about the revival, swapping horror stories about the smothering 1960s, and seeking to reassure themselves that those days are gone forever. All winter and spring the press has been crowded with reports of clearances and rehabilitations of writers, artists and actors falsely charged with producing

[7] Article entitled "Peking Love Song," by James Aronson, journalist and professor of communication, Hunter College; Peking correspondent. *Nation*. p 111–13. Ag. 11–18, '79. © 1979 by the Nation Associates, Inc. Reprinted by permission.

"poisonous weeds," as collaborators of "the dictatorship of the sinister line in literature and art."

Last spring, obviously in response to petitions and protests all over China, the organization and propaganda departments of the Communist Party and the Ministry of Culture met in a national forum with the All-China Federation of Literature and Art to discuss ways and means to hasten the process of clearance. There were thousands upon thousands of victims. Those being processed are already working again, but they want full public recognition that they were falsely charged, and an official statement to that effect.

Publishing

New publications are sprouting and old ones reappearing after a forced absence of ten or more years. The magazine *Popular Cinema* is back, with articles on current films, plans for the Chinese film industry, an article on Chaplin and one on *The Next Generation,* the American television sequel to *Roots.* So is the academic journal *Culture and History,* with an invitation to scholars from the mainland, Macao, Taiwan and Hong Kong to contribute. Reappearing also are the *Literature Review, Women of China* (in English) , *Teaching History* and *Chess*—devoted to the ancient Chinese game denounced during the Cultural Revolution as a "bourgeois pastime."

In February the *People's Daily* published for the first time in full the text of a 16,000-word address in 1961 by Premier Zhou Enlai [Chou En-lai] to a forum "On the Questions Related to Literature and Art." In essence it was an argument against substituting political slogans for art, a challenge to the professionals in the audience to "dare to think, to speak, to act." There was an eighteen-year delayed echo in March, when a similar forum gathered and concluded that many of China's artists still had not taken up the second and third parts of the challenge.

But they are beginning to. In its first issue of 1979, the magazine *Fine Arts* published an editorial denouncing the distortion of history and the "deification of the individual." It did not leave the reference vague. Under the Gang of Four, it said, Mao appeared in paintings with only the blue sky as a backdrop "with shining complexion, and always in the center, high above the people, high above the mountains." These, said the editorial, were the conventions of classical religious paintings: historical paintings must be true to history.

Theater

Of all the arts in China, the theater perhaps has taken up Zhou's challenge most vigorously. The plays I have seen are first rate, matching the best in the United States in direction and acting, and certainly deeper in content. In Peking, the sixth theater festival in celebration of the thirtieth anniversary of the founding of the People's Republic has presented, among others, *Tea House,* by the novelist and playwright Lao She, who committed suicide during the Cultural Revolution. He is the author also of the novel published in the United States under the title *Rickshaw Boy* in the 1940s—a seminal book on China for many Americans.

Tea House depicts old China in three stages: the reform movement of 1898, the time of the clashes among the warlords and the Kuomintang rule after the Japanese occupation. Three main characters (there are seventy) age and decline with the tea house. They are the hard-working tea house owner, a capitalist, and a worker, all of them sympathetic characters rendering China's history with high humor and satire.

Also being presented is a Chinese version of Brecht's *Galileo,* to which the Chinese style lends itself admirably; and *Yanzhi,* a Shaoxing opera adapted from the novel *Strange Stories From a Chinese Studio,* a denunciation of bureaucracy wonderfully free of political posturing. The opera, the critics say, applies the principle of "seeking truth from facts," an interesting phrase which I would further interpret as good old-fashioned investigative reporting.

Films

The state of the cinema unfortunately is far less healthy. The flawless revolutionary hero persists: handsome, wholesome, pure—and dull. One film I saw, *Silver Flower,* tells of a beautiful battered Mongolian slave girl who turns nomad and ends up as an Eighth Route Army brigade commander. Typical scene: our heroine dismounting, uniform spotless and smooth after a hard day's ride over the Mongolian plains, and delivering a tide-turning speech to a crowd of landlord-deceived Mongols and Hans. I assigned the film for review as an exercise in news writing for my class at the Institute of Journalism in Peking. The class numbers seventeen. There were seventeen negative reviews. One student concluded that the film suffered acutely from "intellectual malnutrition." All had some tart advice for the film industry.

Film makers are feeling the hot breath of national disapproval. The heads of the eleven studios met in March to announce fifty new feature films for 1979, but more importantly to set in motion a program to overhaul all aspects of film production. Administrators, directors, actors and scenarists discussed ways to "blaze new trails," to discard monotonous themes and replace them with the reality of contemporary life. The *People's Daily* recently published a full page of articles and letters attesting to the sad state of the industry. It promised more.

Music and Art

On his return from China with the Boston Symphony Orchestra, Harold Schonberg wrote (the New York *Times,* April 1) that "it is hard to get close to painters in China." I have not found it so. Perhaps because my wife, Grambs Miller, is an artist and illustrator with a special interest in Chinese painting, we have encountered no barriers. In addition to meeting artists at exhibits, we have visited with them in their homes and studios.

The art scene here is volatile. There is a rebellion

against political poster painting but not, as Schonberg indicated, against traditional painting. Quite the contrary; many painters, old and young, have gone back to the traditional style, some traveling deep into the mountains to paint and perhaps to reflect on the scars of the recent past, as did the artist-pilgrims of dynastic China. Several know and have studied the works of Matisse, Picasso, van Gogh and Monet.

One leading painter, Liu Jiyou, famous for his animals, had studied in Czechoslovakia, where he formed a great admiration for Albrecht Dürer. The son of a painter, his two daughters and son are also studying painting. The younger daughter hopes to study at an art school in the United States. Liu showed us his fastidious earlier work to emphasize his freer contemporary brush. Then he went to his table and, as we watched, painted a marvelous rabbit from his storehouse memory. His first stroke was an ear in two colors.

The Chinese love music—their own lilting tunes and folk music of the world. They missed the classical music of the West during the period of inane prohibition. Some of this was repaired with the visit of the Boston Symphony, which had a television audience of millions. They were followed by the Lyons Symphony which, in addition to appearing on TV, played for 15,000 persons in eight concerts in Shanghai and Peking.

In a note in the New York *Times,* pianist Walter Hautzig reported that after a recital in China students in the audience refused to meet with him privately backstage for fear of getting into trouble. He spoke of a "lingering police-state paranoia." No doubt the past lingers, but paranoia is much too strong a word. Anxiety would be more apt, and among most of the young people I have met there is not even that. For example, a student at the Conservatory of Music, near where we live, seems to have adopted us. Two or three times a week, in daylight and dusk, she bikes to our little walled house in Noisy Market Street. The other day she invited us to the conservatory's auditorium for an afternoon concert by students seeking a place in the International Chopin Competition.

As is the theater, the music world is becoming more daring. Ly Ji, chairman of the union of musicians, recently urged his fellow artists to "smash the mental shackles" of the recent past and write "what people want to hear." Life is rich and colorful, with all kinds of themes, he said, "contemporary revolutionary ones, historical ones and everyday life." None is indispensable, anything poetic and beautiful could be made into a good song. "Love," he said, "did not cease to exist just because our love songs were banned."

Literature

Everyone reads. China has 940 journals with a combined circulation of 112 million. Those concerned with nature, science and children's themes have the biggest circulations. China's two major publishers of children's books plan to bring out 300 new titles by the end of 1979 to mark the International Year of the Child. All told, there will be 1,000 titles available by June 1, 1980. The Guangming *Daily,* which appeals mainly to professionals and intellectuals, has a circulation of 1.4 million, up from 200,000 during the Cultural Revolution. Bookstores are constantly crowded. Book publishers from the United States have just begun arriving to inaugurate a two-way sales arrangement with China.

In the midst of the ferment, the past—the "feudal-fascist" past, many call it—is unearthed and examined. "Shocking Literary Exposé," says a headline in the *People's Daily.* Below it appears an article about the "Three Family Village," a grim story of the fate of three writers for the Peking *Evening News* who produced a popular column titled "Notes From the Three Family Village" and "Evening Chats in Yanshan." Deng Tuo, Wu Han and Liao Mosha were their names. With gusto they dealt with social problems, often basing their incisive criticism and satire on letters from readers complaining about bureaucracy, bungling and injustice. One column cautioned readers against high-sounding empty talk. They lampooned the slogan, "The east wind is our benefactor and the west wind is our enemy."

In the late 1960s, after an inquisition into their work, they were charged with launching a "flagrant attack on the scientific Marxist statement" that "the east wind prevails over the west wind," and therefore were attacking Mao Zedong thought. All three were officials of the Peking municipal government, in addition to being writers. Two were hounded to their deaths. Liao Mosha survived to testify before a commission which recently cleared them of any wrongdoing.

Listen to the painter Huang Zhou—noted for his animals and particularly his donkeys—on the madness of the time:

> If I painted a donkey turning its head back, I was accused of longing for the past. If there was one donkey in my picture, the Gang said I was promoting individualism. If it contained many donkeys, I was calling socialism backward. If my donkeys were running west, I was supporting western society. If they were running toward the viewer, they were charging on socialism and attacking it. If they were going north, it was because I liked Soviet revisionism. I was branded a black painter (*heihuajia*) with a deep hatred for the Communist Party. Who could paint under such circumstances?

The answer, of course, is: "Nobody in his or her right mind." Nor write, nor compose, nor act, nor sing nor dance. Then in the post-Cultural Revolution era, when so much has already changed, are there limits still to cultural endeavor and creation? Yes, there are limits—but they are defined now not by Jiang Qing but by the legacy of Zhou Enlai. Where Jiang Qing once banned a dance of one of the Chinese nationalities because the head movements irritated her, Zhou Enlai denounced bureaucratic dictatorship of art form and content.

And the overall limits are set by the system of socialism itself. Art or literature that attacks Chinese socialism is not permitted. It follows then that advocacy of another system likewise is forbidden. Within the socialist system, the Chinese are free to express themselves as they will. The recent developments affecting Democracy Wall are pertinent here. The Wall stands (I pass it two or three times daily) ; new big-character posters go up all the time and the little dissident publications are still sold. But the somewhat vague strictures about the posters have filtered down, and they are observed. Yet, at the same time, and again within the system, the media are vigorously pressing the campaigns against injustice, corruption, inefficiency and bureaucracy. Where the wall was largely symbolic, the media are tangible and widely effective.

There are other limits. Lack of paper holds down the press runs of the new publications. That is socialist reality. The dark stage, the closed study, the uninhabited studio crippled creativity for almost a generation; new writers must be trained and tested, new actors taught, new painters encouraged. That too is real. An editor of a new social studies quarterly told me the first issue had to be postponed some months because the contributors had nothing to write about: they were busy catching up with developments they had missed in a dozen years of isolation.

To this observer's eye, the vast majority of the Chinese are intensely loyal to their system. They do not seek the freedom to overthrow it. What they seek—particularly the people in the arts with whom I have talked at length—is the freedom from fear that the gross distortion of socialism which took place in the Jiang Qing dynasty will reassert itself.

Could it happen again? The first step, they answer, is to try to find out how and why it happened. They do not yet know; they are still trying to sort it out. They do not want it to become nonhistory. But even as they sift through the past, they live vigorously in the present. And they are mindful of another stricture from Zhou Enlai: "The past not forgotten is a guide to the future."

A CHURCH THAT WOULD NOT DIE[8]

In 1966 Red Guards burned Bibles in the streets of Shanghai for several afternoons. When boredom set in, the surviving stock was sent off to a pulping plant. In Xiamen

[8] Article from *Time*. p 48–9. S. 10, '79. Reprinted by permission from *Time*, The Weekly Newsmagazine; Copyright Time Inc. 1979.

(Amoy), a similar burning took place but with a sinister twist: Y.M.C.A. and Y.W.C.A. workers were forced to kneel by the books until their cheeks and hands blistered from the fire. All over China, church buildings were pillaged, closed down or turned into warehouses. Chinese Christians were often tortured or killed if they did not repudiate their beliefs. At the height of the 1966–69 Cultural Revolution, the last eight Western Christian workers in China, Roman Catholic nuns from a school for diplomats' children in Peking, were hounded across the border into Hong Kong by jeering Red Guards. Their crude expulsion seemed to symbolize Communist China's last judgment on four centuries of Western missionary endeavor.

That was 13 years ago. Since then, the death of Mao Tse-tung and a political convulsion have brought to power a more outward looking regime led by Hua Guofeng and Deng Xiaoping. Last week China seemed intent on showing the rest of the world a newer, more tolerant face toward Christianity—and other religions as well. As official Chinese delegates to the Third Assembly of the World Conference on Religion and Peace in Princeton, N.J., eight Chinese religious leaders arrived in the U.S. for the ten-day meeting. The group included Buddhists, Muslims and Christians, among them Anglican Bishop Ding Guangxun (K. H. Ting), 64, who 13 years ago was removed from his house and lost his job as president of Nanjing Theological Seminary after the place was abruptly shut down. It was only the second time in three decades that any Chinese Christian leaders had been permitted to visit the U.S.

Bishop Ding's arrival was the latest in a series of moves by Chinese authorities to extend the hand of recognition to China's Christians and other religious believers. In January the Religious Affairs Bureau, dormant for years, was revived in Peking, along with units in Shanghai and Canton. In February a national-level conference in Kunming, capital of Yunnan province, established an eight-year plan for government-sponsored academic research on religion. Shanghai's Catholic Bishop Gong Binmei (Kung Pin-mei), 77, and Protestant Evangelist Wang Mingdao (Wang Mingtao) , 79, both imprisoned for over 20 years, have reportedly been released. The *People's Daily* declared that China's government would "staunchly and consistently" uphold article 46 of China's 1978 constitution. Article 46 guarantees that the people have "freedom to believe in religion and freedom not to believe in religion."

Characteristically, the article takes back with the left hand what it gave with the right. A further clause guarantees freedom "to propagate atheism." Despite the new "soft line," Peking has never abandoned its Marxist hostility to all religion. It believes that, after suitable "atheistic education," the Chinese will "throw off the various kinds of spiritual shackles." The new thaw is essentially an expression of a "united front" policy toward China's primary problem: modernization. The government is determined to attract wide support both at home and abroad for its ambitious new economic and social goals.

There has also been an implicit recognition of a perplexing reality. The harsh 1966–76 drive to expunge major religions from the national consciousness was a failure. According to China's religious leaders in the U.S. last week, Islam's 10 million adherents have held on, Buddhism's 100 million believers are "lingering." Christianity, according to Bishop Ding, has actually gained "new converts." The official count back in 1954 was 700,000 baptized Protestants and about 3 million Roman Catholics. Today there are no accurate statistics. But it is clear that persecution has created thousands of small, self-contained Christian communities, which operate in secret, mostly without an ordained minister, often without scriptures.

A picture of these small but highly evangelical Chinese congregations has been emerging from recent accounts by Overseas Chinese visitors to close Christian friends and relatives. Jonathan Chao, of Hong Kong's Chinese Church Research Center, says that in the late 1960s the first clandestine groups met in threes and fours in private homes. As the pressures lessened somewhat, the numbers grew from 30 to 50 at each meeting. They would sing, pray, study Bible passages painstakingly copied by hand, and listen to a "sermon" from one of their own. Numbers grew swiftly, especially after reports that physical and mental illnesses were cured by prayer.

In Hong Kong last week one Christian newly arrived from China told *Time*'s Hong Kong Correspondent Bing Wong about a large meeting. Her story:

There were 800 of us gathered in a masonry barn near a coastal city in Guangdong. It was warm, and there was no breeze, so the barn became stuffy at times. As no chairs or benches were available, everybody stood. The leader played the rickety piano and led the congregation in singing hymns. After the sermon we prayed: "Lord, be with us and protect our meeting from being interrupted." Nobody had a Bible, a hymn book or a prayer script.

In an obvious attempt to assert party control over this religious revival, Chinese authorities are now trying to reconstitute the Chinese Three-Self Patriotic Movement, a sort of Protestant superchurch originally set up in the 1950s to cut off all links to foreign churches and unite Protestants in one government-controlled group. The "Three-Selfs" stood for self-government, self-propagation and self-support. But the organization is still mistrusted by Christians; they remember the old days when it sowed suspicion in congregations in order to sabotage the influence of independent-minded church leaders.

While courting their country's Protestants, China's Communist authorities have not neglected the much larger Roman Catholic community. Late in July the Catholic Patriotic Association, China's "autonomous" Catholic church, which was forced to break with Rome in 1957, elected a new "bishop," Michael Fu Tieshan, 47. The appointment was the first since the death of Yao Guangyu in 1964. Chinese Catholics have been cut off from Rome and from the reforms of the Second Vatican Council. (At the only legally open Catholic church, in Peking, the Mass is still said in Latin.) The Vatican has refused to recognize Fu's election. But when Pope John Paul II recently spoke of those ties to the Chinese Catholic community that "never have been broken spiritually," he was implicitly offering to open diplomatic relations again. Peking quickly responded.

As a final sweetener in the attempt to attract Christians to official church programs, the government is planning to print a revised edition of the Bible, the so-called "Union" translation of 1919. The New Testament portion is promised for next spring. That news should be encouraging to American evangelicals, who have had a special feeling for China as a missionary field for more than a century. How many copies will ever reach China's Christians remains a question. Meanwhile, one observer of the scene in Hong Kong remained optimistic about the Chinese church. Citing a Chinese proverb, he said: "In no prairie fire do seeds perish; see, their new blades shoot forth amidst the spring breezes."

HAS JUSTICE A FAIRER FUTURE IN CHINA?[9]

The accused, with head slightly bowed, stood in the center of the spare but freshly painted courtroom of Shanghai's Puto District. Flanked by prosecutor and defender, he faced the panel of four—a judge, two assessors, and a clerk —that would try him. When asked by the judge, he identified himself as Tsao Chung-fa, 34, a worker in the Chekiang Province light bulb factory.

The charges against him were read: In violation of the anti-corruption law, Tsao had persisted in embezzling industrial copper and stealing timber even after he had received a formal warning for an earlier offense. Tsao immediately admitted his guilt. The testimony of three witnesses, two of whom were also implicated in the thefts; an eloquent plea for leniency by one of Tsao's co-workers who blamed the ideas of the Gang of Four for leading Tsao

[9] Article by Jerome Alan Cohen, associate dean and director of East Asian legal studies, Harvard Law School. *Asia.* 1:3–7. Ja./F. '79. Reprinted by permission of *Asia* and the author. Copyright 1979 The Asia Society.

astray; and an older worker's expression of indignation at Tsao's laziness and repeated violations punctuated Tsao's own detailed recitation of his many offenses. The last speaker to step forward was Tsao's wife, who begged for mercy not so much for her husband, she said, as for the father of her children—a petition that barely left a dry eye in the house. With the facts established, the prosecutor and defender debated Tsao's responsibility for his guilt—was he really the chief culprit or merely a victim of the anarchic influence of the Gang of Four?

The panel recessed. Twenty minutes later it returned with its decision: Tsao was sentenced to two years in prison, but because he had confessed and repented, the sentence was suspended; he was ordered to work under the supervision of the masses in his factory for a three-year probationary period.

Was this trial—the first I had been allowed to see in five visits to China since 1972—staged? Although the case was undoubtedly authentic, not the product of a Chinese Agatha Christie, I believe the proceedings had been painstakingly rehearsed to assure a smooth performance. Trials such as this have hardly been typical of the administration of justice in China, especially over the past two decades. But they are now being held with increasing frequency as the post-Mao leadership seeks to demonstrate a sensitivity to "socialist legality" that has long been absent in Peking.

Mao's successors are engaged in a comprehensive campaign to restore the morale, enthusiasm, and productivity of the articulate segments of the nation whose active efforts are essential if China is to fulfill its ambition to become a modern, powerful socialist state. Not only intellectuals but also bureaucrats and workers who have lived through the successive campaigns against "counter-revolutionaries," the "anti-rightist" movement, the Cultural Revolution, the purge of Lin Piao's followers, and the tyranny of the Gang of Four want reassurance about their personal security. So long as fear of arbitrary action persists—and the Peking media concede that fear has been rampant for years—one cannot expect officials to take bold initiatives, scientists to innovate, teachers to present new ideas, and workers to criticize the bureaucracy.

Recognition of Individual Rights

The current leaders have made it clear that the relationship between economic development and individual rights is not an either/or proposition. As they see the issue, certain minimum guarantees of individual rights are essential to promote China's development, to liberate "the socialist activism of all the people"—a view similar to the one adopted by Soviet leaders after Stalin's death. Public trials are an important symbol of the state's guarantee of these rights.

Rehearsed or spontaneous, such trials demonstrate that, prior to stigmatizing and punishing a citizen, the state has notified him or her of the charges, presented its supporting evidence, given the accused at least a minimal opportunity for rebuttal, deliberated over the evidence and an appropriate sanction, and stated the reasons for its judgment. All this takes place in a setting that may not be "public" in the sense that anyone can walk in off the street to attend the proceedings but that nevertheless provides for the presence of the defendant's family, those who have suffered from the offense, certain neighbors or co-workers of the victim and the accused, and possibly some of their friends, thereby assuring the people most immediately affected that the state has not acted arbitrarily.

The current emphasis on "legality" seems to foreshadow another effort to develop a formal legal system—with promulgated law codes, a court hierarchy, and legal education—similar to that which the People's Republic sought to create in the mid-1950s, following the early revolutionary years of kangaroo courts and other drastic methods. The evolution of this system was cut short by the "anti-rightist" movement of 1957–58, which phased out lawyers and reduced the role of the courts to rubber-stamping sentences recommended by the police and the party for those formally stigmatized as criminals. The Cultural Revolution of 1966–69 went even further, seeking to smash the police and party bureaucracy as well as the courts and the procuracy, a prosecutor's office that was supposed to investigate illegal acts, whether committed by government officials or others. Reflecting the radical ideology of the day, the *People's Daily* published an editorial, "In Praise of Lawlessness," that condemned law as a bourgeois restraint upon the natural enthusiasm of the revolutionary masses.

When Mao died in September 1976 and his widow and her three Shanghai colleagues (the Gang of Four) were arrested a few weeks later, China had an administrative system for maintaining public order rather than a conventional formal legal system. The country of almost one billion people had no lawyers. Most judges had little legal training. For a decade no significant legislation had been published. All judicial decisions had to be cleared with the party.

But was this "justice?" The question immediately confronted Mao's successors. Millions of Chinese, including the powerful Teng Hsiao-ping, had suffered the abuses of this administrative system, and current leaders now seem determined to provide individuals with greater protections against arbitrary action.

Constitutional Reform

Thus far the most tangible evidence of the new leadership's concern with law reform has been the Constitution promulgated in March 1978, little more than three years after its predecessor. It resurrects the rights of an accused to make a defense and to have a public trial, as had been provided in the long-ignored 1954 Constitution. It reestablishes the procuracy and revives the requirement that police obtain the approval of either the procuracy or the judiciary before making a formal arrest. Once again China is considering the enactment of legal codes.

Yet Peking is not about to establish the "rule of law" in the sense that government and party officials must uniformly operate within the confines of promulgated norms. Politics will continue to take command in China, and the

legal system will continue to be regarded as an instrument
for suppressing the enemies of the regime as well as protect-
ing "the people."

The 1978 Constitution makes clear that the guiding
principle of government is party control of all state organs,
including the judiciary. It does not reintroduce the principle of judicial independence of political authority that the
1954 Constitution had imported from the USSR. Nor does
it bring back that document's promise of equality before
the law.

Unlike the Soviet Union, which declared an end "to class
struggle" in the wake of de-Stalinization, China has re-
affirmed the need for the "dictatorship of the proletariat"
over those who still bear the constitutionally enshrined
labels of "reactionary capitalist," "landlord," and "rich
peasant," as well as over "counterrevolutionaries" and "bad
elements." Indeed, Peking has just added yet another vague
category to the list of adversaries—"newborn bourgeois elements," persons of good class status who, because of their
opposition to the party line, remove themselves from "the
people" and become the enemy. Constitutional rights, it is
clear, are only to be enjoyed by "the people." Moreover, in
the campaign to weed out supporters of the Gang of Four,
the Chinese leadership is committing some of the very
abuses with which the Gang is charged.

Yet even if China should succeed in moving beyond the
experimental stage to the establishment of a nationwide
public trial system, this in itself would not alter the character of its criminal procedure, which is the nearest thing to
the Inquisition in the contemporary world. In China a person accused of a serious crime is detained and cut off from
any outside contact while police interrogation and investigation run their course. He sees no lawyer, no friend, no family, even if his case takes years to process. Usually, he is
given only a subsistence diet that leaves him slightly hungry
and on edge. He is frequently kept in a cell with other
prisoners who seek to improve their own prospects by pressuring him to confess and reveal the involvement of others.

He is subjected to long periods of interrogation, often late at night, by officials who understand the uses of intimidation, ruses, and various psychological techniques to elicit his cooperation.

There is no presumption of innocence. On the contrary, the presumption is that he would not have been detained unless he had done something wrong, and it is up to him to tell the police all about it instead of awaiting specific accusations. Without the privilege against self-incrimination, stubborn refusal to talk can result in his being put in leg irons or handcuffs, or a term in solitary confinement. Although torture and coerced confessions are forbidden, angry cellmates have been known to assault the obdurate. There is currently no effective outside institutional restraint, whether by procurators, judges, legislators, or others, upon either the duration or conditions of police detention. The fate of the accused is entirely in the hands of the jailers.

In dealing with those suspected of being "class enemies," the Chinese Communist Party, like the Inquisition, views the criminal process as an official inquiry into an evil that must be stamped out. In these circumstances it would be absurd, China's leaders believe, to conduct that inquiry as a contest between equals with the judiciary playing the role of umpire, ensuring that if the police and prosecution violate the rules, they lose the game. The state, they maintain, cannot be neutral in the struggle against evil. All its agencies must cooperate in, not interfere with, that struggle.

China has no belief that it is better to let many guilty people go free than to convict a single innocent person. This is not to say that the Chinese are indifferent to accuracy. Their criminal law seeks to identify and punish offenders, isolate them from society when necessary, rehabilitate those who are susceptible, and deter and educate the populace. To the extent that the guilty go free, these purposes cannot be achieved. Nor can they be achieved to the extent that the innocent are convicted.

The Chinese are aware that their inquisitorial process increases the likelihood of eliciting not only true confessions but also false ones. But they believe that through outside investigation and repeated careful interrogation of the suspect, followed by internal review within the police and verification by the newly recreated procuracy as well as the judiciary, there is, on balance, a higher probability of reaching accurate results than if they employ a more adversarial, more public process that offers the suspect greater procedural safeguards. Such protections could be taken advantage of by "class enemies" to hide the truth and thereby frustrate justice.

The State Represents the People

According to PRC ideology, moreover, there is no need to protect a suspect by rules based upon mistrust of the state because, unlike the situation in bourgeois countries, there is no fundamental inconsistency between the interests of the Chinese state and those of the people. A member of "the people" who is detained for investigation should simply cooperate and tell all, as Tsao did. He can be confident, the Chinese Communists claim, that the state will do the right thing, for it has his interests at heart.

After all, if a parent returns home to find that his children have destroyed the furniture, he does not say: "Children, you are under suspicion, but you are under no obligation to tell me anything about what happened, anything you say may be used against you, you have a right to counsel, and you are free to go where you wish." Parents often privately interrogate their children, comparing the answers and demeanor of each with those of the others and drawing appropriate inferences if anyone refuses to answer. In other words, if parents want to know whether a child has done something, they ask the child in circumstances calculated to elicit a response. Because the child is supposed to know his parents have his best interests at heart, our society generally accepts the practice as a reasonable way to proceed. The People's Republic adopts a similar attitude toward its allegedly wayward citizens. Because he seemed genuinely repentant, Tsao was treated sympathetically and encouraged to reform.

The attitude is not a new one in China. Traditionally, the family was taken as the model for relations between government and people, and the county magistrate, the imperial official closest to the people, was called the *fu-mu kuan,* "the father and mother official." Sir George Staunton noted in 1810 that

[T]he vital and universally operating principle of the Chinese government is the duty of submission to parental authority, whether vested in the parents themselves, or in their representatives. . . .

Indeed, the many similarities between the contemporary criminal process and its Manchu predecessor are striking. The conception of judges as ordinary civil servants rather than special officials independent of political authority, the frequently long detention of a suspect in a coercive environment, the presumption of his guilt, the lack of a privilege against self-incrimination, the absence of counsel, the inadequate opportunity to make a defense, and the emphasis on confession are as noticeable today as they were to the first Americans to visit China almost two centuries ago.

China's Legal Tradition

Yet, despite these similarities, it would be wrong to over-generalize and assume that China's legal tradition is wholly without support for due process values. As one might expect of the nation that invented bureaucracy two millennia ago, China developed a legal system by the seventh century under the T'ang dynasty that was the world's most sophisticated and that served as a model for neighboring Korea, Viet Nam, and even Japan. Although we lack sufficient records to generalize with confidence about the actual application of the law to concrete cases in that distant era, the Manchu dynasty, which began 1,000 years later and endured until the revolution of 1911, has left us numerous samples of its judicial decisions.

To be sure, the Confucian heritage preferred moral indoctrination to legal restraint as the principal means of running the empire; but these cases—and the comprehensive criminal code they interpret—make clear the large extent to which the imperial system relied on law to reinforce dominant moral values and make people conform to the state's needs. The elaborate distinctions of the written law, the reasoned opinions judges were required to write in support of their decisions, and the lengthy review procedures in cases involving major sanctions reflect an overriding concern to curb arbitrary actions in the administration of justice.

The Chinese tradition emphasized the group and the government rather than the individual, and duties to society rather than individual rights, but the legal system was an institutional and intellectual construct that plainly recognized and enforced limits beyond which officials were not permitted to go in dealing with suspected offenders. Even torture, which was allowed in court but not elsewhere to extract a confession from an obdurate accused, was carefully regulated both with respect to duration and the types of instruments that could be used.

The theory that underlay these restraints was not a philosophy of individualism and the rights of man but one that focused on duties and the needs of good government. Yet it was premised on certain beliefs about what was fair, just, and acceptable to the Chinese people. Officials were obligated to those they ruled to behave properly according to prevailing standards.

The Censor

Of course, like any other legal system, that of imperial China was not in fact congruent with the norms and procedures found in its statutes and reported decisions. Corruption and arbitrary departures from prescribed practices often plagued the administration of justice, especially during periods of dynastic decline, as 19th-century China made foreigners all too aware. Yet the records reveal continuing concern over this situation and periodic efforts to improve it. Certain institutions, particularly the censorate, which enjoyed a roving mandate to inspect the legality of official conduct and which must have made the concept of the procuracy easier for contemporary Chinese to understand, were designed to cope with these problems. And a carefully articulated code of administrative punishments existed to deter arbitrary official actions.

It was the duty of a censor to admonish even the emperor if he departed from the standards associated with his role. Although the emperor theoretically enjoyed absolute power, tradition circumscribed his discretion in practice. According to the Confucian ethic, an emperor was to act as an emperor should, just as a county magistrate was to act as a county magistrate should—that is, each was to fulfill his obligations to those he ruled. Ever since the earliest recorded dynasty—Shang of 3,500 years ago—China's rulers have had to live with the idea that government must be benevolent toward the people. A sovereign who treated his subjects arbitrarily risked losing the Mandate of Heaven that justified his right to rule. In fact, widespread dissatisfaction with the administration of justice proved to be one of the classic signs of dynastic decline, as contemporary China's historically-minded rulers and people are well aware.

The People's Republic is at the moment popularizing the more positive aspects of imperial Chinese law rather than its repressive features. All over China, on both stage and screen, the traditional-style Chinese opera *Fifteen Strings of Cash*—banned by Mao's wife for a decade—is again delighting audiences with the dramatic story of how an upright judicial official reversed the unjust conviction of innocent persons tortured into false confessions. On two separate 1978 visits to China, I attended performances of this opera before large and enthusiastic audiences. I asked a number of Chinese whether any contemporary significance should be attached to the recent revival of this superb entertainment, which had been seen and approved by Chairman Mao and Premier Chou En-lai in 1956, shortly after it had been created to contribute to the law reform atmosphere of that era. Their answers were similar.

"Isn't it obvious? It means that the Chinese people will no longer tolerate arbitrary official acts, that torture is wrong, that confessions may not be coerced, that officials must go down among the people to get the facts and must weigh evidence carefully."

Of course, this theme ties in with the campaigns to discredit the Gang of Four, to popularize the new government's asserted respect for fundamental fairness, and to check abuses of power by corrupt and arrogant officials. Undoubtedly, there is an element of scapegoating in the attempt to make the Gang exclusively responsible for the widespread abuses during the past generation. But whatever the accuracy of the claims that only the Gang and its followers violated the rights of the Chinese people, these accusations plainly acknowledge that governments should not behave in this way and that people have a right to complain about such treatment.

As China's leaders know from experience, there will be costs as well as benefits if they proceed to establish a more formal legal system. To the extent that China, a poor developing country, allocates resources to educate and employ the personnel necessary to operate such a system, it will have fewer to devote to its other needs, whether they be training engineers, hiring agricultural economists, or purchasing weapons.

The political costs are also likely to be significant. Politicians and bureaucrats prefer to be unfettered. A legal system, even one dominated by the party, imposes standards and procedures that circumscribe their freedom and inevitably prove irritating, if not frustrating. The previous PRC effort to introduce socialist legality led to profound tensions between those who were "red" and those who were "expert"—that is, between party faithfuls who continued to believe that shortrun political expediency should govern the outcome of concrete cases and party faithfuls (and others) who wanted legal norms and professional judicial considerations to prevail.

Nevertheless, there will be serious costs if the party should fail to implement the promised reforms, for this would handicap the regime's program for reenlisting the loyalty of its most talented groups and replacing fear with personal security, cynicism and apathy with enthusiasm and pride. Can Chairman Hua Kuo-feng and Vice Chairman Teng Hsiao-ping have it both ways, reaping the advantages of a legal system while minimizing its disadvantages? They seem determined to try.

CHINA'S FIVE BELIEF SYSTEMS[10]

Five "pure" belief systems compete for adherents in contemporary China. For the sake of simplicity, these can be labeled traditional, revolutionary, bureaucratic, technological and totalitarian systems. To be sure, these beliefs do not exist in the material world; they only reside in the minds of the Chinese people. Moreover, few Chinese have a single, systematic ideology; rather, most Chinese, the top leaders included, have various, often conflicting, beliefs. In a sense, therefore, the five coherent sets of beliefs described below are analytical constructs illuminating a complex situation but having no "objective" existence.

The Traditional System

The traditional culture incorporated many diverse philosophies. Indeed, as wide a spectrum of beliefs existed in the Chinese as in the Western tradition. Hence, when we speak of traditional beliefs, we do not refer solely to Confucianism, Taoism or Buddhism, but rather to a widely held amalgam of many philosophies.

Pivotal concepts in this traditional philosophy are: the premium placed upon an ordered, hierarchical society; the value attached to harmony, loyalty and propriety; the belief that man should live in harmony with nature; and the central role assigned to family. According to the traditional credo, man achieves spiritual fulfillment through social

[10] Chapter entitled "China's Five Belief Systems," by Michel Oksenberg, assistant professor of political science and research associate, East Asian Institute, Columbia University. *China, the Convulsive Society.* Headline Series, no. 203. p 5–19. D. '70. Foreign Policy Association. Reprinted by permission.

action. But his proper social role is severely circumscribed. Man should not remold his society, but rather should play the roles expected of him. Each person is born into a net of obligations which he must honor. A person who properly meets his obligations, in theory, obtains great satisfaction and moreover secures the obligations of others. When enough people in society abide by the roles assigned them, then the society will be peaceful and well regulated. Through personal example and discipline of the realm, the national leader is responsible for insuring that his people know virtue and act upon it.

Several aspects of this tradition stand out. Overt conflict is considered unpleasant and avoidable. Knowing how and when to yield to preserve a facade of harmony is a valued art. Interdependence is encouraged; independence, discouraged. Excellence in interpersonal relations earns praise; boldness wins scorn. Conformity, not initiative, is prized. Men aspire to be social engineers, not to explore the earth. Ideally, the educational system yields cultured generalists, not technical specialists.

The essence of the traditional system, fostering social stability and continuity, was recorded in an interview with a poor Chinese servant woman:

The generations stretch back thousands of years to the great ancestor parents. They stretch for thousands of years into the future, generation upon generation. Seen in proportion to this great array, the individual is but a small thing. But on the other hand, no individual can drop out. Each is a link in the great chain. No one can drop out without breaking the chain. A woman stands with one hand grasping the generations that have gone before and with the other, the generations to come.

Such notions made old China a society built for the ages. Each family generation subordinated itself to the memory of its ancestors and identified with the welfare of its descendants. Rather than demanding immediate gratification, efforts seemed rewarded if they promised a better position for the family line. These are values tied to an impoverished, relatively stagnant economic system. People did not expect annual improvement in their welfare; they only hoped that in time their family might obtain a larger piece of the existing pie.

The coming of the West in the 1800s challenged these beliefs. Indeed, by the May Fourth movement of 1919 [student uprising against Japanese] few Chinese intellectuals believed that traditional values were relevant to China's new situation. But, for several reasons, the deeply ingrained beliefs and customs did not disappear. While intellectuals and some businessmen may have searched abroad for values that seemed more suitable, millions of Chinese in the hinterlands could only draw inspiration from native ideas. In addition, these values were still congruent with the interests of certain sectors of society, particularly the upper classes in rural areas and the elderly. Moreover, while many Chinese rejected their traditions on the conscious level, they retained them unconsciously. Psychologically, it has proven difficult for many Chinese to reject their proud heritage; rather, they have attempted to salvage portions of their tradition while convincing themselves that much which they accept from the West already existed in China anyway. Finally, traditional Chinese values persist because the factors which gave rise to them persist: certain distinctive childhood rearing practices, poverty and a densely populated agrarian society vulnerable to the vagaries of nature. For all of these reasons, the traditional belief system remains a vital force in present-day China, particularly in the countryside.

Although no major political figure openly advocates the traditional belief system in China today, its continuing influence is revealed in concrete practices. For example, the pivotal role of Mao is, in many ways, similar to that of the emperors of old. As with previous rulers, supposedly he embodies virtue, and his example and discipline orders the realm. Deified, his picture appears in peasant homes where idols previously were kept, and peasants officially are urged to bow before his likeness while orally pledging their loyalty to him. But tradition is seen less in officially sanctioned policy than in the persistence of old customs, especially in more remote rural areas: extended families, arranged marriages and traditional commercial practices.

Revolutionary Beliefs

A revolutionary strand of thought has long coexisted with the dominant traditional strand. It came to the fore during China's periodic peasant revolts and in the early 20th century was reinforced by the importation of populist and anarchist beliefs from the West and Japan. Mao has added to its vitality by eloquently articulating, publicizing and acting upon much of this doctrine.

The revolutionary credo supports an egalitarian redistribution of wealth and opportunity. It places great confidence in man's ability, through sheer will and energy, to remold his society; it considers the Chinese masses, particularly the peasants, to be the motive force of history and dismisses the necessity of having an elite to lead society. It emphasizes the need for a spiritual transformation of mankind, not a technical transformation of man's environment. It considers the root evil on earth to be exploitation of man by other men and traces such other evils as poverty and illness to it. It attacks those segments of society which it deems exploitative, particularly merchants, bureaucrats, intellectuals and urban dwellers. It calls for society to be restructured and, more importantly, for man to transform his desires, so that he no longer would seek to profit at another's expense.

How to change man's attitudes thus becomes a central concern of the revolutionary doctrine. In essence, this ideology distrusts organization and champions spontaneity. The rationale behind this particular aspect of the belief system deserves explanation. The discipline and control of organizations often prevent liberating experiences. Participation in spontaneous collective movements, on the other hand, supposedly severs a person's ties to his past, enabling him to achieve a sense of community with his contemporaries. Losing his old individual identity, he partakes of the greater spirit of the group and thereby achieves a spiritual transformation. Mao calls this submergence of the individual to the group, "Putting public ahead of self." (The induced spontaneity of the Red Guard movement, as we shall see, is a specific example of the experience which Mao believes can produce a spiritual transformation.)

The utopia which this doctrine envisions is therefore a classless society, for only in such a society will exploitation cease. As soon as classes emerge, some profit at the expense of others. Hence, specialization and narrow professional loyalties are undesirable. The psychic barriers between farmers, industrial workers and intellectuals must be removed, and differences between urban and rural areas kept at a minimum. When uniformity is achieved—when everybody is more or less the same—loneliness and exploitation will be eliminated and true community attained.

One other aspect of the revolutionary ideology in China should be made explicit: its provincialism. It rejects the relevance of the outside world to China's current needs. It emphasizes the innate capacity of the Chinese people to transform their own society while denigrating the value or necessity of foreign assistance. Accordingly, a watchword of current Chinese foreign policy is *tzu-li keng-sheng*, meaning "self reliance" or, more precisely, "regeneration through our own efforts."

Further, the revolutionary vision of the good society is applied globally. Ideally, the nations of the world should be united through shared values, not through interdependence. Peace can come to the world only when nations are culturally, economically and militarily independent, and therefore can deal with each other as equals. Hence, the revolutionary doctrine predisposes its Chinese adherents to turn inward, to shun trade and aid, cultural exchanges or entangling military alliances, and to pride themselves on self sufficiency.

Revolutionary beliefs are reflected in many specific policies in China. Bureaucrats periodically must engage in hard labor to break down the barriers between "mental" and "physical" work. Small rural industries are developed to eliminate differences between urban and rural areas. The Chinese military apparatus does not have a formal ranking system. Attempts are made constantly to reduce wage differentials. The regime judges people as much on their attitudes as on their competence. The educational system and the propaganda apparatus aim more at changing attitudes than at teaching proficiency. These policies clearly give China a radical, experimental air.

Mao, as previously noted, certainly embraces these revolutionary ideas and programs, but not as completely as some of his supporters. Above all, it must be remembered, Mao is a dialectician. His quest is for synthesis. He is attempting to build a society which will truly reconcile many contradictory but equally desirable elements: democracy and freedom; discipline and freedom; with unity of will and individuality. Hence, intellectually, Mao embraces both revolutionary beliefs and their opposites. Believing in the dialectic, Mao prefers not to choose one ethic over another, but rather to search for a synthesis. But emotionally, Mao is predisposed toward revolutionary values.

What remain to be explained are the reasons for the strength of revolutionary beliefs. Their support by Mao obviously is a crucial factor. Yet, since these beliefs were powerful in China before Mao, reference simply to Mao is insufficient. Rather, we must ask: Why do revolutionary beliefs elicit such support? A crucial consideration is that populist, egalitarian and antibureaucratic impulses seem to elicit a response from the rural poor. Indeed, around the world, peasants appear to have dual tendencies—usually conservative but also capable of conversion to violent, short lived, radical movements. And in China upon occasion, peasants enthusiastically have responded to calls to remake their harsh world—for example, the T'ai-p'ing Rebellion of the 1850s and the Boxer Rebellion of the 1890s. The Chinese Communists, after all, came to power through peasant support, and a significant portion of Chinese officials just below the top echelons were recruited into the Chinese Communist party (CCP) as illiterate, impoverished peasant youths. Is it any wonder, then, that some of the values of the social classes which brought about the sweeping upheaval in China would continue to have such force only 20 years after the revolution?

But the revolutionary ideology has strength for another reason. The industrialization process generates its own opposition. Indeed, the consequences of industrialization spread unevenly through society, with many people feeling its harmful effects before enjoying its benefits. The father of Lin Piao, the party's vice-chairman, provides a handy example. A relatively well-off manufacturer of handlooms at the turn of the century, his business suffered from the development of a modern weaving industry, and he became a purser on a steamship. The young Lin witnessed the misfortunes of his father. Is it possible that, in part, Lin was swept into the tide of anti-Westernism in the early 1920s precisely because his memories of his father's fate predisposed him to look upon it favorably?

The Technological Ethic

The technological ethic advocates man's triumph over nature. Man, through science, can control and transform his material environment and, thereby, eliminate poverty and disease. Further, according to this optimistic assessment of man's ability to dominate the earth, technological change provides man with the capacity, indeed the need, to initiate social and political change. The technological ethic, therefore, generates policies which hasten scientific development, industrialization and production; it encourages skepticism, bold experimentation and individual initiative and achievement. Competition and conflict, which stimulate research and social change, are preferred to the stifling effect of harmony and compromise. The ethic judges men more on their technical competence and accomplishments than on their personality, morality or background. Rather than encouraging man to fulfill social obligations, it calls upon him to realize his full potential through the manipulation of material things.

Man's crowning achievement, the place where he has built an environment in which he is free to give full reign to his intellectual creativity, is the city. Even the choice of words reflects the preference for the city: "urbane" and "cosmopolitan" are equated with culture; and "bucolic" or "rustic" are often equated with coarseness.

When the technological ethic holds sway, people expect and strive for swift economic improvements, and the society becomes expansive and innovative. The technological ethic also encourages an empirical approach to problems. Choices tend to be made on narrow, technical grounds, and the raising of more profound, time-consuming ideological considerations tends to be discouraged. Arguments supported by production, wage and budget data tend to be more persuasive than metaphysical or moralistic arguments.

The belief in technology is relatively recent in China; it is primarily the result of the Western impact. The technological ethic won converts initially because military power demonstrably accrued to those states accepting it. Gradually, moreover, people whose interests often coincide with the technological ethic—scientists, engineers, factory managers, professional military officers, to an extent skilled industrial workers, and so on—began to acquire influence in China. In addition, it seems that the industrial ethic has its exponents among the top leadership. Premier Chou En-lai seems in many ways to be its most articulate spokesman, but other leaders, particularly those in charge of the nation's economy, have defended technical values against attacks from the supporters of the other value systems.

Certainly, the signs are plentiful that China as a nation —Mao included—is committed to the transformation of China into an industrial power in the world. Thus, China is pushing its development of nuclear weapons and modern delivery systems. In the past 20 years many large industrial centers have sprung up in the interior: Paotow, Chengchow, Lanchow, Taiyuan, Chengtu. Top flight scientists are partially shielded from political turmoil. The land is scoured for its natural resources, which are abundant. The number of engineering and technical personnel has been soaring: 164,000 in 1952; 449,000 in 1956; approximately 1.1 million in 1960; and well over 1.5 million in 1964. The social and material basis to support a technological ethic is gaining in China, but in a basically agrarian society of 750 million people, without an indigenous belief system on which it can be grafted, this ethic has not yet become dominant.

Bureaucratic Ethic

The bureaucratic ethic, unlike traditional or revolutionary beliefs, does not encompass a total view of the ideal society. Rather, recognizing that the means affect ends, it focuses more upon the necessary mechanisms and procedures for maintaining and developing society. The bureaucratic ideology emphasizes that man's welfare depends upon his ability to undertake complex tasks. This in turn requires subdividing the tasks into manageable work assignments, distributing the tasks among individuals and developing ongoing institutions to coordinate the effort. Institutions demand from their members subordination, routine and specialization.

The bureaucratic ethic, then, encourages virtues which facilitate effective organization: loyalty, collegiality, obedience and efficiency. In addition, life within the organization becomes an important source of personal satisfaction. As a result, concern with rewards distributed within the organization—salary, rank and so on—and with the prestige and power of one's organization in society are inextricably part of the ethic. This set of beliefs leads its adherents to develop elaborate doctrine about the pivotal aspects of bureaucracy: recruitment, indoctrination into the norms of the organization, promotion and discipline.

Ideally, the bureaucratic ethic fosters rule through written law. These laws define the tasks of bureaucratic positions and require others to obey the edicts originating from these designated positions, regardless of which individual holds the position. That is, power resides in institutions, not men. At its best, the bureaucratic vision protects citizens from the arbitrary exercise of power. A politically neutral

civil service dutifully administers legal codes which reflect
the popular will. But at its worst, the bureaucratic ethic
leads to empire building, buck passing, blundering officials,
rigid rules, inertia and venality.

The bureaucratic ethic, both good and bad, has long
prospered in China. Even under the Communists, particularly in the mid-1950s, there was widespread advocacy of
establishing a codified legal system, and significant steps
were taken to create a professional civil service system. Indeed, a unified China requires an ideology that endorses
the existence of a large bureaucracy. Only a complex governmental organization could hold the country together,
given its diverse local traditions and cultures; the lack, until
recently, of modern communications and transportation
system; the segmented rather than nationally integrated economic system; and the huge population. Not surprisingly,
the Western ideology which emerged dominant out of the
chaotic warlord period in China was Leninism—essentially
an ideology of organization.

Also not surprisingly, under Communist rule the bureaucratic ethic has been elaborated and supported primarily
by bureaucrats, particularly those responsible for running
the Chinese Communist party apparatus. Foremost among
these was Liu Shao-ch'i, once designated Mao's successor
but purged during the Cultural Revolution. Essentially,
one of the "crimes" for which Mao condemned Liu was his
taking power away from Mao and lodging it in the party
organization—that is, of ruling through institutions rather
than men. Liu supposedly also championed other bureaucratic interests: hierarchy, discipline, career, recruitment
based on merit. Although Liu has departed from the scene,
a central concern of China's rulers in 1970 remained the
problem to which Liu had devoted his life: how to build
an effective party organization.

Totalitarian Beliefs

Yet one other belief system demands attention—totalitarianism. This creed deals with the ideal relationship be-

tween state and society. It advocates a total penetration of society by the government, with no areas of autonomy and freedom remaining. A willful dictator makes use of all the control levers at his disposal—political parties, the propaganda apparatus, the police and army, the educational network, commercial enterprises—to remake the society in his image. The whole nation comes to reflect its ruler: his fears, his hopes, abilities and emotions. "Politics takes command" is how Lin approvingly describes this situation.

Advocates of the totalitarian state have two basic aims. They desire to pulverize their society, isolating each individual so he becomes vulnerable to political control. This is achieved by creating an atmosphere of uncertainty, fear or terror, thereby making people feel helpless against the state. Second, they desire to build a strong state, particularly an omnipotent executive. These two aims focus upon power; indeed, the essence of the totalitarian mentality is its unquenchable thirst for power. Lin reflected this mentality in a remarkably candid speech:

Never forget political power—always have it in mind. Once you forget political power, you forget politics and the fundamental views of Marxism. Consequently you swerve toward economism [the technological ethic in our terms], anarchism [the revolutionary ethic in our terms], and daydreaming . . .

What is political power? Sun Yat-sen believed it to be the management of the affairs of the masses. But he did not understand that political power is an instrument by which one class oppresses another . . . I would put it as: political power is the power to suppress.

Three types of people appear to support a totalitarian state in China: (1) Those who believe such a political system is the best way to transform the society rapidly. The speeches of Lin suggest he may be, in part, an adherent of this view. Such people derive their inspiration not only from the forced industrialization of the Russian people under Stalin, but also draw upon indigenous doctrines and historical examples of how state power arises and should be organized, particularly the Legalist philosophy and the examples of China under strong, willful emperors. (2) The few bureaucrats whose power is directly enhanced under totalitarian rule tend to support its philosophy. Thus, it is not surprising that the repudiated head of the secret police apparatus, K'ang Sheng, and the head of the public security apparatus, Hsieh Fu-chih, emerged as pivotal supporters of Mao during the Cultural Revolution. (3) The "inner court" —the people closest to the national leader who do not have a power base of their own but who share in his power and glory—has a vested interest in constantly expanding the prerogatives of the chief executive. Perhaps this helps to explain why Mao's wife Chiang Ch'ing, his apparent chief aid, Ch'en Po-ta and ideologues, such as Yao Wen-yüan, who had no independent, high bureaucratic position, have been the most enthusiastic advocates of the adulation of Chairman Mao: changing the party constitution to focus upon Mao; distributing a copy of Mao's sayings to every Chinese citizen; revising the performing arts in China so all plots pay homage to Mao's thought; and so on. By making Mao a demigod, those who are closest to him increase their own power *vis-à-vis* the bureaucracy, and they may be able to trade upon their proximity to Mao to retain influence after his death.

The Distinctiveness of China

These five belief systems come in conflict on some matters, but reinforce each other on others. For example, the traditional and revolutionary systems embody radically different visions of the ideal society, but they both stress that man is a social being, advocate the cultivation of a total man and envision man in nature, not over it. The traditional and technological beliefs envision different ideal relationships between man and nature, but both place a premium on education. The totalitarian and bureaucratic beliefs stress the role of the state in ordering society, but the totalitarian desire for unchecked state power contrasts with the bureaucratic desire for the rule of law.

Note some other ways in which aspects of these sets of values overlap. Both the traditional and bureaucratic beliefs esteem authority, hierarchy and discipline. Both the bureaucratic and technological ethics value specialization, competence and regularity. The traditional, revolutionary and bureaucratic beliefs prize man's capacity to order society through his innate talents. The revolutionary and totalitarian doctrines aim at a radical transformation of society. It is precisely because of the overlap between these beliefs that the adherents of each are able to form coalitions.

So, China contains a mix of these five sets of beliefs. But how does this distinguish China from other countries? First, two belief systems that are strong in the West and in former Western colonies are almost absent in China: (1) theocratic beliefs (except Chinese Buddhism) which stress the importance of the relationship between man and a supernatural being, and (2) liberal democratic beliefs which place a premium upon individual procedural liberties and which value a diverse, pluralistic society. Neither strand of thought flourished in China before the Western impact, and the thin reeds that sprouted from Western seeds were cut by the Communists.

The second distinctively Chinese aspect of these values are the historical memories associated with each. The traditional system is clearly identified with the moments of national greatness and therefore not easily rejected; the technological ethic is identified with the West and therefore only reluctantly accepted—indeed, most easily accepted when shown to be Chinese. Proponents of the revolutionary ideology identify the modern bureaucratic ethic with the conduct of the old Chinese Mandarinate (in fact, they differ), and therefore are deeply suspicious of it. The revolutionary ethic has special appeal to Chinese youth, for it is associated with some of the heroic movements of youth in modern China—the May Fourth movement or the resistance to Japan, for example—and with many of the legendary, romantic heroes of ancient Chinese history. Finally, it is possible that the weakness of the liberal democratic tradition and the lack of familiarity with Hitler's and Stalin's barbarism made totalitarianism somewhat less of a specter to the Chinese—initially, at least, before they personally experienced the harshness of Mao's dictatorship.

This leads to the final distinctive aspect of the five belief systems in China. The "mix" is different. The revolutionary belief system currently enjoys a strength unmatched elsewhere in the world, except perhaps in Algeria and Cuba, where it also receives official support. The continued albeit diminished vitality of the traditional system, although different from the traditional values of other countries, makes China somewhat comparable to other nations embarking upon industrialization. The totalitarian impulse, wedded to the revolutionary ethic, enjoys influence where it counts in the short run: at the top. The bureaucratic ethic was a specific object of attack during the height of the Cultural Revolution in 1966–67, but by 1970, it appeared that the attack upon it had met with failure. And, as for the past hundred years, the world continues to expect the imminent assertion of the technological ethic in China, confident that the signs point to its emergence as a dominant force after the current transition.

What is distinctive about China, then, is that *these* are the major belief systems at present [1970] and, more import, that none is dominant. When we ask about China's future, what we really are asking is: What will be the value-mix in the years ahead?

BIBLIOGRAPHY

An asterisk (*) preceding a reference indicates that the article or part of it has been reprinted in this book.

BOOKS, PAMPHLETS, AND DOCUMENTS

Bachrack, S. D. The committee of one million; "China Lobby" politics, 1953–1971. Columbia Univ. Pr. '76.

Baker, Hugh D. Chinese family and kinship. Columbia Univ. Pr. '79.

Barnett, A. Doak. China and the major powers in East Asia. Brookings Instit. '77.

Beattie, Hilary J. Land and lineage in China. Cambridge Univ. Pr. '79.

Biographical dictionary of republican China. Columbia Univ. Pr. '79.

Chang, Parris H. Power and policy in China. Second edition. Pennsylvania State Univ. Pr. '78.

Chesneaux, Jean. China: The People's Republic, 1949–1976. Pantheon Bks. '79.

Chinese Economic Studies. v 12. Fall/Winter 1978–79. Economic policies and the "four modernizations." M. E. Sharpe Inc. '79.

Chinese women in the great leap forward, 1978. AMS Pr. '78.

Clubb, E. O. 20th Century China. Third edition. Columbia Univ. Pr. '78.

Costello, Mary. Sino-Soviet relations. v 1, no 5. F. 4, '77. Editorial Research Reports.

Costello, Mary. China's opening door. v 2, no 9, S. 8, '78. Editorial Research Reports.

Crook, Isabel and David. Ten Mile Inn; mass movement in a Chinese village. Pantheon Bks. '79.

Dalai Lama XIV. My land and my people. McGraw-Hill. '62.

Donzé, Marie-Ange and Claude Sauvageot. China today. English version by Philip Parks. Hippocrene Bks. 1980.

Encyclopedia of China today. Harper & Row. Eurasia Pr. (NJ) '79.

Fodor, Eugene. Fodor's People's Republic of China. David McKay. '79.

*Foreign Policy Association. Great decisions 1979. Foreign Policy Association. '79.

*Harding, Harry Jr. China and the U.S., normalization and beyond. Foreign Policy Association. '79.

Harris, Nigel. The mandate of heaven; Marx and Mao in modern China. Horizon Press/Quartet Books. '79.

Harrison, S. S. China, oil, and Asia. Columbia Univ. Pr. '77.

Hinton, H. C. An introduction to Chinese politics. Second edition. Holt, Rinehart & Winston. '78.

*Hinton, H.C. The Far East and Southwest Pacific 1979. World Today Series. Stryker-Post Publications. '79.

Kim, Samuel. China, the United Nations, and world order. Princeton Univ. Pr. '79.

*Lautz, Terry E., ed. Asia: Half the human race. Council on International and Public Affairs, in cooperation with China Council of Asia Society. '79.

Li, Dun Jen. The ageless Chinese; a history. Scribner. '78.

Lin, Y. S. The crisis of Chinese consciousness. Univ. of Wisconsin Pr. '79.

Maspero, Henri. China in antiquity. Univ. of Mass. Pr. '79.

Maxwell, Neville, ed. China's road to development. Pergamon Pr. '79.

Meskill, J. M. A Chinese pioneer family. Princeton Univ. Pr. '79.

Metzger, T. A. Escape from predicament; neo-Confucianism and China's evolving political culture. Columbia Univ. Pr. '77.

Middleton, Drew. The duel of the giants: China and Russia in Asia. Scribner. '78.

Moulder, Frances. Japan, China and the modern world economy. Cambridge Univ. Pr. '77.

Mydans, Carl and Michael Demarest. China; a visual adventure. Simon and Schuster. '79.

National Foreign Assessment Center. Central Intelligence Agency. China: economic indicators. ER 78-10750. Photoduplication Service, Library of Congress. D. '78.

*National Foreign Assessment Center, Central Intelligence Agency. China: in pursuit of economic modernization. ER 78-10680. Photoduplication Service. Library of Congress. D. '78.

*Oksenberg, Michel. China, the convulsive society. Headline series, no. 203. Foreign Policy Association. D. '70.

Orleans, Leo A., ed. Chinese approaches to family planning. M. E. Sharpe, Inc. '78, '79.

Peterson, G. B. Across the bridge to China. Elsevier/Nelson Bks. '79.

Salisbury, C. Y. China diary: after Mao. Walker & Co. '79.

Saunders, Hilliard. The complete travel guide to China. China Publishing Co. (CA) '79.

Schaller, Michael. The U.S. crusade in China, 1938–1945. Columbia Univ. Pr. '79.

Schell, O.H. China. Gollancz. '78.

Schell, O.H. In the People's Republic. Random House. '78.

Selden, Mark, ed. The People's Republic of China; a documentary history of revolutionary change. Monthly Review Pr. '79.

Sutter, Robert. China-watch; Sino-American reconciliation. Johns Hopkins Univ. Pr. '78.

Teiwes, Frederick C. Politics and purges in China; rectification and the decline of party norms 1950–1965. M. E. Sharpe, Inc. '79.

Terrill, Ross, ed. The China difference. Harper & Row. '79.

Terrill, R. G. The future of China. Delacorte Pr. '78.

Townsend, James R., comp. The People's Republic of China: a basic handbook. China Council of the Asia Society in cooperation with Council on International and Public Affairs. '79.

Wilson, Richard W. and others. Value change in Chinese society. Holt, Rinehart & Winston. '79.

Yahuda, M. B. China's role in world affairs. St. Martins Pr. '78.

PERIODICALS

America. 141:105. S. 15, '79. New China, new Church.

*Art In America. 67:9–25. Mr./Ap. '79. Report from China. Ann-Marie Rousseau and others.

*Asia. 1:3–7. Ja./F. '79. Has justice a fairer future in China? J. A. Cohen.

Asia. 1:33–7. Mr./Ap. '79. For Tibetans, an end to the long exile? Paul Grimes.

Asia. 2:30–7. My./Je. '79. Seeking love's proper place in China. Orville Schell.

*Asia. 2:4–7+. Jl./Ag. '79. Beijing's overseas Chinese connection: these Horatio Algers are supplying their Communist partners with contracts—and capital. Louis Kraar.

Asian Affairs. 10:42–50. F. '79. China's key schools: a new educational mandate. Eli Seifman.

Atlas World Press Review. 26:52. Je. '79. China decentralizes management. John Elliot.

Atlas World Press Review. 26:48. Ag. '79. Inside the Peking daily. Piero Ostellino.

Aviation Week and Space Technology. 110:26–7. My. 28, '79. China beginning manned space effort.

Aviation Week and Space Technology. 110:167–8. Je. 11, '79. China's aerospace market eyed warily. R. R. Ropelewski.

Aviation Week and Space Technology. 110:77+. Je. 25, '79. U.S. team tours China space facilities. Craig Covault.

*Business Week. p 132-3. My. 28, '79. China's long road to large-scale trade. Lewis Young.

Business Week. p 34-5. Jl. 9, '79. Candid new figures have a conservative look.

Business Week. p 39. Jl. 9, '79. Wave of dissidence sweeps China's youth. H. Ellithorpe and L. H. Young.

*Business Week. p 42+. Ag. 6, '79. China: what went wrong with the modernization plan.

China Business Review. p 28+. My./Je. '79. China's participation in international organizations. Natalie Lichtenstein.

China Quarterly. 78:274-95. Je. '79. Relevance of border-region experience to nation-building in China, 1949-52. R. C. Keith.

China Quarterly. 78:296-323. Je. '79. Mao Tun and the wild roses: a study of the psychology of revolutionary commitment. Y. S. Chen.

Christian Science Monitor. p 9. Jl. 23, '79. Tibetans in Bhutan want out. Sarah Pramar.

Christian Science Monitor. p 11. Jl. 25, '79. Peking invests in overseas banking. V. G. Kulkarni.

*Commonweal. p 133+. Mr. 16, '79. Our China "tilt": how about peace now? Peter Kovler.

Crosscurrents. Spr. '75. Mao Tse-tung: the long march. Thomas Berry.

Current History. 76:209-13. My. '79. U.S. trade with China. J. S. Prybyla.

Current History. 77:49-52+. S. '79. China's economic outreach. J. B. Starr.

Current History. 77:53-6+. S. 79. China and Asia: the year of the China-Vietnam war. B. D. Larkin.

Current History. 77:62-5+. S. '79. Industrial modernization in China. S. H. Chou.

Current History. 77:74-8+. S. '79. Implications of China's liberalization. Merle Goldman.

Department of State Bulletin. 79:13. Mr. '79. Pinyin—the new Chinese system of romanization.

Department of State Bulletin. 79:14-17. Mr. '79. China—A profile.

Department of State Bulletin. 79:18. Mr. '79. China trade by area and selected countries.

Department of State Bulletin. 79:40. Ag. '79. U.S.-P.R.C. sign claims agreement: text of agreement, May 11, 1979.

Economist. 270:11. F. 24, '79. China acts.

Economist. 271:42. My. 19, '79. Coming closer.

Encore. 8:8. F. 5, '79. China and the new world order. Ida Lewis.

Encore. 8:8. Mr. 19, '79. China in the Middle East. Ida Lewis.

Encore. 8:9. Ap. 2, '79. China in Africa: an alternative super-power? Ida Lewis.

Environment. 21:4–5+. Je. '79. China; view from abroad. R. A. Luken.

*Far Eastern Economic Review. p 73–4. My. 25, '79. U.S. and Peking find a way. Melinda Liu.

Far Eastern Economic Review. 104:10–11. Je. 8, '79. Peking's divided leaders: hint of a new purge. David Bonavia.

Far Eastern Economic Review. p 59–60. O. 5, '79. Coming years may erase memories of leaner times. Bennet Lee.

*Far Eastern Economic Review. p 61–2. O. 5, '79. One is fine, two is more than adequate. Stewart Fraser.

Far Eastern Economic Review. p 71–2. O. 5, '79. Modern teaching is based on outdated curriculums. Susan Rifkin.

Forbes. 123:37. Ap. 16, '79. Poor country learns about modernization. M. S. Forbes Jr.

Foreign Affairs. 157:125–37. Fall '78. The new thrust in China's foreign policy. Chalmers Johnson.

Foreign Affairs. 157:1090–1110. Summer '79. Japan, China and the United States. Saburo Okita.

Horizon. 22:62–5. Ag. '79. After the Gang of Four. Schuyler Chapin.

*Human Behavior. 8:18–23. Ap. '79. Curbing the urge in Red China. Alfred Messer.

*Human Nature. 1:63–8. N. '79. The failure of Western medicine. Arthur Kleinman.

Humanist. 39:24–7. S. '79. Another view of China. Y. H. Lee.

Mankind. 14:18–19. Mr. '79. Not merely players: drama, art and ritual in traditional China. B. E. Ward.

Nation. 228:201–3. F. 24, '79. Chinese checkmate: the Taiwan question. O. Edmund Clubb.

*Nation. 228:257+. Mr. 17, '79. China's historical hegemony. Owen Lattimore.

Nation. 228:295–7. Mr. 24, '79. Blunder in Vietnam: China drops a stone on its own foot. O. Edmund Clubb.

*Nation. 228:228–30. Mr. 31, '79. War talk in Peking. James Aronson.

Nation. 228:524–5. My. 12, '79. Broken treaty; Sino-Soviet friendship treaty. Albert Resis.

*Nation. 229:111–13. Ag. 11, '79. Peking love song. James Aronson.

National Geographic. 156:536–62. O. '79. Scenic Guilin links China's past and present.

*National Review. 31:348–50. Mr. 16, '79. The break with Taiwan; is it worth the price we paid? Robert Elegant.

National Review. 31:423. Mr. 30, '79. The Taiwan connection.

New Leader. 62:8–9. F. 12, '79. India and China start talking. A. G. Noorani.

New Republic. 180:5–6. Ja. 6, '79. The China card.

New Republic. 180:8–10. Ja. 6, '79. Carter and China. John Osborne.

New Republic. 180:21–3. Ja. 20, '79. All the peanuts in China. Murray Sayle.

New Republic. 180:10–12. F. 10, '79. Twinkles from Beijing.

New York Review of Books. 26:41–5. Ap. 3, '79. Women and education in China: how much progress? Nick Eberstadt.

New York Review of Books. 26:33–40. Ap. 19, '79. Has China failed? Nick Eberstadt.

New York Review of Books. 26:39–44. My. 3, '79. China: how much success? Nick Eberstadt.

New York Times. p A12. Ap. 5, '79. Chinese, mindful of the economy, shift back to traditional teaching.

New York Times. p A14. Ap. 5. '79. China's leaders start to crack down on witchcraft, democracy and other social evils. Fox Butterfield.

New York Times. p A8. Jl. 26, '79. For Tibet, a thin Chinese veneer. Fox Butterfield.

*New York Times. p 1+. Jl. 29, '79. China's elderly find good life in retirement. Fox Butterfield.

New York Times. 4:4. Jl. 29, '79. Assignment Tibet—and many Chinese don't like it. Fox Butterfield.

New York Times. p A9. Jl. 31, '79. Peking says it sent 300,000 men to aid Hanoi in war with U.S.

New York Times. p A5. Ag. 1, '79. Peking preparing a drive against corrupt officials. Fox Butterfield.

New York Times. p 5. Ag. 4, '79. China rehabilitates critics of Mao.

New York Times. p A3. Ag. 9, '79. 400 ragged provincials in Peking stage a sit-in for justice and jobs.

New York Times. p 12. Ag. 12, '79. China discovers the sweet smell of money in the perfume trade. James Sterba.

New York Times. p A4. Ag. 13, '79. Chinese will try to halt growth of population by end of century. James Sterba.

New York Times. p A1. S. 24, '79. Chinese ready to begin talks with Russians. Craig Whitney.

*New York Times. P A1 and A5. O. 8, '79. China restores small businesses to provide jobs. Fox Butterfield.

New York Times. p A2. O. 11, '79. 2,000 students in Peking protest army's use of campus. Fox Butterfield.

New York Times. p A3. O. 17, '79. Leading Chinese dissident gets 15-year prison term. Fox Butterfield.

New York Times. p A1. O. 18, '79. U.S. starts an appeal to overturn judge's ruling on Taiwan Pact. Graham Hovey.

New York Times. p 1. O. 20, '79. Peking permits once-banned exhibit of new art.

New York Times. p A1+. O. 24, '79. Chinese trade pact is sent to Congress.

New Yorker. p 127–50. S. 10, '79. When the snow thaws. David Finkelstein.

Newsweek. 94:50. Jl. 30, '79. Blacks accuse China of racism. Fay Willey and James Pringle.

Newsweek. 94:35. S. 10, '79. A diplomatic tilt toward China? Fay Willey and Barry Cane.

*Outlook. p 7–8. F. '79. China: A first look through the open door. Alexander Taffel.

Saturday Review. 6:16+. Mr. 17, '79. China: rushing to join the world. Horace Sutton.

Social Forces. 57:384–418. D. '78. Reflections on the Chinese model of development. B. M. Frolic.

*Time. p 48–9. S. 10. '79. A church that would not die.

U.S. News & World Report. 86:55–6. Ja. 15, '79. China's "new course"—an Australian perspective.

U.S. News & World Report. 86:15–18. Ja. 22, '79. China: really a bonanza for U.S. business?

U.S. News & World Report. 86:37–8. Ja. 22, '79. What China's Teng wants from U.S.

U.S. News & World Report. 86:38. Ja. 22, '79. Through a Senator's eyes. Patrick Leahy.

U.S. News & World Report. 86:43–4. Ja. 22, '79. China's shift: "dramatic, ambitious—and realistic." A. Doak Barnett.

U.S. News & World Report. 86:45–6, 48. Ja. 22, '79. Another war over Indo-China for U.S.?

U.S. News & World Report. 86:24. F. 12, '79. Teng face-to-face. Joseph Fromm.

U.S. News & World Report. 86:21–3. Mr. 5, '79. Why China shakes its fist.

U.S. News & World Report. 86:27–30. Mr. 12, '79. Now China learns a lesson in Vietnam.

U.S. News & World Report. 86:28. Mr. 19, '79. China-Vietnam peace—just a facade.

U.S. News & World Report. 87:16. Jl. 9, '79. Behind the shift in Carter's Asian policy.

U.S. News & World Report. 87:7. Ag. 13, '79. China's boast: how it fought U.S.

U.S. News & World Report. 87:53. S. 10, '79. Mondale offers more carrots to China.

Wall Street Journal. 193:1+. Mr. 6, '79. Pause in Peking: after
    hectic months, China slows its talks with western firms. Barry
    Kramer.
*Wall Street Journal. p 1+. Ag. 22, '79. Tibetans' observance of
    Buddhism returns after long repression. Frank Ching.
*Washington Post. p A15. D. 21, '78. A price for Taiwan. George
    Will.
*Washington Post. Op-ed p 15. F. 11, '79. China ties and the
    U.S.-Soviet balance. John Armitage.